T0226237

Lecture Notes in Computer Science 10478

Commenced Publication in 1973
Founding and Former Series Editors:
Gerhard Goos, Juris Hartmanis, and Jan van Leeuwen

More information about this series at http://www.springer.com/series/7409

Prasenjit Majumder · Mandar Mitra
Parth Mehta · Jainisha Sankhavara (Eds.)

Text Processing

FIRE 2016 International Workshop
Kolkata, India, December 7–10, 2016
Revised Selected Papers

 Springer

Editors
Prasenjit Majumder
DAIICT
Gujarat
India

Parth Mehta ⓘ
DAIICT
Gujarat
India

Mandar Mitra
Indian Statistical Institute
Kolkata
India

Jainisha Sankhavara
DAIICT
Gujarat
India

ISSN 0302-9743   ISSN 1611-3349   (electronic)
Lecture Notes in Computer Science
ISBN 978-3-319-73605-1   ISBN 978-3-319-73606-8   (eBook)
https://doi.org/10.1007/978-3-319-73606-8

Library of Congress Control Number: 2017963769

LNCS Sublibrary: SL3 – Information Systems and Applications, incl. Internet/Web, and HCI

Printed on acid-free paper

This Springer imprint is published by Springer Nature
The registered company is Springer International Publishing AG
The registered company address is: Gewerbestrasse 11, 6330 Cham, Switzerland

Preface

We are happy to present the current edited volume on "Advances in Text Processing." This volume comprises 16 papers from the seven tracks offered at FIRE 2016: Consumer Health Information Search (CHIS), Detecting Paraphrases in Indian Languages (DPIL), Information Extraction from Microblogs Posted During Disasters, Persian Plagiarism Detection (PersianPlagDet), Personality Recognition in Source Code (PR-SOCO), Shared Task on Mixed Script Information Retrieval (MSIR), and Shared Task on Code Mix Entity Extraction in Indian Languages (CMEE-IL).

Persian language text processing was a significant inclusion this year, in addition to the major Indian languages. FIRE was enriched by including an annotated Persian corpora and five papers. The next major contribution in this volume is on the DPIL task. Data on four Indian languages were presented – Tamil, Malayalam, Hindi, and Punjabi – and four papers on these languages are included in this volume. We included two papers on CHIS and MSIR each. Moreover, included one paper for each of the following tracks: the PR-SOCO, CMEE-IL, and Microblog track.

We invited top teams to submit their papers for this book and received 19 papers. All submissions underwent a review process after which 16 papers were selected for inclusion. We would like to thank the track organizers and reviewers for helping us in the selection process with their insightful opinion and feedback.

November 2017

Prasenjit Majumder
Mandar Mitra
Parth Mehta
Jainisha Sankhavara

Organization

FIRE 2016, the Forum for Information Retrieval Evaluation, was organized by the Indian Statistical Institute, Kolkata.

General Chairs

Mandar Mitra	Indian Statistical Institute Kolkata, India
Prasenjit Majumder	Dhirubhai Ambani Institute of ICT, India

Program Committee

Habibollah Asghari	ICT research Institute, Iran
Somnath Banerjee	Jadavpur University, India
Debasis Ganguly	Dublin City University, Ireland
Saptarshi Ghosh	Indian Institute of Technology Kharagpur, India
Kripabandhu Ghosh	Indian Institute of Technology Kanpur, India
Mark Michael Hall	Edge Hill University, UK
Ben Heuwing	Universität Hildesheim, Germany
Gareth Jones	Dublin City University, Ireland
Anand Kumar M.	Amrita Vishwa Vidyapeetham, India
Sobha Lalitha	AU-KBC Research Centre, India
Johannes Leveling	Elsevier, Germany
Mihai Lupu	Vienna University of Technology, Austria
Debapriyo Majumdar	Indian Statistical Institute Kolkata, India
Thomas Mandl	Universität Hildesheim, Germany
Parth Mehta	Dhirubhai Ambani Institute of ICT, India
Henning Müller	University of Applied Sciences Western Switzerland, Switzerland
Jiaul Paik	Indian Institute of Technology Kharagpur, India
Girish Palshikar	Tata Research Development and Design Centre, India
Swapan K. Parui	Indian Statistical Institute Kolkata, India
Paulo Quaresma	Universidade de Evora, Portugal
Nitin Ramrakhiyani	Tata Research Development and Design Centre, India
Pattabhi Rao	AU-KBC Research Centre, India
Paolo Rosso	Universitat Politècnica de València, Spain
Rishiraj Saha Roy	Max Planck Institute for Informatics, Germany
Jainisha Sankhavara	Dhirubhai Ambani Institute of ICT, India
Manjira Sinha	Conduent Labs, India
Jerome White	New York University, Abu Dhabi
David Zellhoefer	Berlin State Library, Germany

Contents

PAN@FIRE: Overview of the PR-SOCO Track on Personality Recognition in SOurce COde

Francisco Rangel[1(✉)], Fabio González[2], Felipe Restrepo[2], Manuel Montes[3], and Paolo Rosso[4]

[1] Autoritas Consulting, Valencia, Spain
`francisco.rangel@autoritas.es`
[2] MindLab Research Group, Universidad Nacional de Colombia, Bogotá, Colombia
`{fagonzalezo,ferestrepoca}@unal.edu.co`
[3] INAOE, Puebla, Mexico
`mmontesg@inaoep.mx`
[4] PRHLT Research Center, Universitat Politècnica de València, Valencia, Spain
`prosso@dsic.upv.es`

Abstract. Author profiling consists of predicting an author's demographics (e.g. age, gender, personality) from her writing. After addressing at PAN@CLEF mainly age and gender identification, and also personality recognition in Twitter (http://pan.webis.de/), in this PAN@FIRE track on Personality Recognition from SOurce COde (PR-SOCO) we have addressed the problem of predicting an author's personality from her source code. In this paper, we analyse 48 runs sent by 11 participants. Given a set of source codes written in Java by students who answered also a personality test, participants had to predict big five traits. Results have been evaluated with two complementary measures (RMSE and Pearson product-moment correlation) that have allowed to identify whether systems with low error rates may work due to random chance. No matter the approach, openness is the trait that allowed to obtain the best results for both measures.

Keywords: Personality recognition · Source code · Author profiling

1 Introduction

Personality influence most, if not all, of the human activities, such as the way people write [6,25], interact with others, and the way people make decisions, for instance in the case of developers the criteria they consider when selecting a software project they want to participate [22], or the way they write and structure their source code. Personality is defined along five traits using the Big Five Theory [7], which is the most widely accepted in psychology. The five traits are: extroversion (E), emotional stability/neuroticism (S), agreeableness (A), conscientiousness (C), and openness to experience (O).

Personality recognition may have several practical applications, for example to set up high performance teams. In software development, not only technical

© Springer International Publishing AG 2018
P. Majumder et al. (Eds.): FIRE 2016 Workshop, LNCS 10478, pp. 1–19, 2018.
https://doi.org/10.1007/978-3-319-73606-8_1

skills are required but also soft skills such as communication or teamwork. The possibility of using a tool to predict personality from source code, in order to know whether a candidate may fit in a team, may be very valuable for the recruitment process. Also in education, to know students' personality from their source codes may help to improve the learning process by customising the educational offer.

In this PAN@FIRE track on Personality Recognition from SOurce COde (PR-SOCO) we have addressed the problem of predicting an author's personality from her source code. Given a source code collection of a programmer, the aim is to identify her personality traits. In the training phase participants have been provided with source codes in Java of computer science students together with their personality traits. At test, participants will be given source codes of a few programmers and they will have to predict their personality traits. The number of source codes per programmer will be small reflecting a real scenario such as the one of a job interview: the interviewer could be interested in knowing the interviewee degree of conscientiousness by evaluating just a couple of programming problems.

We suggested participants to investigate beyond standard n-grams based features. For example, the way the code is commented, the variables naming or indentation may also provide valuable information. In order to encourage the investigation of different kinds of features, several runs per participant were allowed. In this paper, we describe the participation of 11 teams that sent 48 runs.

The reminder of this paper is organised as follows. Section 2 covers the state of the art, Sect. 3 describes the corpus and the evaluation measures, and Sect. 4 presents the approaches submitted by the participants. Sections 5 and 6 discuss results and draw conclusions respectively.

2   Related Work

Pioneers investigations in personality recognition were carried out by Argamon *et al.* [27], who focused on the identification of extroversion and emotional stability. They used support vector machines with a combination of word categories and relative frequency of function words to recognize these traits from self-reports. Similarly, Oberlander and Nowson [21] focused on personality identification of bloggers. Mairesse *et al.* [20] analysed the impact of different set of psycholinguistic features obtained with LIWC[1] and MRC[2], showing the highest performance on openness to experience trait.

Recently, researchers have focused on personality recognition from social media. In [5,14,24], the authors analysed different sets of linguistic features as well as friends count or daily activity. In [18], the authors reported a comprehensive analysis on features such as the size of the friendship network, the number of uploaded photos or the events attended by the user. They analysed

---

[1] http://www.liwc.net/.

[2] http://www.psych.rl.ac.uk/.

more than 180,000 Facebook users and found correlations among these features and the different traits, specially in case of extroversion. With the same Facebook dataset and similar set of features, Bachrach *et al.* [1] reported high results predicting extroversion automatically.

In [26], the authors analysed 75,000 Facebook messages of volunteers who filled a personality test and found interesting correlations among words usage and personality traits. According to them, extroverts use more social words and introverts more words related to solitary activities. Emotionally stable people use words related to sports, vacation, beach, church or team whereas neurotics use more words and sentences referring to depression.

Due to the interest on this field and with the aim at defining a common framework of evaluation, some shared tasks have been organised. For example, *(i)* the Workshop on Computational Personality Recognition [6]; or *(ii)* the Author Profiling task at PAN 2015 [25] with the objective of identifying age, gender and personality traits of Twitter users.

Regarding programming style and personality, in [3] the authors explored the relationship between cognitive style, personality and computer programming style. Recently, the authors in [16] also related personality to programming style and performance. Whereas the 2014 [10] and 2015 [11] PAN@FIRE tracks on SOurce COde (SOCO) where devoted to detect reuse, in 2016 we aimed at identifying personality traits from source code.

3 Evaluation Framework

In this section we describe the construction of the corpus, covering particular properties, challenges and novelties. Finally, the evaluation measures are described.

3.1 Corpus

The dataset is composed of Java programs written by computer science students from a data structures class at the Universidad Nacional de Colombia. Students were asked to upload source code, responding to some functional requirements of different programming tasks, to an automated assessment tool. For each task, students could upload more than one attempted solution. The number of attempts per problem was not limited/discouraged in any way. There are very similar submissions among different attempts and also some of them contain compilation-time or runtime errors.

Furthermore, in most of the cases students uploaded the right Java source code file, but some of them erroneously uploaded the compiler output, debug information or even the source code in other programming language (e.g.: Python). A priori this seems to be noise for the dataset and the and a sensible alternative could have been to remove these entries. However, we decided to keep them due to the following reasons: firstly, teams could remove them easily if they decide to do so; secondly, it is possible that this kind of mistakes is related to some personality traits, so this information can be used as a feature as well. Finally, although we encouraged the students to write their own code, some of them could reuse some pieces of code from other exercises or even looked for code excerpt on books or Internet.

In addition each student answered a Big Five personality test that allowed us to calculate a numerical score for each one of the following personality traits: extroversion, emotional stability/neuroticism, agreeableness, conscientiousness, and openness to experience.

Overall, the dataset consists of 2,492 source code programs written by 70 students along with the scores of the five personality traits for each student, which are provided as floating point numbers in the continuous range [20, 80]. The source code of each student were organized on a single text file with all her source codes together with a line separator among them. The dataset was split in training and test subsets, the first one containing the data for 49 students and the second one the data of the remaining 21. Participants only have access to the personality trait scores of the 49 students in the training dataset.

3.2 Performance Measures

For evaluating participants' approaches we have used two complementary measures: Root Mean Square Error (RMSE) and Pearson Product-Moment Correlation (PC). The motivation to use both measures is to try to understand whether a committed error is due to random chance.

We have calculated RMSE for each trait with Eq. 1.

$$RMSE_t = \sqrt{\frac{1}{n} \sum_{1}^{n} (y_i - \hat{y}_i)^2} \tag{1}$$

Where $RMSE_t$ is the Root Mean Square Error for trait t (neuroticism, extroversion, openness, agreeableness, conscientiousness); y_i and $\hat{y}_i$ are the ground truth and predicted value respectively for author i.

Also for each trait, PC is calculated following Eq. 2.

$$r = \frac{\sum_{i=1}^{n} (x_i - \bar{x})(y_i - \bar{y})}{\sum_{i=1}^{n} (x_i - \bar{x})^2 \sum_{i=1}^{n} (y_i - \bar{y})^2} \tag{2}$$

Where each x_i and y_i are respectively the ground truth and the predicted value for each author i; $\bar{x}$ and $\bar{y}$ the average values.

4 Overview of the Submitted Approaches

Eleven teams participated in the Personality Recognition in SOurce COde[3] shared task. They sent 48 runs with different approaches, and 9 of them have submitted the working notes describing their approaches. Following, we briefly highlight the different systems.

---

[3] http://www.autoritas.es/prsoco/.

- *besumich* [23] experimented with two kinds of features, bag of words and character n-grams (with n = 1, 2, 3). In both cases, they experimented with lowercase and original case, and three representations, binary (presence/absence), term frequency (TF) and TF-IDF. The authors trained linear regression, ridge regression and Lasso. The final configuration used to send their runs combined lowercased unigrams weighted with TF-IDF (with and without space characters) with different values for the alpha parameter of Lasso regression.
- *bilan* [2] started with analysing the code structure with the Antlr Java Code Analyzer[4]: it parses the program code and produces a parse tree of it. Then, they use each single node of the output tree (nodes represent different code categories, like classes, loops or variables) and count the frequency distribution of these nodes (around 200 features are taken into consideration). Apart from the Antlr, they obtain a set of custom features for the source code, such as the length of the whole program, the average length of variable names, the frequency of comments, their length, what indentation the programmer is using and also look at the distribution and usage of various statements and decorators. They also extract features from the comments such as the type/token ratio, usage of punctuation marks, average word length and a TF-IDF vector. They trained their models with two approaches, learning from each individual source code, and from the whole set of source codes per author.
- *castellanos* [4] used also Antlr with the Java grammar to obtain different measures from the analysis of the source code. For example, the amount of files, the average lines of code, the average number of classes, the average number of lines per class, average attributes per class, average methods per class, average static methods, and so on, combined with Halstead metrics [15] such as bugs delivered, difficulty, effort, time to understand or implement or volume. They have experimented with support vector regression, extra trees regression and support vector regression on averages.
- *delair* [8] have combined style features (e.g. code layout and formatting, indentation, headers, Javadoc, comments, whitespaces) with content features (e.g. class design problems, method design problem, annotations, block checks, coding, imports, metrics, modifiers, naming, conventions, size violations). They trained support vector machine for regression, gaussian processes, M5, M5 rules and random tree.
- *doval* [9] approached the task with a shallow Long Short Term Memory (LSTM) recurrent neural network. It works at the byte level, meaning that at each time step a new byte from the input text is processed by the network in an ordered manner. Bytes belonging to a particular source code package in an input text file are considered as a sequence, where the processing of some byte at time step t is influenced by the previous time steps $t - 1, t - 2, \ldots, 0$ (initial time step). The network learning criterion is a smoothed mean absolute error which uses a squared term if the absolute element-wise error falls below 1.

---

[4] https://github.com/antlr.

– *gimenez* [13] propose two different approaches to tackle this task. On the one hand, each code sample from each author was taken as an independent sample and vectorized using word n-grams; on the other hand, all the codes from an author was taken as a unique sample vectorized using word n-grams together with hand-crafted features (e.g. number of codes that implemented the same class, the appearance of pieces of code suspicious of plagiarism, number of developed classes, number of different classes). Regardless of the approach, a regression model was trained.

– *hhu* [19] extracted structure (e.g. number of methods per class, length of function names, cyclomatic complexity) and style (e.g. length of methods per class, number of comments per class) features but ignored layout features (e.g. indentation) because they may be easily modifiable by the programming IDE. They used variance and range besides mean to aggregate the frequencies and then, constructed a separate model for each trait training both linear regression and nearest neighbour models.

– *kumar* [12] have used multiple linear regression to model each of the five personality traits. For each personality trait, they have used four features: *(i)* The number of genuine comment words in multi-line comments, i.e., between */** and **/* found in the program code; *(ii)* The number of genuine single-line comment words in single line comments, i.e., comments following "//". Both in the previous feature and in this one, they have not considered the cases where lines of code are commented and the feature value is normalized by dividing it by the total number of words in the program file; *(iii)* The number of lines containing non-existent spaces, e.g., $for\,(int\,i\,=\,1;\,i\,\leq\,cases;\,i++)$ as opposed to $for\,(int\,i\,=\,1;\,i\,\leq\,cases;\,i++)$, since the presence of spaces is supposed to be a good programming practice. This feature value is normalized by dividing it by the total number of lines in the program file; *(iv)* The number of instances where the programmer has imported the specific libraries only (e.g. cases of import java.io.FileNotFoundException as opposed to import java.io.*) as this is supposed to be a good programming practice. This feature value also is normalized with respect to the total number of lines in the program file.

– *uaemex* [28] obtained three types of features related with: *(i)* Indentation: space in code, space in the comments, space between classes, spaces between source code blocks, space between methods, spaces between control sentences and spaces in clustering characters "( ), [ ], { }"; *(ii)* Identifier: the presence of underscore, uppercase, lowercase and numbers characters in the identifier and the length of the identifier. These characteristics were extracted for each class, method and variable names. Also, the percentage of number of initialized variables was extracted; and *(iii)* Comments: the presence of line and block comments, the size of the comments and the presence of comments with all letters in uppercase. They have experimented with symbolic regression, support vector machines, k-nearest neighbour and back propagation neural networks.

Although *montejo* have not sent a working note, they sent us a brief description of their system. They have used ToneAnalyzer[5], an IBM Watson module that proposes a value for each big five trait for a given text. The authors used ToneAnalyzer with the source code as it is and rescaled the output to fit the right range for the traits. Similarly, *lee* sent us the description of their system. They set a hypothesis that according to the personality, there will be differences in the steps of the source codes. Given a *ith* coder and n source codes for a coder c_i, the authors sort codes by length and naming c_i^0 to c_i^{n-1}. They transform each code to a vector v_i^j using skip-thought encoding [17], then calculate $n-1$ difference vectors d_i^j using equation $d_i^j = v_i^{j+1} - v_i^j$. The authors plot each coder to a feature space $Sum(d_i)$ and $Avg(d_i)$, and then apply logistic regression algorithm to train a model.

Furthermore, we have provided with two baselines:

- *bow:* a bag of character 3-grams with frequency weight.
- *mean:* an approach that always predicts the mean value observed in the training data.

5   Evaluation and Discussion of the Submitted Approaches

Results are presented in Table 1 in alphabetical order. Below the participants' results, a summary with the common descriptive statistics is provided for each trait. In the bottom of the table, results for the baselines are also provided. Figures 11, 12 and 13 show the distribution of the two measures: RMSE and Pearson correlation for all the participants except the baselines. In Fig. 11 we can appreciate that there are many runs with anomalous RMSE values (outliers), whereas in Fig. 12 we have removed these outliers. Looking at these figures and at the table of results, we can observe that:

- The mean is between 10.49 and 12.75 (a difference of 2.26), corresponding the lowest value to openness and the highest one to neuroticism.
- The median is between 8.14 and 10.77 (a difference of 2.63), corresponding again the lowest value to openness and the highest one to neuroticism.
- The lowest difference between mean and median was obtained for conscientiousness (1.75), followed by neuroticism (1.98). The highest difference was obtained for extroversion (2.72), agreeableness (2.36) and openness (2.35).
- In all the cases, the mean is higher than the median, and also than the 3rd quartile (q3), showing the effect of the outliers.
- The minimum and maximum values were obtained for openness trait (6.95 and 33.53 respectively).
- When removing outliers, the maximum value was obtained for extroversion (16.67).

---

[5] https://tone-analyzer-demo.mybluemix.net/.

Table 1. Participants' results in root mean square error and Pearson product moment correlation.

Team	Run	Neuroticism	Extroversion	Openness	Agreeableness	Conscientiousness
besumich	1	10.69/0.05	9.00/0.14	8.58/−0.33	9.38/−0.09	8.89/−0.14
	2	10.69/0.05	9.00/0.14	8.58/−0.33	9.38/−0.09	8.89/−0.14
	3	10.53/0.05	9.05/0.10	8.43/−0.33	9.32/−0.07	8.88/−0.17
	4	10.53/0.05	9.05/0.10	8.43/−0.33	9.32/−0.07	8.88/−0.17
	5	10.83/0.10	**8.60**/0.38	9.06/−0.31	9.66/−0.10	8.77/−0.06
bilan	1	10.42/0.04	8.96/0.16	7.54/0.10	9.16/0.04	8.61/0.07
	2	10.28/0.14	9.55/−0.10	7.25/0.29	9.17/−0.12	8.83/−0.31
	3	10.77/−0.12	9.35/−0.07	7.19/0.36	8.84/0.21	8.99/−0.11
	4	12.06/−0.04	11.18/−0.35	7.50/0.35	10.89/−0.05	8.90/0.16
	5	11.95/0.06	11.69/−0.37	7.46/0.37	11.19/−0.05	9.10/0.11
castellanos	1	11.83/0.05	9.54/0.11	8.14/0.28	10.48/−0.08	8.39/−0.09
	2	10.31/0.02	9.06/0.00	7.27/0.29	9.61/−0.11	8.47/−0.16
	3	10.24/0.03	9.01/0.01	7.34/0.30	9.36/0.01	9.99/−0.25
delair	1	19.07/0.20	25.22/0.08	23.62/**0.62**	21.47/−0.15	22.05/**0.33**
	2	26.36/0.19	16.67/−0.02	15.97/0.19	23.11/−0.13	21.72/0.10
	3	18.75/0.20	25.22/0.08	20.28/0.54	21.47/−0.15	22.05/**0.33**
	4	17.55/0.29	20.34/−0.26	16.74/0.27	21.10/−0.06	20.90/0.14
	5	26.72/0.18	23.41/−0.11	16.25/0.13	27.78/−0.19	15.53/0.27
doval	1	11.99/−0.01	11.18/0.09	12.27/−0.05	10.31/0.20	8.85/0.02
	2	12.63/−0.18	11.81/0.21	8.19/−0.02	12.69/−0.01	9.91/−0.30
	3	10.37/0.14	12.50/0.00	9.25/0.11	11.66/−0.14	8.89/0.15
	4	29.44/−0.24	28.80/**0.47**	27.81/−0.14	25.53/**0.38**	14.69/0.32
	5	11.34/0.05	11.71/0.19	10.93/0.12	10.52/−0.07	10.78/−0.12
gimenez	1	10.67/−0.22	8.75/0.31	7.85/−0.12	9.29/0.03	9.02/−0.23
	2	10.46/−0.07	8.79/0.28	7.67/0.05	9.36/0.00	8.99/−0.19
	3	10.22/0.09	9.00/0.18	7.57/0.03	**8.79**/0.33	8.69/−0.12
	4	10.73/−0.15	8.69/0.28	7.81/−0.05	9.62/−0.03	8.86/−0.09
	5	10.65/−0.16	8.65/0.30	7.79/−0.02	9.71/−0.06	8.89/−0.12
hhu	1	11.65/0.05	14.28/−0.31	7.42/0.29	12.29/−0.28	8.56/0.13
	2	9.97/0.23	9.60/−0.10	8.01/0.02	11.91/−0.30	**8.38**/0.19
	3	11.65/0.05	14.28/−0.31	7.42/0.29	11.50/−0.32	8.56/0.13
	4	9.97/0.23	9.22/−0.20	7.84/0.07	11.50/−0.32	**8.38**/0.19
	5	10.36/0.13	9.60/−0.10	8.01/0.02	11.91/−0.30	8.73/−0.05
	6	13.91/−0.10	25.63/−0.05	33.53/0.24	12.29/−0.28	14.31/0.16
kumar	1	10.22/**0.36**	**8.60**/0.35	7.16/0.33	9.60/0.09	9.99/−0.20
	2	10.04/0.27	10.17/0.04	7.36/0.27	9.55/0.11	10.16/−0.13
lee	1	10.19/0.10	9.08/0.00	8.43/0.00	9.39/0.06	8.59/0.00
	2	12.93/−0.18	9.26/0.26	9.58/−0.06	9.93/−0.02	9.18/0.21
	3	**9.78** /0.31	8.8/0.25	8.21/−0.36	8.83/0.24	9.11/0.05
	4	12.20/−0.19	8.98/0.31	8.82/−0.04	9.77/0.07	9.03/0.26
	5	12.38/−0.16	8.80/0.31	9.22/−0.15	9.70/0.02	9.05/0.31
montejo	1	24.16/0.10	27.39/0.10	22.57/0.27	28.63/0.21	22.36/−0.11
uaemex	1	11.54/−0.29	11.08/−0.14	**6.95**/0.45	8.98/0.22	8.53/0.11
	2	11.10/−0.14	12.23/−0.15	9.72/0.04	9.94/0.19	9.86/−0.30
	3	9.84/0.35	12.69/−0.10	7.34/0.28	9.56/0.33	11.36/−0.01
	4	10.67/0.04	9.49/−0.04	8.14/0.10	8.97/0.29	8.82/0.07
	5	10.25/0.00	9.85/0.00	9.84/0.00	9.42/0.00	10.50/−0.29
	6	10.86/0.13	9.85/0.00	7.57/0.00	9.42/0.00	8.53/0.00
Min		9.78/−0.29	8.60/−0.37	6.95/−0.36	8.79/−0.32	8.38/−0.31
q1		10.36/−0.08	9.00/−0.10	7.54/−0.05	9.38/−0.11	8.77/−0.14
Median		10.77/0.05	9.55/0.08	8.14/0.07	9.71/−0.03	8.99/−0.01
Mean		12.75/0.04	12.27/0.06	10.49/0.09	12.07/−0.01	10.74/−0.01
q3		12.20/0.14	12.23/0.21	9.58/0.28	11.66/0.07	9.99/0.14
Max		29.44/0.36	28.80/0.47	33.53/0.62	28.63/0.38	22.36/0.33
		Neuroticism	Extroversion	Openness	Agreeableness	Conscientiousness
Baseline	Bow	10.29/0.06	9.06/0.12	7.74/−0.17	9.00/0.20	8.47/0.17
	Mean	10.26/ 0.00	9.06/0.00	7.57/0.00	9.04/0.00	8.54/0.00

- The lowest quartiles, both 1st and 3rd quartiles (q1 and q3), correspond to openness (7.54 and 9.58 respectively).
- The narrowest inter quartile range corresponds to conscientiousness (1.22), followed by neuroticism (1.84) and openness (2.04). The widest correspond to extroversion (3.23), followed by agreeableness (2.28).

In Fig. 13 the distribution of the Pearson correlations is shown. Looking at this figure and at the table of results, we can observe that:

- There is only one outlier in agreeableness trait (0.38). Regretfully, this correlation corresponds to a high RMSE (25.53).
- The mean is between −0.01 and 0.09 (a difference of 0.10), corresponding the lowest value to conscientiousness and agreeableness, and the highest one to openness. In any case, values very close to the random chance.
- The median is between −0.03 and 0.08 (a difference of 0.11), corresponding the lowest value to agreeableness and the highest one to extroversion.
- The lowest difference between mean and median was obtained for conscientiousness (0), followed by neuroticism (0.01), and extroversion, agreeableness and openness (0.02).
- The mean is higher than the median in case of openness (0.09 vs. 0.07) and agreeableness (−0.01 vs. −0.03). The other occurs in case of neuroticism (0.04 vs. 0.05), extroversion (0.06 vs. 0.08) and conscientiousness (−0.01 in both).
- The minimum value was obtained for extroversion (−0.37), very close to openness (−0.36), and the maximum for openness (0.62), followed by extroversion (0.47), agreeableness (0.38), neuroticism (0.36) and conscientiousness (0.33).
- Nevertheless the goodness of the maximum values, they correspond in most cases with high RMSE: openness (23.62), extroversion (28.80), agreeableness (25.53), and conscientiousness (22.05). Only in case of neuroticism the maximum Pearson correlations corresponds to a low value of RMSE (10.22).
- The highest q3 corresponds to openness (0.28) and extroversion (0.21), followed by conscientiousness (0.14 and neuroticism (0.14). The lowest one corresponds to agreeableness (0.07).
- The narrowest inter quartile range corresponds to agreeableness (0.18), followed by neuroticism (0.22), conscientiousness (0.28), extroversion (0.31) and openness (0.33).

We can conclude that, in general, systems work quite similar in terms of Pearson correlation for all the traits. However, there seem to be higher differences with respect to RMSE, where the systems obtained better results for openness than for the rest. The distributions show that the lowest sparsity occurs with conscientiousness in case of RMSE and agreeableness in case of Pearson correlation, meanwhile the highest sparsity occurs with extroversion in case of RMSE and openness in case of Pearson correlation.

Results for **neuroticism** are plotted in Fig. 1. This figure represents each system's results by plotting its RMSE in x axis and Pearson correlation in y axis. It is worth to mention that the system proposed by *delair* in their 4th run obtained one of the highest values for Pearson correlation (0.29) although with

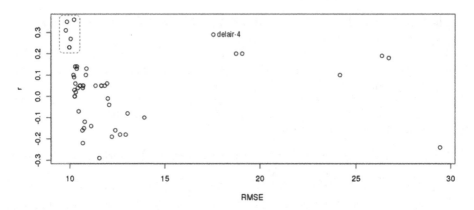

Fig. 1. RMSE vs. PC for neuroticism.

a high RMSE (17.55). This system consists in a combination of style features (code layout and formatting, indentation...) and content features (class design, method design, imports...), trained with random tree. We can observe a group of five (actually six due to two systems that obtained the same results) in the upper-left corner of the chart. These systems obtained the highest correlations with the lowest error, and they are detailed in Fig. 2. We can see that all of them (except *lee* which used skip-thought encoding) extracted specific features from the source code, such as the number of methods, the number of comments per class, the type of comments (/* */ vs. inline), type of naming variables, and so on. We can see that some of these teams obtained similar results for two of

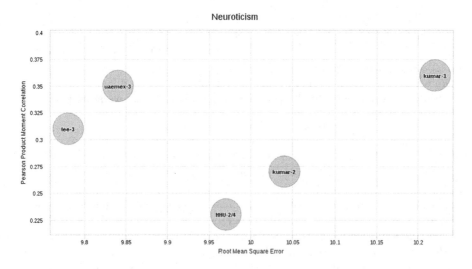

Fig. 2. RMSE vs. PC for neuroticism (detailed).

their systems. For example, *kumar* with their 1st and 2nd runs (they used linear regression for both runs, but they tried to optimise run 2 by removing from the training set the three files which obtained the highest error in training), or *hhu* that obtained the best results for their 2nd and 4th run (they both used k-NN with a different combination of features). *Uaemex* obtained their best result with run 3 that used back propagation neural network. We can conclude that for neuroticism, specific features extracted from the code (*kumar, hhu, uaemex*) worked better than generic features such as n-grams (*besumich*, that obtained low RMSE but without correlation in most cases), byte streams (*doval*, that obtained low RMSE but with negative correlations in most cases) or text streams (*montejo*, that obtained high RMSE with low correlations).

In Fig. 3 results for **extroversion** are shown. We can see that *doval* in their 4th run obtained both the highest Pearson correlation (0.47) but with the worst RMSE (28.80). They trained a LSTM recurrent neural network by converting the input at byte level, that is, without the need of performing feature engineering. In the upper-left corner of the figure we can see the group of the best results both in RMSE and Pearson correlation, that is detailed in Fig. 4. We can highlight the superiority of *besumich* run 5 (lowercased character unigrams weighted with TF-IDF and training a Lasso regression algorithm with alpha 0.01), which obtained a correlation of 0.38 with a RMSE of 8.60, and *kumar* run 1 (code specific features with logistic regression without optimisation), with a correlation of 0.35 and a RMSE of 8.60. It is worth to mention that *lee* obtained high results with four of their approaches that use skip-thought encoding, and similar occurred with *gimenez*. The last one used a combination of word n-grams with specific features obtained from the code (the number of code that implemented the same class, the appearance of pieces of code suspicious of plagiarism, the number of classes developed, and the number of different classes developed), trained with ridge runs 1 (8.75/0.31) and 2 (8.79/0.28), and logistic regression run 4 (8.69/0.28). In case of extroversion we can see that common features such as n-grams (*besumich*) obtained good results. Also *gimenez* used word n-grams in combination to other

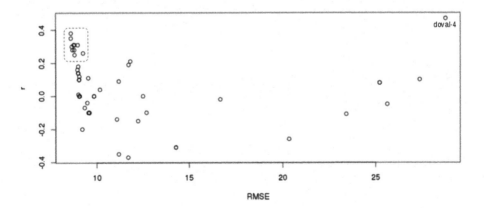

Fig. 3. RMSE vs. PC for extroversion.

features, what supports this conclusion. However, byte streams (*doval*) again produced high RMSE with high correlation, or text streams (*montejo*) produced high RMSE but with low correlation. In some cases, specific features obtained low RMSE but with negative correlation (*bilan, hhu, uaemex*). Although the *bow-based baseline* is not in the top performing methods, it obtained low RMSE (9.06) with over the median correlation (0.12).

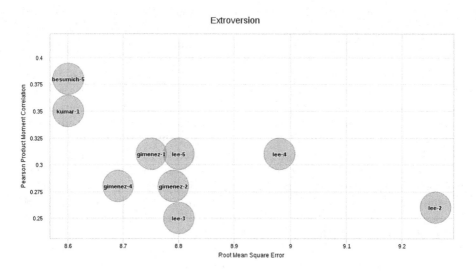

Fig. 4. RMSE vs. PC for extroversion (detailed).

Similarly, **openness** results are presented in Fig. 5. It is noticeable that two systems presented by *delair* obtained the highest correlations but with quite high RMSE. Concretely, run 1 obtained the highest correlation (0.62) with high

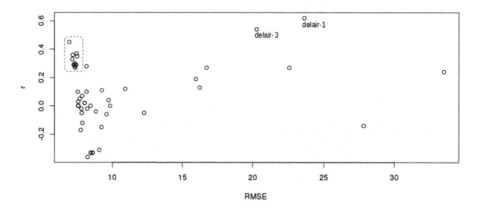

Fig. 5. RMSE vs. PC for openness.

RMSE (23.62), and run 3 obtaining the second highest correlation (0.54) with a little lower RMSE (20.28). They used M5rules and M5P respectively. Systems in the upper-left corner are shown in detail in Fig. 6. We can see that the best result for both RMSE and Pearson correlation was obtained by *uaemex* in their 1st run. This run was generated using symbolic regression with three types of features: indentation, identifiers and comments. The authors optimised this run by eliminating the source codes of five developers according to the following criteria: the person who had high values in all the personality traits, the person who had a lower values in all the personality traits, the person who had an average values in all the personality traits, the person who had more source codes and the person who had few source codes. They also obtained high results with their 3rd run, where they trained a back propagation neural network with the whole set of training codes. Systems presented by *bilan* also obtained high results in different runs. Concretely, using Antlr parser to obtain features in combination with features extracted from comments and so on, they trained gradient boosted regression and multinomial logistic regression. Similarly, *castellanos* who used also Antlr combined with Halstead measures and trained extra trees regressor (run 2) and support vector regression on averages (run 3); *kumar* with combinations of structure and style features trained with linear regression (2nd run optimised by eliminating training files); and *hhu* also with combinations of structure and style features with k-NN in both runs. For openness the best performing teams used specific features extracted from the code (*uaemex, kumar, hhu*), even with the help of code analysers such as Antlr (*castellanos, bilan*). Common features seem to obtain good level of RMSE but with low (or even negative) correlations (*besumich, bow-based baseline*).

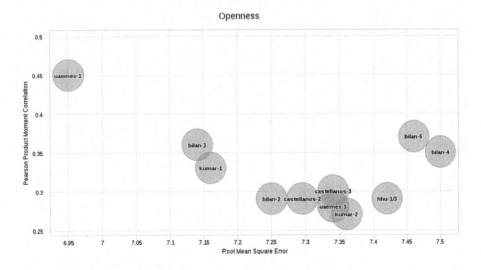

Fig. 6. RMSE vs. PC for openness (detailed).

In case of **agreeableness**, as shown in Fig. 7 we can see that *doval* with their 4th run obtained the highest correlation (0.38), but with a high RMSE (25.53). Systems in the upper-left corner are shown in detail in Fig. 8. We can say that the best result in both measures was obtained by *gimenez* in their 3rd run. The team used ridge to train their model with a subset of code style features. It is worth mentioning that the provided baseline consistent in character n-grams appears as one of the top performing methods for this trait. For this trait is more difficult to differentiate between common and specific features since there are many different teams that, although obtained low RMSE, have negative correlations. For example *besumich* with character n-grams, *bilan* and *castellanos* with specific features obtained with Antlr (among others), or *delair* with a

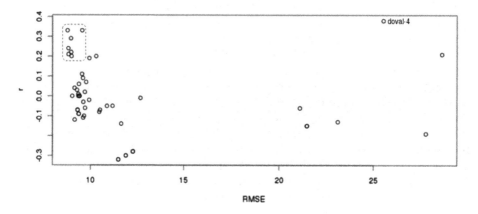

Fig. 7. RMSE vs. PC for agreableness.

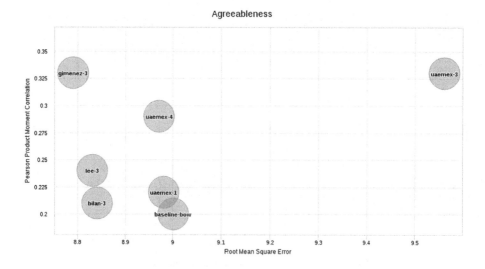

Fig. 8. RMSE vs. PC for agreableness (detailed).

combination of style and content features. However, it is worth to mention that the *bow baseline* obtained top results both in RMSE and Pearson correlation.

Finally, with respect to **conscientiousness** results are depicted in Fig. 9. We can see that four runs obtained high values for Pearson correlation but also obtained high RMSE. Concretely, *delair* obtained the highest correlation (0.33) with the second highest RMSE (22.05) with their 1st and 3rd runs (M5rules and M5P respectively), and also a high correlation (0.27) with a little lower RMSE (15.53) with their 5th run (support vector machine for regression). Similarly, *doval* with their 4th run obtained high correlation (0.32) but with high RMSE (14.69) by using LSTM recurrent neural network with a byte level input. Systems in the upper-left corner are represented in Fig. 10. In this case, the best results in terms of RMSE are not the best ones in terms of Pearson correlation: with respect to the first ones, *hhu* with runs 1, 2 and 3 or *uaemex* with run 1. With respect to the second ones, lee with runs 2, 4 and 5, *bilan* with runs 4 and 5 and *doval* with run 3. It is noticeable that again the provided *baseline* obtained one of the best results. In this case the second better RMSE with one of the top 5 correlations. In case of conscientiousness, systems that used *n*-grams (*besumich*, *gimenez*), byte streams (*doval*) and text streams (*montejo*) performed worst in case of Pearson correlation, with negative values in most cases, whereas the best results were achieved by combinations of structure, style and comments (*hhu*, *uaemex*) or features obtained by analysing the codes (*bilan*). However, again the *bow baseline* achieved top positions, specially in RMSE.

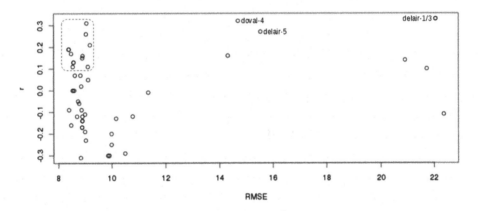

Fig. 9. RMSE vs. PC for conscientiousness.

To sum up, depending on the trait, generic features such as *n*-grams obtained different results in comparison with specific features obtained from the code. In case of generic features, their impact is specially on correlation: they may obtain good levels of RMSE but without a good correlation. As it was expected, the mean-based baseline obtained no correlation, since it seems more a random value. However, its RMSE was better than the average results and the median results in most cases. This result supports the need of using also a measure like Pearson correlation in order to avoid low RMSE due to random chance.

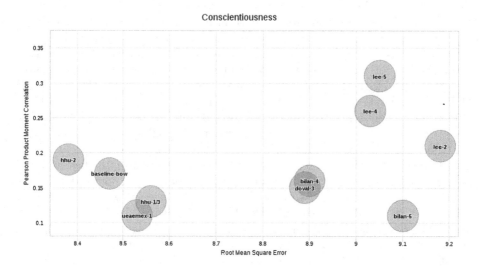

Fig. 10. RMSE vs. PC for conscientiousness (detailed).

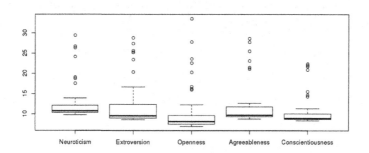

Fig. 11. RMSE distribution.

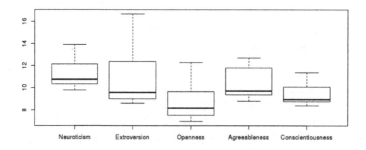

Fig. 12. RMSE distribution (without outliers).

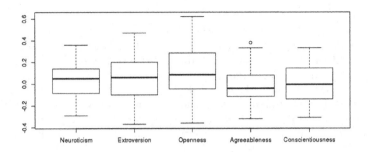

Fig. 13. Pearson correlation distribution.

6   Conclusion

This paper describes the 48 runs sent by 11 participants to the PR-SOCO shared task at PAN-FIRE 2016. Given a set of source codes written in Java by students who answered a personality test, the participants had to predict values for the big five traits.

Results have been evaluated with two complementary measures: RMSE, which provides an overall score of the performance of the system, and Pearson product-moment correlation, which indicates whether the performance is due to the random chance. In general systems showed to work quite similarly in terms of Pearson correlation for all traits. Higher differences where noticed with respect to RMSE. The best results were achieved for openness (6.95), as previously was reported by Mairesse *et al.* [20], as well as this was one of the traits with the lower RMSE at PAN 2015 [25] for most languages.

Participants have used different kinds of features: from general ones such as word or character n-grams to specific ones obtained by parsing the code, analysing its structure, style or comments. Depending on the trait, generic features obtained competitive results compared with specific ones in terms of RMSE. However, in most cases the best RMSE obtained with these features obtained low values of the Pearson correlation. In these cases, some systems seemed to be less robust, at least for some of the personality traits.

Finally, in line with the above comments, it is worth mentioning that approaches that took advantage of the training distributions (such as the baseline based on means did), obtained low RMSE. However, this may be due to random chance. This supports the need of using complementary measures to RMSE such as Pearson correlation, in order to avoid misinterpretations due to a biased measure.

Acknowledgments. Our special thanks go to all of PR-SOCO participants. The work of the first author was partially supported by Autoritas Consulting and by Ministerio de Economía y Competitividad de España under grant ECOPORTUNITY IPT-2012-1220-430000. The work of the fifth author was partially supported by the SomEMBED TIN2015-71147-C2-1-P MINECO research project and by the Generalitat Valenciana under the grant ALMAMATER (PrometeoII/2014/030).

References

1. Bachrach, Y., Kosinski, M., Graepel, T., Kohli, P., Stillwell, D.: Personality and patterns of Facebook usage. In: Proceedings of the ACM Web Science Conference, pp. 36–44. ACM, New York (2012)
2. Bilan, I., Saller, E., Roth, B., Krytchak, M.: CAPS-PRC: a system for personality recognition in programming code - notebook for PAN at FIRE16. In: Working Notes for PAN-PRSOCO at FIRE 2016. Workshops Proceedings of the 8th International Forum for Information Retrieval Evaluation (Fire 2015), Kolkata, India (2016)
3. Bishop-Clark, C.: Cognitive style, personality, and computer programming. Comput. Hum. Behav. **11**(2), 241–260 (1995)
4. Castellanos, H.A.: Personality recognition applying machine learning techniques on source code metrics. In: Working Notes for PAN-PRSOCO at FIRE 2016. Workshops Proceedings of the 8th International Forum for Information Retrieval Evaluation (Fire 2015), Kolkata, India (2016)
5. Celli, F., Polonio, L.: Relationships between personality and interactions in Facebook. In: Social Networking: Recent Trends, Emerging Issues and Future Outlook, pp. 41–54. Nova Science Publishers, Inc. (2013)
6. Celli, F., Lepri, B., Biel, J.-I., Gatica-Perez, D., Riccardi, G., Pianesi, F.: The workshop on computational personality recognition 2014. In: Proceedings of the ACM International Conference on Multimedia, pp. 1245–1246. ACM (2014)
7. Costa, P.T., McCrae, R.R.: The revised NEO personality inventory (NEO-PI-R). In: The SAGE Handbook of Personality Theory and Assessment, vol. 2, pp. 179–198. Sage Publications Inc., Thousand Oaks (2008)
8. Delair, R., Mahajan, R.: Personality recognition in source code. In: Working Notes for PAN-PRSOCO at FIRE 2016. Workshops Proceedings of the 8th International Forum for Information Retrieval Evaluation (Fire 2015), Kolkata, India (2016)
9. Doval, Y., Gómez-Rodríguez, C., Vilares, J.: Shallow recurrent neural network for personality recognition in source code. In: Working Notes for PAN-PRSOCO at FIRE 2016. Workshops Proceedings of the 8th International Forum for Information Retrieval Evaluation (Fire 2015), Kolkata, India (2016)
10. Flores, E., Rosso, P., Moreno, L., Villatoro-Tello, E.: PAN@ FIRE: overview of SOCO track on the detection of SOurce COde Re-use. In: Notebook Papers of FIRE 2014, FIRE-2014, Bangalore, India (2014)
11. Flores, E., Rosso, P., Moreno, L., Villatoro-Tello, E.: PAN@ FIRE 2015: overview of CL-SOCO track on the detection of cross-language SOurce COde Re-use. In: Proceedings of the Seventh Forum for Information Retrieval Evaluation (FIRE 2015), Gandhinagar, India, pp. 4–6 (2015)
12. Ghosh, K., Kumar-Parui, S.: Indian Statistical Institute, Kolkata at PR-SOCO 2016: a simple linear regression based approach. In: Working Notes for PAN-PRSOCO at FIRE 2016. Workshops Proceedings of the 8th International Forum for Information Retrieval Evaluation (Fire 2015), Kolkata, India (2016)
13. Giménez, M., Paredes, R.: PRHLT at PR-SOCO: a regression model for predicting personality traits from source code - notebook for PR-SOCO at FIRE 2016. In: Working Notes for PAN-PRSOCO at FIRE 2016. Workshops Proceedings of the 8th International Forum for Information Retrieval Evaluation (Fire 2015), Kolkata, India (2016)
14. Golbeck, J., Robles, C., Turner, K.: Predicting personality with social media. In: CHI 2011 Extended Abstracts on Human Factors in Computing Systems, pp. 253–262, ACM (2011)

15. Halstead, M.H.: Elements of Software Science. Operating and Programming Systems Series, vol. 2. Elsevier, New York (1977)
16. Karimi, Z., Baraani-Dastjerdi, A., Ghasem-Aghaee, N., Wagner, S.: Links between the personalities, styles and performance in computer programming. J. Syst. Softw. **111**, 228–241 (2016)
17. Kiros, R., Zhu, Y., Salakhutdinov, R.R., Zemel, R., Urtasun, R., Torralba, A., Fidler, S.: Skip-thought vectors. In: Advances in Neural Information Processing Systems, pp. 3294–3302 (2015)
18. Kosinski, M., Bachrach, Y., Kohli, P., Stillwell, D., Graepel, T.: Manifestations of user personality in website choice and behaviour on online social networks. Mach. Learn. **95**, 1–24 (2013)
19. Liebeck, M., Modaresi, P., Askinadze, A., Conrad, S.: Pisco: a computational approach to predict personality types from Java source code. In: Working Notes for PAN-PRSOCO at FIRE 2016. Workshops Proceedings of the 8th International Forum for Information Retrieval Evaluation (Fire 2015), Kolkata, India (2016)
20. Mairesse, F., Walker, M.A., Mehl, M.R., Moore, R.K.: Using linguistic cues for the automatic recognition of personality in conversation and text. J. Artif. Intell. Res. **30**(1), 457–500 (2007)
21. Oberlander, J., Nowson, S.: Whose thumb is it anyway?: classifying author personality from weblog text. In: Proceedings of the COLING/ACL on Main Conference Poster Sessions, pp. 627–634. Association for Computational Linguistics (2006)
22. Paruma-Pabón, O.H., González, F.A., Aponte, J., Camargo, J.E., Restrepo-Calle, F.: Finding relationships between socio-technical aspects and personality traits by mining developer e-mails. In: Proceedings of the 9th International Workshop on Cooperative and Human Aspects of Software Engineering, pp. 8–14. ACM (2016)
23. Phani, S., Lahiri, S., Biswas, A.: Personality recognition working note: team BESUMich. In: Working Notes for PAN-PRSOCO at FIRE 2016. Workshops Proceedings of the 8th International Forum for Information Retrieval Evaluation (Fire 2015), Kolkata, India (2016)
24. Quercia, D., Lambiotte, R., Stillwell, D., Kosinski, M., Crowcroft, J.: The personality of popular Facebook users. In: Proceedings of the ACM 2012 Conference on Computer Supported Cooperative Work, pp. 955–964. ACM (2012)
25. Rangel, F., Rosso, P., Potthast, M., Stein, B., Daelemans, W.: Overview of the 3rd author profiling task at PAN 2015. In: Cappellato, L., Ferro, N., Jones G., San Juan, E. (eds.) CLEF 2015 Labs and Workshops, Notebook Papers. CEUR Workshop Proceedings, vol. 1391. CEUR-WS.org (2015)
26. Schwartz, H.A., Eichstaedt, J.C., Kern, M.L., Dziurzynski, L., Ramones, S.M., Agrawal, M., Shah, A., Kosinski, M., Stillwell, D., Seligman, M.E., et al.: Personality, gender, and age in the language of social media: the open-vocabulary approach. PLoS ONE **8**(9), 773–791 (2013)
27. Argamon, S., Dhawle, S., Pennebaker, J.W.: Lexical predictors of personality type. In: Proceedings of the Joint Annual Meeting of the Interface and the Classification Society of North America (2005)
28. Vázquez-Vázquez, E., González-Brito, O., Armeaga-García, J., García-Calderón, M., Villada-Ramírez, G., Serrano-León, A.J., García-Hernández, R.A., Ledeneva, Y.: UAEMex system for identifying traits personality in source code. In: Working Notes for PAN-PRSOCO at FIRE 2016. Workshops Proceedings of the 8th International Forum for Information Retrieval Evaluation (Fire 2015), Kolkata, India (2016)

Microblog Retrieval During Disasters: Comparative Evaluation of IR Methodologies

Moumita Basu[1,2]([⊠]), Kripabandhu Ghosh[3], Somenath Das[1],
Somprakash Bandyopadhyay[4], and Saptarshi Ghosh[1,5]

[1] Indian Institute of Engineering Science and Technology, Shibpur, Howrah, India
moumitabasu0979@gmail.com
[2] University of Engineering and Management, Kolkata, India
[3] Indian Institute of Technology, Kanpur, Kanpur, India
[4] Indian Institute of Management, Calcutta, Kolkata, India
[5] Indian Institute of Technology, Kharagpur, Kharagpur, India
saptarshi@cse.iitkgp.ernet.in

Abstract. Microblogging sites are important sources of situational information during any natural or man-made disasters. Hence, it is important to design and test Information Retrieval (IR) systems that retrieve information from microblogs during disasters. With this perspective, a track was organized at the 8th meeting of Forum for Information Retrieval Evaluation (FIRE) 2016, focused on microblog retrieval during disaster events. A collection of about 50,000 microblogs posted during the Nepal Earthquake in April 2015 was released, along with a set of seven pragmatic information needs during a disaster situation. The task was to retrieve microblogs relevant to these information needs. Ten teams participated in the task, and fifteen runs were submitted. Evaluation of the performances of various microblog retrieval methodologies, as submitted by the participants, revealed several challenges associated with microblog retrieval. In this chapter, we describe our experience in organizing the FIRE track on microblog retrieval during disaster events. Additionally, we propose two novel methodologies for the said task, which perform better than all the methodologies submitted to the FIRE track.

Keywords: Microblog retrieval · FIRE microblog track · Disasters
Word embedding · Word2vec

1 Introduction

In a disaster situation, access to situational information is crucial [29], since such information helps in reducing casualties, preventing secondary disasters, economic losses, and social disruption [3]. In recent times, microblogging sites such as Twitter have played important roles as information media in disaster management [12, 27, 28]. However, in such forums, important information is often obscured by a lot of personal opinions, emotion, and sentiment (e.g., prayers

© Springer International Publishing AG 2018
P. Majumder et al. (Eds.): FIRE 2016 Workshop, LNCS 10478, pp. 20–38, 2018.
https://doi.org/10.1007/978-3-319-73606-8_2

and sympathy for the victims of the disaster). Thus, automated IR techniques are sought to extract precise, meaningful situational information from a large amount of social media text. There have been a few recent studies on identifying specific types of microblogs (or tweets) during disaster situations [1, 27] (see Sect. 2). All these works have used their own datasets, and there has not been much effort till now to develop a standard test collection on which microblog retrieval methodologies can be compared empirically.

The FIRE (Forum for Information Retrieval Evaluation) 2016 Microblog track [10] was motivated by the TREC Microblog Track [19] which aims to evaluate microblog retrieval methodologies. In contrast, the FIRE 2016 Microblog Track focused on microblog retrieval in a disaster situation. The goal of FIRE 2016 Microblog track were two-fold – (i) to develop a benchmark dataset for evaluation of microblog retrieval methodologies during disaster situations, and (ii) to evaluate and compare the performances of various IR methodologies on the benchmark dataset.

In the FIRE 2016 Microblog track, a collection of about 50,000 microblogs posted during a recent disaster – the Nepal Earthquake in April 2015 – was released along with topics reflecting seven realistic information needs during disaster situations (obtained through discussion with agencies who respond to disasters). Minutiae about the collection are specified in Sect. 3. The task was to retrieve microblogs pertinent to the information requirements. Ten teams took part in the task and 15 runs were submitted that are described in Sect. 4. Standard measures of Precision and MAP were used to evaluate the run against the gold standard developed by human annotators. This book chapter describes our experience in organizing the FIRE 2016 Microblog track.

Additionally, in this chapter, we also propose two novel word embedding based retrieval models (using word2vec [17]) for the said task. We also apply two strategies for query expansion via pseudo relevance feedback – the standard Rocchio expansion, and an expansion strategy based on word embeddings (details in Sect. 5). The proposed methodologies perform better than all the methodologies submitted to the FIRE 2016 Microblog track (evaluation results in Sect. 6).

To summarize, our primary contributions are – (i) we develop a test collection for evaluating IR systems for microblog retrieval in disaster situations. (ii) we perform comparative evaluation of several diverse microblog retrieval methodologies, including methodologies involving Natural Language Processing, word embedding, and so on, and (iii) we also propose two novel methodologies for the said task, based on word embeddings, and demonstrate that our proposed methodologies perform better than all the submitted runs in the FIRE 2016 track. In general, we establish that word embedding based retrieval is a promising approach for dealing with the short, noisy nature of microblogs.

2   Related Work

2.1   Developing Test Collections for Evaluating IR Strategies

The Text REtrieval Conference (TREC – http://trec.nist.gov/) was perhaps the first endeavour to present testbeds for standard evaluation of IR systems. They advocated the Cranfield style [6] which states that an IR test collection should comprise three components – (1) Text representations of information needs, called *topics*, (2) A static set of documents, and (3) Relevance status of the documents with respect to a query, called *relevance assessments*. We also adopt this style while preparing our dataset.

The TREC Microblog Track [19] (introduced in 2011) focuses on the evaluation of microblog retrieval strategies in general. Various microblog retrieval tasks have also been organized as part of CLEF[1] and NTCIR.[2] However, to our knowledge, the FIRE 2016 task described in this chapter is the first task designed specifically for microblog retrieval in a real-life disaster situation.

2.2   IR on Microblogs Posted During Disasters

There has been lot of recent interest in addressing various challenges on microblogs posted during disaster events, such as classification, summarization, event detection, and so on. The reader is referred to [12] for a survey on these prior works.

Some datasets of social media posts during disasters have also been developed [7], but they are primarily meant for evaluating methodologies for classification among different types of posts (and not for retrieval methodologies).

Few methodologies for retrieving specific types of microblogs have also been proposed, such as tweets asking for help, and tweets reporting infrastructure damage [1,27]. However, all such studies have used different datasets. To our knowledge, there is no standard test collection for evaluating strategies for microblog retrieval in a disaster scenario; this chapter describes attempts to develop such a test collection.

3   Dataset

In this section, we discuss the procedure for developing the test collection. As stated earlier, we follow the Cranfield style [6] for developing the test collection. The formation of topics (information needs), document set (here, microblogs or tweets) collection and relevance assessment to prepare the gold standard necessary for evaluation of IR methodologies are explained in this section.

---

[1] http://clef2016.clef-initiative.eu/.

[2] http://research.nii.ac.jp/ntcir/index-en.html.

Table 1. Seven topics of interest to agencies who respond to disasters such as earthquakes or floods. Each topic is written following the format used in TREC tracks. The challenge is to retrieve microblogs relevant to each of these topics.

<num> **Number: FMT1** <title> **What resources were available** <desc> Identify the messages which describe the availability of some resources. <narr> A relevant message must mention the availability of some resource like food, drinking water, shelter, clothes, blankets, human resources like volunteers, resources to build or support infrastructure, like tents, water filter, power supply and so on. Messages informing the availability of transport vehicles for assisting the resource distribution process would also be relevant. However, generalized statements without reference to any resource or messages asking for donation of money would not be relevant.
<num> **Number: FMT2** <title> **What resources were required** <desc> Identify the messages which describe the requirement or need of some resources. <narr> A relevant message must mention the requirement / need of some resource like food, water, shelter, clothes, blankets, human resources like volunteers, resources to build or support infrastructure like tents, water filter, power supply, and so on. A message informing the requirement of transport vehicles assisting resource distribution process would also be relevant. However, generalized statements without reference to any particular resource, or messages asking for donation of money would not be relevant.
<num> **Number: FMT3** <title> **What medical resources were available** <desc> Identify the messages which give some information about availability of medicines and other medical resources. <narr> A relevant message must mention the availability of some medical resource like medicines, medical equipments, blood, supplementary food items (e.g., milk for infants), human resources like doctors/staff and resources to build or support medical infrastructure like tents, water filter, power supply, ambulance, etc. Generalized statements without reference to medical resources would not be relevant.
<num> **Number: FMT4** <title> **What medical resources were required** <desc> Identify the messages which describe the requirement of some medicine or other medical resources. <narr> A relevant message must mention the requirement of some medical resource like medicines, medical equipments, supplementary food items, blood, human resources like doctors/staff and resources to build or support medical infrastructure like tents, water filter, power supply, ambulance, etc. Generalized statements without reference to medical resources would not be relevant.
<num> **Number: FMT5** <title> **What were the requirements / availability of resources at specific locations** <desc> Identify the messages which describe the requirement or availability of resources at some particular geographical location. <narr> A relevant message must mention both the requirement or availability of some resource, (e.g., human resources like volunteers/medical staff, food, water, shelter, medical resources, tents, power supply) as well as a particular geographical location. Messages containing only the requirement / availability of some resource, without mentioning a geographical location would not be relevant.
<num> **Number: FMT6** <title> **What were the activities of various NGOs / Government organizations** <desc> Identify the messages which describe on-ground activities of different NGOs and Government organizations. <narr> A relevant message must contain information about relief-related activities of different NGOs and Government organizations in rescue and relief operation. Messages that contain information about the volunteers visiting different geographical locations would also be relevant. However, messages that do not contain the name of any NGO / Government organization would not be relevant.
<num> **Number: FMT7** <title> **What infrastructure damage and restoration were being reported** <desc> Identify the messages which contain information related to infrastructure damage or restoration. <narr> A relevant message must mention the damage or restoration of some specific infrastructure resources, such as structures (e.g., dams, houses, mobile tower), communication infrastructure (e.g., roads, runways, railway), electricity, mobile or Internet connectivity, etc. Generalized statements without reference to infrastructure resources would not be relevant.

3.1   Topics for Retrieval

In this track, our goal was to develop a test collection to evaluate IR methodologies for extracting information (from microblogs) that can essentially help Government agencies and other responding organizations to undertake any disaster situation such as an earthquake or a flood more competently. To this end, we conferred with members of several NGOs like, Doctors For You[3] and SPADE,[4] who regularly work in disaster-affected regions. Our aim was to know what are the conventional information requirements during a humanitarian relief operation. The NGO members helped us to figure out some specific information requirements, such as, what resources are required/available (especially medical resources), what infrastructure damages are being reported, the situation at specific geographical locations, the ongoing activities of various NGOs and government agencies (so that the operations of various responding agencies can be coordinated), and so on. Based on their opinion, *seven* pertinent topics (information needs) were identified.

The topics, developed as a part of the test collection, are written in the format typically used for TREC topics in Table 1. Each topic contains an identifying number (num), a textual representation of the information need (title), a brief description (desc) of the same and a more detailed narrative (narr) explaining what type of documents (tweets) will be considered relevant to the topic, and what type of tweets would not be considered relevant.

3.2   Tweet Dataset

A destructive earthquake occurred in Nepal and parts of India on 25th April 2015. Tweets related to the Nepal earthquake, posted during the two weeks following the earthquake, were extracted through the Twitter Search API [26], using the keyword 'nepal'. In total, we collected 100 K tweets written in English (where the language recognition is done by Twitter itself).

It is known that some tweets are usually retweeted/reposted by multiple users [25], especially during events like a disaster. Thus, there is likely to be a considerable presence of duplicates and near-duplicates in the set of tweets. However, the presence of duplicates can result in over-estimation of the performance of an IR methodology. Hence, it is preferred that duplicates should not be present in a test collection for IR. Moreover, while developing the gold standard, the occurrence of duplicate documents also leads to overwork for human annotators [14]. Therefore, we removed duplicate and near-duplicate tweets using a simplified version of the methodologies illustrated in [25], as follows. Initially, tweets are pre-processed by excluding standard English stopwords and URLs. Subsequently considering each tweet as a bag of words, the similarity between two tweets was measured as the Jaccard similarity between the two corresponding bags (sets) of words. Two tweets were considered as near-duplicates if the Jaccard similarity between two tweets was measured to be greater than a threshold value (0.7). The longer tweet (potentially more informative) was retained in the collection.

After eliminating duplicates and near-duplicates, we obtained a set of 50,068 tweets, which was used as the test collection for the track.

---

[3] http://doctorsforyou.org/.

[4] http://www.spadeindia.org/.

3.3 Developing Gold Standard for Retrieval

The gold standard or ground truth judgment of relevance is a principal requirement in the evaluation of any IR methodology. We involved a set of three human
annotators in developing the gold standard. Each of the annotators is a regu-
lar user of Twitter, has proficiency in English and has preceding experience of
working with social media content posted during disasters. The gold standard
was developed in three phases.

Phase 1: Each annotator was given the set of 50,068 tweets, and the seven
topics (in TREC format, as stated in Table 1). Each annotator was instructed to
identify all tweets relevant to each topic, separately, i.e., without conferring with
the other annotators. The tweets were indexed using the well-known Indri IR
system [24], to aid the annotators to search for tweets containing specific terms.
For each topic, The annotators were instructed to figure out appropriate search
terms for each topic, retrieve tweets containing those search terms (using Indri),
and to manually judge the relevance of the retrieved tweets.

After the first phase, it is observed that the set of tweets identified to be
relevant to the same topic by different annotators was notably dissimilar. This
difference was because different annotators used different search terms to retrieve
tweets.[5] Thus, a second phase was conducted.

Phase 2: In the second phase, for each topic, we considered the tweets that were
judged relevant in the first phase by *at least one* of the annotators. The judgment
on the topic-wise relevance of the tweet was confirmed through discussion among
all the annotators and mutual agreement.

Phase 3: This phase used standard pooling [23] over all runs submitted to
the FIRE 2016 track (as commonly done in TREC tracks) - for each topic the
top ranked 30 tweets of all the submitted runs were pooled and annotated. In
the third phase, all annotators were judging a common set of tweets; hence
inter-annotator agreement could be measured. There was agreement among all
annotators for over 90% of the tweets; for the rest, the relevance was decided
through discussion among all the annotators and mutual agreement.

The final ground truth judgment of relevance includes the tweets pertinent
to the seven topics. For each topic, number of relevant tweets and corresponding
examples are illustrated in Table 2.

3.4 Insights from the Gold Standard Development Process

Through the process of developing the ground truth, we realize that for any of
the topics, there are numerous tweets which are definitely relevant to the topic,
but hard to retrieve even by manual annotation. This is apparent from the fact
that, many of the relevant tweets could initially be retrieved by only one out of
the three annotators (in the first phase), but when the tweets were shown to the

---

[5] Since the different annotators potentially judged different sets of tweets, reporting
inter-annotator agreement would not be meaningful under these circumstances.

Table 2. Final ground truth judgment of relevance pertinent to the seven topics.

Topic	Relevant tweets	Example tweets
FMT1	589	Bharat Sevashram Sangha started relief work in earthquake hit Nepal. Cooked food being distributed in the outskirts of Kathmandu
FMT2	301	#SoulVultures: Pickaxes, shovels and earth-moving equipment required in Nepal. [url]
FMT3	334	mount of supplies may be used for more than 7 days. Mobile Hospital is equipped to even perform a surgery. #earthquake #Nepal #Kathmandu
FMT4	112	THT - Hospitals may face shortage of oxygen and medicine [url]
FMT5	189	RT @Goal_Nepal Sahara Club Sends Bottled Water, Noodles To Gorkha, Lamjung For Earthquake Victims READ: [url]
FMT6	377	We @CFCT_INDIA are collecting Blankets for Nepal earthquake victims. please contact ......[mobile-no] [url]
FMT7	254	#NBC #News Runway Damage Closes Nepal Airport to Heavy Planes: Earthquake-struck Nepal has been forced to clos... [url]

other annotators (in the second phase), they unanimously agreed that the tweet was relevant. These observations highlight the challenges in microblog retrieval.

It is to be noted that our process of developing the gold standard is dissimilar from the approach used in TREC tracks, where the gold standard is normally developed by annotating few top-ranked documents, retrieved by different submitted systems. In other words, only the standard pooling phase (as described in Phase 3) is applied in TREC tracks.

Given that it is challenging to identify many of the tweets relevant to a topic (as discussed above), annotating only a relatively small pool of documents retrieved by IR methodologies has the potential risk of missing many of the relevant documents which are more difficult to retrieve. We believe that our approach, where the annotators searched through the entire dataset instead of a relatively small pool, is likely to be more robust, and is expected to have resulted in the development of a complete gold standard which is irrespective of the performance of any IR methodology.

4 Baseline Methodologies Submitted to the FIRE 2016 Track

The participants of the FIRE 2016 track were given the tweet collection and the seven topics described earlier.[6] The participants were invited to develop IR

---

[6] Note that the Twitter terms and conditions prohibit direct public sharing of tweets. Hence, only the tweet-ids of the tweets were distributed among the participants, along with a Python script using which the tweets can be downloaded via the Twitter API.

methodologies for retrieving tweets relevant to each of the seven topics, and submit a ranked list of tweets that they judge relevant to each topic. The ranked list was evaluated based on the gold standard (developed as described earlier).

The track invited three types of methodologies – (i) *Automatic*, where both query formulation and retrieval are automated, and (ii) *Semi-automatic*, where manual intervention is involved in the query formulation stage (but not in the retrieval stage), and (iii) *Manual*, where manual intervention is involved in both query formulation and retrieval stages.

Ten teams participated in the FIRE 2016 Microblog track, submitting 15 runs in total, out of which, one run was fully automatic, while the others were semi-automatic. A summary of the methodologies used by each team is discussed in this section.

dcu_fmt16 [13]: This team participated from ADAPT Centre, School of Computing, Dublin City University, Ireland and applied WordNet[7] for query expansion. It submitted the following two runs:

1. *dcu_fmt16_1:* This is an *Automatic* run. The initial query was created from the words in *title* and *narr*, from which the stopwords were removed. For each word in the query thus formed, the expanded query was frormed by adding the synonyms using WordNet. This expanded query was used for retrieval based on the BM25 model [21].
2. *dcu_fmt16_2:* This is a *Semi-automatic* run. An initial ranked list was created from the original topic. From the top retrieved 30 tweets, 1–2 relevant tweets were manually identified from which query expansion was done. This expanded query was expanded further using WordNet like *dcu_fmt16_1* and used for retrieval.

iiest_saptarashmi_bandyopadhyay [2]: This team participated from Indian Institute of Engineering Science and Technology, Shibpur, India. It submitted one *Semi-automatic* run described below:

- *iiest_saptarashmi_bandyopadhyay_1:* The relevance score for a given topic-tweet pair was determined by the correlation between the topic words and the tweet. The Stanford NER tagger[8] was applied to identify the LOCATION, ORGANIZATION and PERSON names in the tweets. For each topic, a number of tools (e.g., PyDictionary, NodeBox toolkit etc.) was applied on some manually selected keywords. These were used to find the corresponding synonyms, inflectional variants etc. The bag of words were converted into a vector using Word2Vec package.[9] The relevance score was computed from the correlation between the vector representations of the topic words and the tweet text.

---

[7] https://wordnet.princeton.edu/.

[8] nlp.stanford.edu/software/Stanford-ner-2015-04-20.zip.

[9] https://deeplearning4j.org/word2vec.

JU_NLP [8]: This team participated from Jadavpur University, India. It submitted three *Semi-automatic* runs described as below:

1. *JU_NLP_1:* For each topic, relevant words were hand-picked. Query expansion was done with the synonyms obtained from NLTK WordNet toolkit. Past, past participle and present continuous forms of verbs were obtained using the NodeBox library for Python. For the topics FMT5 and FMT6, Stanford NER tagger was used to identify the location and organization information. GloVe [20] model was trained on the twitter collection. For a tweet-query pair, a tweet vector and a query vector was formed by taking the normalized summation of the GloVe vector of the constituent words. For each pair, the similarity score was computed by the cosine similarity of the corresponding vectors.
2. *JU_NLP_2:* This run is similar to *JU_NLP_1* except that here word bags were split categorically. Then, average similarity between the tweet vector and the split topic vectors was calculated.
3. *JU_NLP_3:* This is identical to *JU_NLP_2*.

iitbhu_fmt16 [22]: This team participated from Department of Computer Science and Engineering, Indian Institute of Technology (BHU) Varanasi, India. It submitted one *Semi-automatic* run – *iitbhu_fmt16_1* described as follows:

- *iitbhu_fmt16_1:* The run was generated using the Lucene[10] default similarity model, which combines Vector Space Model (VSM) and probabilistic models (e.g., BM25). StandardAnalyzer was used to handle names, email address, lowercasing of each token and removal of stopwords and punctuations. Manual intervention was done in the the query formulation stage.

daiict_irlab [18]: This team participated from DAIICT, Gandhinagar, India and LDRP, Gandhinagar, India. It submitted two *Semi-automatic* runs described as follows:

1. *daiict_irlab_1:* In this run, the 5 most similar words and hashtags from the Word2vec model, trained on the tweet corpus, were added to the original query. Equal weight was assigned to each term.
2. *daiict_irlab_2:* This run was produced in the same way as *daiict_irlab_1* except that different weights were assigned to the expanded terms than the original terms. Higher weights were assigned to the words like *required* and *available*. Query expansion was also done using WordNet.

trish_iiest [9]: This team participated from Indian Institute of Engineering Science and Technology, Shibpur, India. It submitted two *Semi-automatic* runs described below:

---

[10] https://lucene.apache.org/ (2016, August 20).

1. *trish_iiest_ss:* The similarity score between a query and a tweet was computed from the word-overlap between them and then normalized by the query length. For each topic, the query was formed by the nouns, identified by the Stanford Part-Of-Speech Tagger. Higher weight was assigned to the words like *availability* or *requirement.*
2. *trish_iiest_ws:* In this run, the overlap score was calculated using the synsets of each term obtained from WordNet.

nita_nitmz [4]: This team participated from National Institute of Technology, Agartala, India and National Institute of Technology, Mizoram. It submitted one *Semi-supervised* run described as below:

- *nita_nitmz_1:* Apache Nutch 0.9 was used for this run to perform search using the different combination of words present in the query. The final result was obtained by merging the results generated by different combinations of query.

Helpingtech [5]: This team participated from Indian Institute of Technology, Patna, Bihar, India and submitted the following *Semi-automatic* run (on 5 topics only):

- *Helpingtech_1:* For this run, relationships entities and action verbs were defined through manual inspection. The ranking score was calculated on the basis of the presence of these relationships in the tweet for a given query. Higher consideration was given to a tweet which indicated immediate action than a one which suggested a proposed action for future.

GANJI [15]: This team participated from Èvora University, Portugal. It submitted retrieval results for the first three topics only using *Semi-automatic* methodology, described below:

- *GANJI:* Keywords were extracted using Part-of-speech tagger, Word2Vec (to obtain the *nouns*) and WordNet (to obtain the *verbs*). Retrieval was performed on Terrier[11] using the BM25 model. SVM classifier was used to classify the retrieved tweets into *available*, *required* and *other* classes.

relevancer_ru_nl [11]: This team participated from Radboud University, the Netherlands and submitted the following *Semi-automatic* run:

- *relevancer_ru_nl:* A tool *Relevancer* was used to generate this run. First, the tweet collection was clustered to identify *coherent* clusters. Each *coherent* cluster was manually labelled by some experts as "relevant" or "not relevant". This training data was fed into a Naive Bayes classifier. The test tweets, which were predicted as relevant by the classifier, were submitted.

From the above descriptions, it is evident that a wide variety of methodologies were applied, including traditional IR methodologies, methodologies using NLP, as well as methodologies based on recent advances like word embeddings.

---

[11] http://terrier.org.

5   Proposed Methodology

In addition to the methodologies submitted by the FIRE 2016 participants (described in the previous section), we now propose a novel methodology for the microblog retrieval task.

We start by observing that the topics FMT1, FMT2, FMT3, FMT4 and FMT7 are more general, and any tweet containing suitable information would be relevant to these topics. However, the topics FMT5 and FMT6 need some special consideration. In case of FMT5, relevant tweets should have a reference of location (in addition to the context of need and availability), and for FMT6, the relevant tweets must contain the reference to an organization (Government organization/NGO). Hence, we first describe a general IR methodology for the topics FMT1, FMT2, FMT3, FMT4 and FMT7, and then later describe the distinct methodology for FMT5 and FMT6.

5.1   Proposed Methodology for Topics FMT1, FMT2, FMT3, FMT4 and FMT7

For the topics FMT1, FMT2, FMT3, FMT4 and FMT7, we consider three stages in the retrieval – (i) generating a query from the topic, (ii) retrieving and ranking microblogs with respect to the query, and (iii) expanding the query, and subsequently retrieving and ranking microblogs with respect to the expanded query. These steps are described next.

Query generation from topics: For a given topic, we consider the query to be a set of terms (unigrams) extracted from the text of the topic (stated in Table 1). Specifically, terms are extracted from the narrative part of the topic, as follows.

For all the topics, a standard set of English stopwords are ignored, and terms which appear in the narrative of at least four out of the five topics (e.g., 'message', 'mention') are ignored. Additionally, the last sentence of the narrative, which mentions what type of tweets would *not* be relevant, is ignored. Next, an English part-of-speech (POS) tagger[12] is applied on the rest of the narrative text, and *nouns, verbs*, and *adjectives* (terms which are tagged as 'NN', 'VB', and 'JJ' by the POS tagger) are extracted.[13] The selected terms are stemmed using the standard Porter stemmer, and the query is considered as a bag of the stemmed terms. Table 3 shows the automatically generated queries (showing the terms obtained after stemming) for the five topics.

Microblog retrieval and ranking: We now describe the proposed methodology of retrieving microblogs for a given query. The tweets are pre-processed by removing a standard set of English stopwords, URLs and punctuation symbols, and all terms whose frequency in the entire corpus is less than 5 are also ignored. The remaining terms are then stemmed using the standard Porter stemmer. Thus, each tweet is considered as a bag/set of terms (stemmed).

---

[12] The POS tagger included in the Python Natural Language Toolkit was used.

[13] We also tried retrieval with other parts of speech, and observed that forming the query out of nouns, verbs, and adjectives, gives the best retrieval performance.

Table 3. Queries for the five topics FMT1, FMT2, FMT3, FMT4 and FMT7. Each query is a set of unigrams selected from the text of the topics, and then stemmed.

Topic	Query terms
FMT1: What resources were available	Avail, blanket, cloth, distribut, drink, process, shelter, transport, vehicl, volunt
FMT2: What resources were required	Blanket, cloth, distribut, need, process, requir, shelter, transport, vehicl, volunt
FMT3: What medical resources were available	Ambul, avail, blood, doctor, equip, infant, item, medic, medicin, milk, staff, supplementari
FMTT4: What medical resources were required	Ambul, blood, doctor, equip, item, medic, medicin, requir, staff, supplementari
FMT7: What infrastructure damage and restoration were being reported	Commun, connect, dam, damag, electr, hous, internet, mobil, railwai, restor, road, runwai, specif, structur, tower

We employ a simplistic word2vec [17] based retrieval model which is suitable for short documents like tweets. We first trained word2vec over the pre-processed set of tweets.[14] Specifically, the continuous bag of words model is used for the training, along with Hierarchical softmax, and the following parameter values – Vector size: 2000, Context size: 5, Learning rate: 0.05. The word2vec model gives a vector (of dimension 2000, as decided by the parameters) for each term in the corpus, which we refer to as *term-vectors*. The term-vector for a particular term is expected to capture the context in which the term has been frequently used.

For a given query (which we consider as a set of terms, as described above), we derive a *query-vector* by summing the term-vectors of all terms in the query. Since the word2vec term-vectors are additive – i.e., they can be added or subtracted to respectively include or exclude the semantic representations of the corresponding terms [17] – we expect the query-vector to capture the collective context of all the terms in the query. For instance, the sum of the vectors for the terms 'need' and 'food' will capture the context of food being needed.

Similarly, for each tweet, we derive a *tweet-vector* by summing the term-vectors of all terms contained in the pre-processed tweet (as described above). For retrieving tweets for a given query, we compute the cosine similarity between the corresponding query-vector and each tweet-vector, and rank the tweets in decreasing order of the cosine similarity.

Query expansion: Query expansion is the process of adding some relevant terms to the query, in an attempt to improve retrieval performance (especially the recall). We consider the *pseudo (or blind) relevance feedback* setting [16] – after documents are retrieved using a particular query, a small number of the

---

[14] The Gensim implementation for word2vec was used – https://radimrehurek.com/gensim/models/word2vec.html.

top-ranked documents are assumed to be relevant, and certain terms are selected from the top retrieved documents to add to the query.

We consider two approaches for query expansion – Rocchio expansion with pseudo relevance feedback [16], and the other based on word2vec, as described below. For both approaches, we consider the 10 top-ranked tweets retrieved by the original query, and select $p = 5$ terms from these 10 top-ranked tweets to expand the query.

Rocchio expansion: For each distinct term in the 10 top-ranked tweets retrieved by the original query, the $tf \times idf$ Rocchio scores are computed, where tf is the frequency of the term among the 10 top-ranked tweets, and idf is the inverse document frequency of the term over the entire corpus. and the top p terms in the decreasing order of Rocchio scores are selected for expanding the query.

Query expansion using word2vec: As stated earlier, the query-vector is expected to capture the overall context of a query. After retrieving tweets using the initial query, we identify a set of terms within the 10 top-ranked tweets, which are most related to the context of the query, and use these terms to expand the query. Specifically, we compute the cosine similarity of the query-vector with the term-vector of every distinct term in the 10 top-ranked tweets, and select those p terms for which the term-vector has highest cosine similarity with the query-vector.

Table 4 states the expansion terms (stemmed) obtained by the two strategies for some of the topics.

Table 4. Expansion terms (stemmed) for the initial queries (stated in Table 3), obtained through Rocchio expansion and word2vec-based expansion.

Topic: FMT1	Topic: FMT2	Topic: FMT7
Query expansion by Rocchio method		
Food, medicin, shelter, tent, water	Food, medicin, need, sanit, water	Beyond, damag, hous, repair, road
Query expansion using word2vec		
Biscuit, hygien, medicin, sanit, tem	Biscuit, hygien, medicin, necess, sanit	Cheaper, inspect, partial, scout, sprint

5.2   Proposed Methodology for Topics FMT5 and FMT6

As stated earlier, we adopted a different approach for the topics FMT5 (what were requirement/availability of resources at specific location) and FMT6 (what were the activities of various NGOs/Government organizations). From Table 1, it is evident that the sets of tweets relevant to these two topics are actually subsets of the combined set of tweets relevant to the topics FMT1, FMT2, FMT3 and FMT4. Specifically, if we consider the combined set of tweets relevant to the topics FMT1, FMT2, FMT3 and FMT4, then the subset of these tweets that contain a specific location would be relevant to FMT5. Similarly, the subset of tweets which contain the name of an organization would be relevant to FMT6.

Hence, we adopted the following strategy for FMT5 and FMT6. First, we considered the combined set of retrieved tweets judged as relevant to the topics FMT1, FMT2, FMT3 and FMT4, by any of the methodologies described earlier, and obtained the top-ranked 4,000 tweets from this set.[15]

Next, we applied the Stanford Named Entity Recognition (NER) tagger[16] on the selected tweets, to identify location and organization references. The Stanford NER tagger labels locations present in a text as LOCATION, and organization names as ORGANIZATION. The tweets which were found to contain a location reference were considered relevant to FMT5, and the tweets which were found to contain the name of an organization were considered relevant to FMT6.

Finally, we rank the tweets that were judged relevant to FMT5/FMT6. A query-vector was formed for FMT5/FMT6 by summing the query-vectors for FMT1, FMT2, FMT3 and FMT4 (considering the expanded queries, following the Rocchio expansion or the word2vec-based expansion strategy). The tweets were ranked according to the cosine similarity of the tweet-vectors and the query-vector, as described earlier.

6   Experimental Results

In this section, we discuss the performance of the methodologies described in the previous sections – the methodologies submitted to the FIRE 2016 Microblog track, and the two proposed methodologies. Ideally, for a given topic, an IR methodology should retrieve only the relevant microblogs (i.e., high precision) and all the relevant microblogs (i.e., high recall). So, we consider the following measures to evaluate the performance of an IR methodology – (i) *Precision at 20* (Prec@20), i.e., what fraction of the top-ranked 20 results are actually relevant according to the gold standard, (ii) *Mean Average Precision* (MAP) considering the full retrieved ranked list.

Table 5 reports the retrieval performance for all the submitted runs, along with our proposed methodologies. It is evident that, among the methodologies which attempted retrieval for all seven topics, our proposed methodologies have outperformed all the other methodologies submitted to the FIRE 2016 Microblog track.

Table 6 represents topic-wise MAP score of submitted and proposed methodologies. The MAP score of proposed methodologies, for a large majority of the topics, are significantly better than all the other methodologies as evident from the Table 6.

In general, we observe that most of the methodologies which performed well, applied query expansion and word embedding techniques (like word2vec and glove). The better performance of such methodologies can probably be explained

---

[15] We had many ties among the rankings, e.g., the top-ranked tweet for FMT1 and the top-ranked tweet for FMT2 both had same rank.

[16] nlp.stanford.edu/software/Stanford-ner-2015-04-20.zip.

Table 5. Comparison among all the methodologies submitted to FIRE 2016 track, and the two proposed methodologies. Methodologies which attempted retrieval only for a subset of the topics are listed separately at the end of the table.

Methodology	Prec@20	MAP	Type	Method summary
Proposed Methodology 1	0.4428	0.1800	Automatic	Word2vec Expansion and Word2vec Ranking, NER tagger
Proposed Methodology 2	0.4357	0.1829	Automatic	Rocchio Expansion and Word2vec Ranking, NER tagger
dcu_fmt16_1	0.3786	0.1103	Automatic	WordNet, Query Expansion
iiest_saptarashmi _bandyopadhyay_1	0.4357	0.1125	Semi-automatic	Correlation, NER, Word2vec
JU_NLP_1	0.4357	0.1079	Semi-automatic	WordNet, Query Expansion, NER, GloVe
dcu_fmt16_2	0.4286	0.0815	Semi-automatic	WordNet, Query Expansion, Relevance Feedback
JU_NLP_2	0.3714	0.0881	Semi-automatic	WordNet, Query Expansion, NER, GloVe, word bags split
JU_NLP_3	0.3714	0.0881	Semi-automatic	WordNet, Query Expansion, NER, GloVe, word bags split
iitbhu_fmt16_1	0.3214	0.0827	Semi-automatic	Lucene default model
relevancer_ru_nl	0.3143	0.0406	Semi-automatic	Relevancer system, Clustering, Manual labelling, Naive Bayes classification
daiict_irlab_1	0.3143	0.0275	Semi-automatic	Word2vec, Query Expansion, equal term weight
daiict_irlab_2	0.3000	0.0250	Semi-automatic	Word2vec, Query Expansion, unequal term weights, WordNet
trish_iiest_ss	0.0929	0.0203	Semi-automatic	Word-overlap, POS tagging
trish_iiest_ws	0.0786	0.0099	Semi-automatic	WordNet, POS tagging
nita_nitmz_1	0.0583	0.0031	Semi-automatic	Apache Nutch 0.9, query segmentation, result merging
Helpingtech_1 (only 5 topics)	0.7700	0.2208	Semi-automatic	Entity and action verbs relationships, Temporal Importance
GANJI (only 3 topics)	0.8500	0.2420	Semi-automatic	Keyword extraction, Part-of-speech tagger, Word2vec, WordNet, Terrier, SVM classification

Table 6. MAP score of different methodologies, for each of the seven topics.

Methodology	FMT1	FMT2	FMT3	FMT4	FMT5	FMT6	FMT7
Proposed Methodology 1	0.3448	0.2073	0.4217	0.0735	0.0369	0.1022	0.0850
Proposed Methodology 2	0.3322	0.2255	0.4151	0.0768	0.0368	0.0934	0.1004
dcu_fmt16_1	0.0569	0.1730	0.2677	0.0599	0.0306	0.0087	0.1753
iiest_saptarashmi _bandyopadhyay_1	0.1571	0.1234	0.2158	0.1212	0.0290	0.0365	0.1046
JU_NLP_1	0.1530	0.1151	0.2374	0.0905	0.0211	0.0369	0.1014
dcu_fmt16_2	0.0596	0.0853	0.2198	0.0791	0.0274	0.0722	0.0269
JU_NLP_2	0.1055	0.1146	0.1468	0.1047	0.0198	0.0196	0.1057
JU_NLP_3	0.1055	0.1146	0.1468	0.1047	0.0198	0.0196	0.1057
iitbhu_fmt16_1	0.1036	0.2102	0.0275	0.1856	0.0212	0.0054	0.0257
relevancer_ru_nl	0.0913	0.0459	0.0586	0.0036	0.0027	0.0414	0.0409
daiict_irlab_1	0.0257	0.0649	0.0281	0.0502	0.0033	0.0030	0.0176
daiict_irlab_2	0.0190	0.0702	0.0086	0.0415	0.0175	0.0004	0.0175
trish_iiest_ss	0.0234	0.0404	0.0064	0.0270	0.0171	0.0200	0.0079
trish_iiest_ws	0.0134	0.0128	0.0088	0.0074	0.0088	0.0137	0.0042
nita_nitmz_1	0.0000	0.0007	0.0087	0.0090	0.0000	-	0.0000
Helpingtech_1	0.1824	0.2516	0.2201	0.2852	-	-	0.1648
GANJI	0.2270	0.3401	0.1588	-	-	-	-

as follows. Short, informally-written microblogs that are relevant to a topic often do *not* contain key terms that are seemingly important for the topic. For instance, we found that a considerable fraction of the microblogs relevant to a topic *do not contain any of the terms in the corresponding query.* In such scenarios, query expansion is useful for inclusion of relevant terms in the query. Additionally, word embedding methods can better match the semantic context of a microblog with the context of the query, even if the same terms are not present in the two.

7   Conclusion

The primary contribution of the FIRE 2016 Microblog track was the creation of a benchmark collection of microblogs posted during disaster events, and comparison among the performance of various IR methodologies over the collection. Additionally, in this book chapter, we have proposed IR methodologies that have performed better than all the methodologies submitted to the FIRE track.

In future, several extensions of the work can be considered:

- Instead of just considering binary relevance (where a tweet is either relevant to a topic or not), graded relevance can be considered, e.g., based on factors like how actionable the information contained in the tweet is, how useful the tweet is likely to be to the agencies responding to the disaster, and so on.

- The work described in this chapter considered a static set of microblogs. But in reality, microblogs are obtained in a continuous stream. The challenge can be extended to retrieve relevant microblogs dynamically, e.g., as and when they are posted.

Furthermore, it can be noted that even the best performing methodology described in this book chapter achieved relatively low MAP scores, which highlights the difficulty and challenges in microblog retrieval during a disaster situation. We hope that the test collection developed in this work will help development of better models for microblog retrieval in future.

Acknowledgement. We thank the FIRE organizing committee for allowing us to run the track, and all participating teams for their participation. This research was partially supported by a grant from the Information Technology Research Academy (ITRA), MeITY, Government of India (Ref. No.: ITRA/15 (58)/Mobile/DISARM/05).

References

1. AIDR - Artificial Intelligence for Disaster Response. https://irevolutions.org/2013/10/01/aidr-artificial-intelligence-for-disaster-response/
2. Bandyopadhyay, S.: Correlation distance based information extraction system at FIRE 2016 Microblog Track. In: Working notes for the 2016 Conference of the Forum for Information Retrieval Evaluation (FIRE), CEUR Workshop Proceedings. CEUR-WS.org, December 2016
3. Basu, M., Bandyopadhyay, S., Ghosh, S.: Post disaster situation awareness and decision support through interactive crowdsourcing. In: Proceedings of International Conference on Humanitarian Technology: Science, Systems and Global Impact (HumTech), Procedia Engineering, pp. 167–173. Elsevier (2016)
4. Bhardwaj, P., Pakray, P.: Information extraction from Microblogs. In: Working Notes for the 2016 Conference of the Forum for Information Retrieval Evaluation (FIRE), CEUR Workshop Proceedings. CEUR-WS.org, December 2016
5. Chakraborty, R., Bhavsar, M.: Information Retrieval from Microblogs during natural disasters. In: Working Notes for the 2016 Conference of the Forum for Information Retrieval Evaluation (FIRE), CEUR Workshop Proceedings. CEUR-WS.org, December 2016
6. Cleverdon, C.: The cranfield tests on index language devices. In: Sparck Jones, K., Willett, P. (eds.) Readings in Information Retrieval, pp. 47–59. Morgan Kaufmann Publishers Inc., San Francisco (1997)
7. CrisisLex: Crisis-related Social Media Data and Tools. http://crisislex.org/
8. Dasgupta, S., Kumar, A., Das, D., Naskar, S.K., Bandyopadhyay, S.: Word embeddings for information extraction from tweets. In: Working notes for the 2016 Conference of the Forum for Information Retrieval Evaluation (FIRE), CEUR Workshop Proceedings. CEUR-WS.org, December 2016
9. Ghorai, T.: An information retrieval system for FIRE 2016 Microblog Track. In: Working Notes for the 2016 Conference of the Forum for Information Retrieval Evaluation (FIRE), CEUR Workshop Proceedings. CEUR-WS.org, December 2016

10. Ghosh, S., Ghosh, K.: Overview of the FIRE 2016 Microblog Track: information extraction from microblogs posted during disasters. In: Working Notes of FIRE 2016 - Forum for Information Retrieval Evaluation, Kolkata, India, pp. 56–61. 7–10 December 2016. http://ceur-ws.org/Vol-1737/T2-1.pdf

11. Hürriyetoğlu, A., van den Bosch, A., Oostdijk, N.: Relevant tweet detection in Nepal earthquake with relevancer. In: Working notes for the 2016 Conference of the Forum for Information Retrieval Evaluation (FIRE), CEUR Workshop Proceedings. CEUR-WS.org, December 2016

12. Imran, M., Castillo, C., Diaz, F., Vieweg, S.: Processing social media messages in mass emergency: a survey. ACM Comput. Surv. **47**(4), 67:1–67:38 (2015)

13. Li, W., Ganguly, D., Jones, G.J.F.: Using WordNet for query expansion: ADAPT@ FIRE 2016 Microblog Track. In: Working Notes for the 2016 Conference of the Forum for Information Retrieval Evaluation (FIRE), CEUR Workshop Proceedings. CEUR-WS.org, December 2016

14. Lin, J., Efron, M., Wang, Y., Sherman, G., Voorhees, E.: Overview of the TREC-2015 Microblog Track. In: Proceedings of Text Retrieval Conference (TREC) (2015). http://trec.nist.gov/pubs/trec24/papers/Overview-MB.pdf

15. Lkhagvasuren, G., Gonçalves, T., Saias, J.: Semi-automatic keyword based approach for FIRE 2016 Microblog Track. In: Working Notes for the 2016 Conference of the Forum for Information Retrieval Evaluation (FIRE), CEUR Workshop Proceedings. CEUR-WS.org, December 2016

16. Manning, C.D., Raghavan, P., Schütze, H.: Introduction to Information Retrieval. Cambridge University Press, New York (2008)

17. Mikolov, T., Yih, W., Zweig, G.: Linguistic regularities in continuous space word representations. In: NAACL HLT 2013 (2013)

18. Modha, S., Mandalia, C., Agrawal, K., Verma, D., Majumder, P.: Real time information extraction from Microblog. In: Working Notes for the 2016 Conference of the Forum for Information Retrieval Evaluation (FIRE), CEUR Workshop Proceedings. CEUR-WS.org, December 2016

19. Ounis, I., Macdonald, C., Lin, J., Soboroff, I.: Overview of the TREC-2011 Microblog Track. In: Proceedings of Text Retrieval Conference (TREC) (2011). http://trec.nist.gov/pubs/trec20/papers/MICROBLOG.OVERVIEW.pdf

20. Pennington, J., Socher, R., Manning, C.D.: Glove: global vectors for word representation. In: Empirical Methods in Natural Language Processing (EMNLP), pp. 1532–1543 (2014). http://www.aclweb.org/anthology/D14-1162

21. Robertson, S.E., Zaragoza, H.: The probabilistic relevance framework: BM25 and beyond. Found. Trends Inf. Retr. **3**(4), 333–389 (2009)

22. Soni, R., Pal, S.: IIT BHU at FIRE 2016 Microblog Track: a semi-automatic Microblog retrieval system. In: Working Notes for the 2016 Conference of the Forum for Information Retrieval Evaluation (FIRE), CEUR Workshop Proceedings. CEUR-WS.org, December 2016

23. Sparck Jones, K., van Rijsbergen, C.: Report on the need for and provision of an ideal information retrieval test collection. Technical report 5266, Computer Laboratory, University of Cambridge, UK (1975)

24. Strohman, T., Metzler, D., Turtle, H., Croft, W.B.: Indri: a language model-based search engine for complex queries. In: Proceedings of ICIA (2004). http://www.lemurproject.org/indri/

25. Tao, K., Abel, F., Hauff, C., Houben, G.J., Gadiraju, U.: Groundhog day: near-duplicate detection on Twitter. In: Proceedings of World Wide Web (WWW) (2013)

26. Twitter Search API. https://dev.twitter.com/rest/public/search
27. Varga, I., et al.: Aid is out there: looking for help from tweets during a large scale disaster. In: Proceedings of ACL (2013)
28. Vieweg, S., Hughes, A.L., Starbird, K., Palen, L.: Microblogging during two natural hazards events: what Twitter may contribute to situational awareness. In: Proceedings of ACM SIGCHI (2010)
29. World Disasters Report 2013 - Focus on technology and the future of humanitarian action (2013). http://www.ifrc.org/PageFiles/134658/WDR2013complete.pdf

Overview of the Mixed Script Information Retrieval (MSIR) at FIRE-2016

Somnath Banerjee[1]([✉]), Kunal Chakma[2], Sudip Kumar Naskar[1], Amitava Das[3], Paolo Rosso[4], Sivaji Bandyopadhyay[1], and Monojit Choudhury[5]

[1] Jadavpur University, Kolkata, India
`sb.cse.ju@gmail.com`, {`sudip.naskar,sbandyopadhyay`}`@cse.jdvu.ac.in`
[2] NIT Agartala, Jirania, India
`kchax4377@gmail.com`
[3] IIIT Sriharikota, Sricity, India
`amitava.santu@gmail.com`
[4] Universitat Politècnica de València, Valencia, Spain
`prosso@dsic.upv.es`
[5] Microsoft Research India, Bengaluru, India
`monojitc@microsoft.com`

Abstract. The shared task on Mixed Script Information Retrieval (MSIR) was organized for the fourth year in FIRE-2016. The track had two subtasks. Subtask-1 was on question classification where questions were in code mixed Bengali-English and Bengali was written in transliterated Roman script. Subtask-2 was on ad-hoc retrieval of Hindi film song lyrics, movie reviews and astrology documents, where both the queries and documents were in Hindi either written in Devanagari script or in Roman transliterated form. A total of 33 runs were submitted by 9 participating teams, of which 20 runs were for subtask-1 by 7 teams and 13 runs for subtask-2 by 7 teams. The overview presents a comprehensive report of the subtasks, datasets and performances of the submitted runs.

Keywords: Mixed Script Information Retrieval
Code Mixed Question Answering · Code-mixed tweets

1 Introduction

A large number of languages, including Arabic, Russian, and most of the South and South East Asian languages like Bengali, Hindi etc., have their own indigenous scripts. However, websites and user generated content (such as tweets and blogs) in these languages are written using Roman script due to various socio-cultural and technological reasons [1]. This process of phonetically representing the words of a language in a non-native script is called transliteration. English being the most popular language of the web, transliteration, especially into the

---

A preliminary non-peer-reviewed version has been published as working notes.

© Springer International Publishing AG 2018
P. Majumder et al. (Eds.): FIRE 2016 Workshop, LNCS 10478, pp. 39–49, 2018.
https://doi.org/10.1007/978-3-319-73606-8_3

Roman script, is used abundantly on the Web not only for documents, but also for user queries that intend to search for these documents. This situation, where both documents and queries can be in more than one script, and the user expectation could be to retrieve documents across scripts is referred to as Mixed Script Information Retrieval (MSIR).

The MSIR shared task was introduced in 2013 as "Transliterated Search" at FIRE-2013 [15]. Two pilot subtasks on transliterated search were introduced as a part of the FIRE-2013 shared task on MSIR. Subtask-1 was on language identification of the query words and subsequent back transliteration of the Indian language words. The subtask was conducted for three Indian languages - Hindi, Bengali and Gujarati. Subtask-2 was on ad hoc retrieval of Bollywood song lyrics - one of the most common forms of transliterated search that commercial search engines have to tackle. Five teams participated in the shared task.

In FIRE-2014, the scope of subtask-1 was extended to cover three more South Indian languages - Tamil, Kannada and Malayalam. In subtask-2, (a) queries in Devanagari script, and (b) more natural queries with splitting and joining of words, were introduced. More than 15 teams participated in the 2 subtasks [7].

Last year at FIRE-2015, the shared task was renamed from "Transliterated Search" to "Mixed Script Information Retrieval (MSIR)" to align it to the framework proposed by [8]. In FIRE-2015, three subtasks were conducted [17]. Subtask-1 was extended further by including more Indic languages, and transliterated text from all the languages were mixed. Subtask-2 was on searching movie dialogues and reviews along with song lyrics. Mixed script question answering (MSQA) was introduced as subtask-3. A total of 10 teams made 24 submissions for subtask-1 and subtask-2. In spite of a significant number of registrations, no run was received for subtask-3.

This year, we hosted two subtasks in the MSIR shared task. Subtask-1 was on classifying code-mixed cross-script question; this task was the continuation of last year's subtask-3. Here Bengali words were written in Roman transliterated Bengali. Subtask-2 was on information retrieval of Hindi-English code-mixed tweets. The objective of subtask-2 was to retrieve the top k tweets from a corpus [6] for a given query consisting of Hind-English terms where the Hindi terms are written in Roman transliterated form.

This paper provides the overview of the MSIR track in the Eighth Forum for Information Retrieval Conference 2016 (FIRE-2016). The track was coordinated jointly by Microsoft Research India, Jadavpur University, Technical University of Valencia, IIIT Sriharikota and NIT Agartala. Details of these tasks can also be found on the website https://msir2016.github.io/.

The rest of the paper is organized as follows. Sections 2 and 3 describe the datasets, present and analyze the run submissions for the Subtask-1 and Subtask-2 respectively. We conclude with a summary in Sect. 4.

2 Subtask-1: Code-Mixed Cross-Script Question Answering

Being a classic application of natural language processing, question answering (QA) has practical applications in various domains such as education, health care, personal assistance, etc. QA is a retrieval task which is more challenging than the task of common search engines because the purpose of QA is to find an accurate and concise answer to a question rather than just retrieving relevant documents containing the answer [11]. Recently, the code-mixed cross-script QA research problem was formally introduced in [2]. The first step of understanding a question is to perform question analysis. Question classification is an important task in question analysis which detects the answer type of the question. Question classification helps not only filter out a wide range of candidate answers but also to determine answer selection strategies [11]. Furthermore, it has been observed that the performance of question classification has significant influence on the overall performance of a QA system.

Let, $Q = \{q_1, q_2, \ldots, q_n\}$ be a set of factoid questions associated with domain D. Each question $q : \langle w_1 w_2 w_3 \ldots w_p \rangle$, is a set of words where p denotes the total number of words in a question. The words, $w_1, w_2, w_3, \ldots, w_p$, could be English words or transliterated from Bengali in the code mixed scenario. Let $C = \{c_1, c_2, \ldots, c_m\}$ be the set of question classes. Here n and m refer to the total number of questions and question classes respectively.

The objective of this subtask is to classify each given question $q_i \in Q$ into one of the predefined coarse-grained classes $c_j \in C$. For example, the question *"last volvo bus kokhon chare?"* (English gloss: "When does the last volvo bus depart?") should be classified to the class 'TEMPORAL'.

2.1 Datasets

We prepared the datasets for subtask-1 from the dataset described in [2] which is the only dataset available for code-mixed cross-script QA research. The dataset described in [2] contains questions, messages and answers from the sports and tourism domains in code-mixed cross-script English–Bengali. The dataset contains a total of 20 documents from two domains, namely sports and tourism. There are 10 documents in the sports domain which consist of 116 informal posts and 192 questions, while the 10 documents in the tourism domain consist of 183 informal posts and 314 questions. We initially provided 330 labeled factoid questions as the development set to the participants after accepting the data usage agreement. The testset contains 180 unlabeled factoid questions. Tables 1 and 2 provide statistics of the dataset. Question class specific distribution of the datasets is given in Fig. 1.

Table 1. MSIR16 Subtask-1 Datasets

Dataset	Questions(Q)	Total words	Avg. words/Q
Trainset	330	1776	5.321
Testset	180	1138	6.322

Table 2. Subtask-1: Question class statistics

Class	Training	Testing
Person (PER)	55	27
Location (LOC)	26	23
Organization (ORG)	67	24
Temporal (TEMP)	61	25
Numerical (NUM)	45	26
Distance (DIST)	24	21
Money (MNY)	26	16
Object (OBJ)	21	10
Miscellaneous (MISC)	5	8

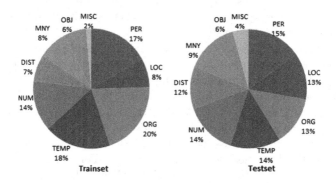

Fig. 1. Classwise distribution of dataset

2.2   Submissions

A total of 15 research teams registered for subtask-1. However, only 7 teams submitted runs and a total of 20 runs were received. All the teams submitted 3 runs except AMRITA_CEN who submitted 2 runs.

AMRITA_CEN [13] team submitted 2 runs. They used bag-of-words (BoW) model for the Run-1, while the Run-2 was based on Recurrent Neural Network (RNN) approach. The initial embedding vector was given to RNN and the output of RNN was fed to logistic regression for training. Overall, the BoW model outperformed the RNN model by almost 7% ons F1-measure.

AMRITA-CEN-NLP [10] team submitted 3 runs. They approached the problem using a Vector Space Model (VSM). A weighted term approach based on the context was applied to overcome the shortcomings of VSM. The proposed approach achieved upto 80% accuracy in terms of F1-measure.

ANUJ [16] also submitted 3 runs. The author used *term frequency inverse document frequency* (TF-IDF) vector as a feature. A number of machine learning algorithms, namely Support Vector Machines (SVM), Logistic Regression (LR), Random Forest (RF) and Gradient Boosting were applied using Grid Search to come up with the best parameters and model. The RF model performed the best among the 3 runs.

BITS_PILANI [4] submitted 3 runs. Instead of applying the classifiers on the code-mixed cross-script data, they convert data into English. The translation was performed using *Google translation API*[1]. Then they applied three machine learning classifiers for each run, namely Gaussian Naïve Bayes, LR and RF Classifier. The Gaussian Nave Bayes classifier was found to outperform the other two classifiers

IINTU [5] was the best performing team. The team submitted 3 runs which were based on machine learning approaches. They trained three separate classifiers namely RF, One-vs-Rest and k-NN, followed by building an ensemble classifier using these 3 classifiers for the classification task. The ensemble classifier took the output label of each of the individual classifiers and selected the majority label as output. In the case of a tie one label was chosen at random as output.

NLP-NITMZ [14] submitted 3 runs of which 2 runs were rule based - a first set of *direct* rules were applied for the Run-1 while a second set of *dependent* rules were used for the Run-3. A total of 39 rules were identified for the rule based runs. Naïve Bayes classifier was used in Run-2 whereas Naïve Bayes updateable classifier was used in Run-3.

IIT(ISM)D used three different machine learning based classification models - Sequential Minimal Optimization, Naïve Bayes Multimodel and Decision Tree FT to annotate the question text. This team submitted their runs after the deadline.

2.3   Results

In this section, we define the evaluation metrics used to evaluate the runs submitted to the subtask-1. Typically, the performance of a question classifier is measured by calculating the *accuracy* of that classifier on a particular test set [11]. We also used this metric to evaluate code-mixed cross-script question classification performance.

$$accuracy = \frac{\text{number of correctly classified samples}}{\text{total number of testset samples}}$$

In addition, we also computed the standard precision, recall and F1-measure to evaluate the class specific performances of the participating systems. The precision, recall and F1-measure of a classifier on a particular class c are defined as follows:

$$precision(P) = \frac{\text{number of samples correctly classified as } c}{\text{number of samples classified as } c}$$

$$recall(R) = \frac{\text{number of samples correctly classified as } c}{\text{total number of samples in class } c}$$

$$F1 - measure = \frac{2.P.R}{P + R}$$

---

[1] https://translate.google.com/.

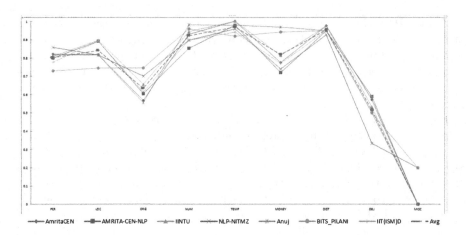

Fig. 2. Subtask-1: F-Measure of different teams for classes (Best run)

Table 3. Subtask-1: Teams performance (*denotes late submission)

Team	Run ID	Correct	Incorrect	Accuracy
Baseline	-	143	37	79.440
AmritaCEN	1	145	35	80.556
AmritaCEN	2	133	47	73.889
AMRITA-CEN-NLP	1	143	37	79.444
AMRITA-CEN-NLP	2	132	48	73.333
AMRITA-CEN-NLP	3	132	48	73.333
Anuj	1	139	41	77.222
Anuj	2	146	34	81.111
Anuj	3	141	39	78.333
BITS_PILANI	1	146	34	81.111
BITS_PILANI	2	144	36	80.000
BITS_PILANI	3	131	49	72.778
IINTU	1	147	33	81.667
IINTU	**2**	**150**	**30**	**83.333**
IINTU	3	146	34	81.111
NLP-NITMZ	1	134	46	74.444
NLP-NITMZ	2	134	46	74.444
NLP-NITMZ	3	142	38	78.889
*IIT(ISM)D	1	144	36	80.000
*IIT(ISM)D	2	142	38	78.889
*IIT(ISM)D	3	144	36	80.000

Table 4. Subtask-1: Class specific performances (NA denotes no identification of a class)

Team	Run ID	PER	LOC	ORG	NUM	TEMP	MONEY	DIST	OBJ	MISC
AmritaCEN	1	0.8214	0.8182	0.5667	0.9286	**1.0000**	0.7742	0.9756	0.5714	NA
AmritaCEN	2	0.7541	0.8095	0.6667	0.8125	**1.0000**	0.4615	0.8649	NA	NA
AMRITA-CEN-NLP	1	0.8000	0.8936	0.6032	0.8525	0.9796	0.7200	0.9500	**0.5882**	NA
AMRITA-CEN-NLP	2	0.7500	0.7273	0.5507	0.8387	0.9434	0.5833	0.9756	0.1818	NA
AMRITA-CEN-NLP	3	0.6939	0.8936	0.5455	0.8125	0.9804	0.6154	0.8333	0.3077	NA
IINTU	1	0.7843	0.8571	0.6333	0.9286	**1.0000**	0.8125	0.9756	0.4615	NA
IINTU	2	0.8077	**0.8980**	0.6552	0.9455	**1.0000**	0.8125	0.9756	0.5333	NA
IINTU	3	0.7600	0.8571	0.5938	0.9455	**1.0000**	0.8571	**0.9767**	0.4615	NA
NLP-NITMZ	1	0.7347	0.8444	0.5667	0.8387	0.9796	0.6154	0.9268	0.2857	0.1429
NLP-NITMZ	2	0.6190	0.8444	0.5667	0.9630	0.8000	0.7333	0.9756	0.4286	0.1429
NLP-NITMZ	3	**0.8571**	0.8163	0.7000	0.8966	0.9583	0.7407	0.9268	0.3333	**0.2000**
Anuj	1	0.7600	0.8936	0.6032	0.8125	0.9804	0.7200	0.8649	0.5333	NA
Anuj	2	0.8163	0.8163	0.5538	**0.9811**	0.9796	0.9677	0.9500	0.5000	NA
Anuj	3	0.8163	0.8936	0.5846	0.8254	**1.0000**	0.7200	0.8947	0.5333	NA
BITS_PILANI	1	0.7297	0.7442	**0.7442**	0.9600	0.9200	0.9412	0.9500	0.5000	**0.2000**
BITS_PILANI	2	0.6753	0.7805	0.7273	0.9455	0.9600	**1.0000**	0.8947	0.4286	NA
BITS_PILANI	3	0.6190	0.7805	0.7179	0.8125	0.8936	0.9333	0.6452	0.5333	NA
*IIT(ISM)D	1	0.7755	0.8936	0.6129	0.8966	0.9412	0.7692	0.9524	**0.5882**	NA
*IIT(ISM)D	2	0.8400	0.8750	0.6780	0.8525	0.9091	0.6667	0.9500	0.1667	NA
*IIT(ISM)D	3	0.8000	0.8936	0.6207	0.8667	**1.0000**	0.6923	0.9500	0.5333	NA
Avg		0.7607	0.8415	0.6245	0.8858	0.9613	0.7568	0.9204	0.4458	NA

Table 3 presents the performance of the submitted runs in terms of accuracy. Class specific performances are reported in Table 4. A baseline system was also developed for the sake of comparison using the BoW which obtained 79.444% accuracy. It can be observed from Table 3 that the highest accuracy (83.333%) was achieved by the IINTU team. The classification performance on the temporal (TEMP) class was very high for almost all the teams. However, Table 4 and Fig. 2 suggest that the miscellaneous (MISC) question class was very difficult to identify. Most of the teams could not identify the MISC class. The reason could be very low presence (2%) of MISC class in the training dataset.

3   Subtask-2: Information Retrieval on Code-Mixed Hindi-English Tweets

This subtask is based on the concepts discussed in [8]. In this subtask, the objective was to retrieve Code-Mixed Hindi-English tweets from a corpus for code-mixed queries. The Hindi components in both the tweets and the queries are written in Roman transliterated form. This subtask did not consider cases where both Roman and Devanagari scripts are present. Therefore, the documents in this case are tweets consisting of code-mixed Hindi-English texts where the

Hindi terms are in Roman transliterated form. Given a query consisting of Hindi and English terms written in Roman script, the system has to retrieve the top-k documents (i.e., tweets) from a corpus that contains Code-Mixed Hindi-English tweets. The expected output is a ranked list of the top twenty (k = 20 here) tweets retrieved from the given corpus.

3.1 Datasets

Initially we released 6,133 code-mixed Hindi-English tweets with 23 queries as the training dataset. Later we released a document collection containing 2,796 code-mixed tweets along with 12 code-mixed queries as the testset. Query terms are mostly *named entities* with Roman transliterated Hindi words. The average length of the queries in the training set is 3.43 words and in the testset it is 3.25 words. The tweets in the training set cover 10 topics whereas the testset cover 3 topics.

3.2 Submissions

This year total 7 teams have submitted 13 runs. The submitted runs for the retrieval task of Code-Mixed tweets mostly adopted preprocessing of the data and then applying different techniques for retrieving the desired tweets. Team Amrita_CEN [9] removed some Hindi/English stop words to declutter useless words. After that, they have tokenized all the tweets. The cosine distance was used to score the relevance of tweets to the query. After that, the top 20 tweets based on the scores were retrieved. Team CEN@Amrita [18] used a Vector Space Model based approach. Team UB [12] adopted three different techniques for the retrieval task. First, they used *Named Entity boosts* where the purpose was to boost the documents based on their NE matches from the query, i.e., the query was parsed to extract NEs and each document (tweet) that matched the given NE was provided a small numeric boost. At the second level of boosting, phrase matching was carried out, i.e. documents that more closely matched the input query phrase were ranked higher than those that did not. The UB team used *Synonym Expansion* and *Narrative based weighting* as the second and third techniques. Team NITA_NITMZ [3] performed stop word removal followed by query segmentation and finally merging. Team IIT(ISM)_D considered every tweet as a document and indexed using uniword indexing on Terrier implementation. Query terms were expanded using the soundex coding scheme. Terms with an identical soundex code were selected as candidate query and included in final queries to retrieve the relevent tweets (documents). Further, they used three different retrieval models BM25, DFR and TF-IDF to measure the similarity. However, this team submitted the runs after the deadline.

3.3 Results

The retrieval task requires that the retrieved documents at higher ranks be more important than the retrieved documents at lower ranks for a given query and we

Table 5. Results for subtask-2 showing mean average precision

Team	Run ID	MAP
UB	1	0.0217
UB	2	0.016
UB	3	0.0152
Anuj	1	0.0209
Anuj	2	0.0199
Amrita_CEN	1	**0.0377**
NLP-NITMZ	1	0.0203
NITA_NITMZ	1	0.0047
CEN@Amrita	1	0.0315
CEn@Amrita	2	0.0168
IIT (ISM)D	1	0.0021
IIT (ISM)D	2	0.0083
IIT (ISM)D	3	0.0021

want our measures to account for that. Therefore, set based evaluation metrics such as Precision, Recall and F-measure are not suitable for this task. Therefore, we used Mean Average Precision (MAP) as the performance evaluation metric for subtask-2. MAP is also referred to as *"average precision* at seen relevant documents". The idea is that, first, *average precision* is computed for each query and subsequently the average precisions are averaged over the queries. MAP is represented as

$$MAP = \frac{1}{N} \sum_{j=1}^{N} \frac{1}{Q_j} \sum_{i=1}^{Q_j} P(doc_i)$$

where Q_j refers to the number of relevant documents for query j, N indicates the number of queries and $P(doc_i)$ represents precision at the ith relevant document.

The evaluation results of the submitted runs are reported in Table 5. The highest MAP (0.0377) was achieved by team Amrita@CEN which is still very low. The very low MAP values in Table 5 suggest that the task of retrieving Code-Mixed tweets against query terms comprising code-mixed Hindi and English words is a difficult task and the techniques proposed by the teams do not produce satisfactory results. Therefore, the problem of retrieving relevant code-mixed tweets requires better techniques and methodologies to be developed for improving system performance.

4   Summary

In this overview, we elaborated on the two subtasks of the MSIR-2016 at FIRE-2016. The overview is divided into two major parts one for each subtask, where the dataset, evaluations metric and results are discussed in detail. A total of 33 runs were submitted from 9 unique teams.

In subtask-1, 20 runs were received from 7 teams. The details of the dataset for subtask-1 are given in Tables 1, 2 and Fig. 1 respectively. The results for subtask-1 are tabulated in Tables 3 and 4 and class specific performance of the best run of the teams is depicted in Fig. 2. The subtask-1 deals with code-mixed Bengali-English language. In the coming years, we would like to include more Indian languages. The participation was encouraging and we plan to continue subtask-1 in subsequent FIRE conferences.

Subtask-2 received a total of 13 run submissions from 7 teams out of which one team submitted after the deadline. The best MAP value achieved was 0.0377 which is rather low. From the results of the run submissions it can be inferred that information retrieval of code-mixed informal micro blog texts such as tweets is a very challenging task. Therefore, the stated problem opens and calls for new avenues of research for developing better techniques and methodologies.

References

1. Ahmed, U.Z., Bali, K., Choudhury, M., Sowmya, V.B.: Challenges in designing input method editors for Indian languages: the role of word-origin and context. In: Advances in Text Input Methods (WTIM 2011), pp. 1–9 (2011)
2. Banerjee, S., Naskar, S.K., Rosso, P., Bandyopadhyay, S.: The first cross-script code-mixed question answering corpus. In: Proceedings of the workshop on Modeling, Learning and Mining for Cross/Multilinguality (MultiLingMine 2016), Co-located with the 38th European Conference on Information Retrieval (ECIR) (2016)
3. Bhardwaj, P., Pakray, P., Bajpeyee, V., Taneja, A.: Information retrieval on code-mixed Hindi-English tweets. In: Working Notes of FIRE 2016 - Forum for Information Retrieval Evaluation, Kolkata, India, 7–10 December 2016, CEUR Workshop Proceedings, December 2016
4. Bhargava, R., Khandelwal, S., Bhatia, A., Sharmai, Y.: Modeling classifier for code mixed cross script questions. In: Working notes of FIRE 2016 - Forum for Information Retrieval Evaluation, Kolkata, India, 7–10 December 2016, CEUR Workshop Proceedings, CEUR-WS.org (2016)
5. Bhattacharjee, D., Bhattacharya, P.: Ensemble classifier based approach for code-mixed cross-script question classification. In: Working notes of FIRE 2016 - Forum for Information Retrieval Evaluation, Kolkata, India, 7–10 December 2016, CEUR Workshop Proceedings, CEUR-WS.org (2016)
6. Chakma, K., Das, A.: CMIR: a corpus for evaluation of code mixed information retrieval of Hindi-English tweets. In: The 17th International Conference on Intelligent Text Processing and Computational Linguistics (CICLING), April 2016
7. Choudhury, M., Gupta, G.C., Gupta, P., Das, A.: Overview of FIRE 2014 track on transliterated search (2014)
8. Gupta, P., Bali, K., Banchs, R.E., Choudhury, M., Rosso, P.: Query expansion for mixed-script information retrieval. In: Proceedings of the 37th International ACM SIGIR Conference on Research & Development in Information Retrieval, pp. 677–686. ACM (2014)

9. Barathi Ganesh, H.B., Anand Kumar, M., Soman, K.P.: Distributional semantic representation for information retrieval. In: Working notes of FIRE 2016 - Forum for Information Retrieval Evaluation, Kolkata, India, 7–10 December 2016, CEUR Workshop Proceedings, December 2016

10. Barathi Ganesh, H.B., Anand Kumar, M., Soman, K.P.: Distributional semantic representation for text classification. In: Working Notes of FIRE 2016 - Forum for Information Retrieval Evaluation, Kolkata, India, 7–10 December 2016, CEUR Workshop Proceedings. CEUR-WS.org (2016)

11. Li, X., Roth, D.: Learning question classifiers. In: Proceedings of the 19th International Conference on Computational Linguistics, vol. 1, pp. 1–7. Association for Computational Linguistics (2002)

12. Londhe, N., Srihari, R.K.: Exploiting named entity mentions towards code mixed IR: working notes for the UB system submission for MSIR@FIRE16 (2016)

13. Anand Kumar, M., Soman, K.P.: Amrita-CEN@MSIR-FIRE2016: code-mixed question classification using BoWs and RNN embeddings. In: Working Notes of FIRE 2016 - Forum for Information Retrieval Evaluation, Kolkata, India, 7–10 December 2016, CEUR Workshop Proceedings, CEUR-WS.org (2016)

14. Majumder, G., Pakray, P.: NLP-NITMZ @ MSIR 2016 system for code-mixed cross-script question classification. In: Working Notes of FIRE 2016 - Forum for Information Retrieval Evaluation, Kolkata, India, 7–10 December 2016, CEUR Workshop Proceedings, CEUR-WS.org (2016)

15. Roy, R.S., Choudhury, M., Majumder, P., Agarwal, K.: Overview and datasets of FIRE 2013 track on transliterated search. In: Fifth Forum for Information Retrieval Evaluation (2013)

16. Saini, A.: Code mixed cross script question classification. In: Working Notes of FIRE 2016 - Forum for Information Retrieval Evaluation, Kolkata, India, 7–10 December 2016, CEUR Workshop Proceedings. CEUR-WS.org (2016)

17. Sequiera, R., Choudhury, M., Gupta, P., Rosso, P., Kumar, S., Banerjee, S., Naskar, S.K., Bandyopadhyay, S., Chittaranjan, G., Das, A., Chakma, K.: Overview of FIRE-2015 Shared Task on Mixed Script Information Retrieval (2015)

18. Singh, S., Anand Kumar, M., Soman, K.P.: CEN@Amrita: information retrieval on CodeMixed Hindi-English tweets using vector space models. In: Working Notes of FIRE 2016 - Forum for Information Retrieval Evaluation, Kolkata, India, 7–10 December 2016, CEUR Workshop Proceedings, December 2016

From Vector Space Models to Vector Space Models of Semantics

H. B. Barathi Ganesh[✉], M. Anand Kumar, and K. P. Soman

Centre for Computational Engineering and Networking (CEN),
Amrita School of Engineering,
Amrita Vishwa Vidyapeetham, Coimbatore, India
barathiganesh.hb@gmail.com, m_anandkumar@cb.amrita.edu,
kp_soman@amrita.edu

Abstract. This paper assesses the performance of frequency and concept based text representation in Mixed Script Information Retrieval and Classification tasks. In text analytics, representation serves as an unresolved research problem to progress further towards different applications. In this paper observations from different text representation methods in text classification and information retrieval are presented. The data set from the Mixed Script Information Retrieval shared task is used in this experiment and the performance of final submitted model is evaluated by task organizers. It is observed that distributional representation performs better than the frequency based text representation methods. The final system attained first place in task 2 and was 3.89% lesser than the top scored system in task 1.

Keywords: Text representation · Vector Space Models
Vector Space Models of Semantics · Text classification
Information retrieval

1 Introduction

Being a major break through in the recent decades, text analytics conquers a major portion in multiple domains like search engine, chat bot, health science, targeted user profiling etc. Even though the application varies widely, commonly it falls under the well known text analytics problems like text classification or information retrieval. Though the problems varies in the application level but the principle component for these text analytics application is representation of text. Henceforth in this paper we have focused more on these text representation methods.

If the vector representation of two texts occurs together or equivalent in the space spanned by those vector, then they tend to share similarity among themselves. By having this general statistical semantic hypothesis, this paper focuses on how Vector Space Models (VSM) has moved towards the Vector Space Models of Semantics (VSMs). This text representation methods evolved over the time to improve the originality of representation. This persuades research

© Springer International Publishing AG 2018
P. Majumder et al. (Eds.): FIRE 2016 Workshop, LNCS 10478, pp. 50–60, 2018.
https://doi.org/10.1007/978-3-319-73606-8_4

direction to move towards the VSMs, which is a concept based representation method. Though there are other methods like set-theoretic Boolean systems, this paper focuses only on VSM and VSMs [1].

In VSM, a vector will be computed to numerically represent the text content. When the elements of this vector is in binary (represents the presence or absence term in a document), the resulting term - document matrix will be a binary matrix. Similarly when the elements of this vector is a real value, the resulting matrix will be Document-Term Matrix (number of times a term occur in the document) or Term Frequency-Inverse Document Frequency (inverse relation between the number of times a word occur in a document and number of times word presence across the documents). Here term represents a word or phrase [2].

A text compromises the properties like usage of word with respect to the context (lexical); combining structure of the words to form a context (syntax) and context of the text (semantic). The atomic symbolic representation of words as a feature in VSM ignores to include the above mentioned properties. Moreover, the Documents-Term Matrix (DTM) is biased towards the count of the word in a class. This may be due to the unbalanced data or uninformative data (text from social media). The Term Frequency-Inverse Document Frequency (TF-IDF) representation method overcomes the cons of the DTM by including the inverse document frequency. Basically it re-weighs the term frequency in the DTM by inverse of the number of time terms present across the other documents available in a text collection [4]. Due to the misspelling, abbreviated words and shortened words, these words get the higher weigh in TF-IDF representation but these words are less informative. This is usual while developing text analytics solutions for the social media texts.

To include lexical and semantic properties of a text, VSMs has been introduced in which the lexical meaning is included by computing co-occurrence of words and semantic information is included by computing the distributional representation of the text. In simple VSMs are achieved by computing VSM based representation, and co-occurrence matrix followed by the Matrix Factorization methods like Non-Negative Matrix Factorization (NMF) and Singular Value Decomposition (SVD) [5,6,11,15]. Finding co-occurrence matrix helps to find the weighed average count for the term present in the VSM matrix. Distributional representation of text is achieved through a matrix factorization, in which it computes the basis vector for the vectors in the co-occurrence matrix [7]. Though it includes the lexical and semantic properties, the order of words or phrases (syntax property) in a text is not included in VSMs. This VSMs based representation also has a well known problem named "Curse of Dimensionality".

The above said three properties of the texts are included in the distributed representation in which, Word Embedding along with the syntax information of the short texts are utilized for representation. The context representation for a single sentence can be represented through this method. The size of the vector also can be controlled to solve the "Curse of Dimensionality" problem. Computation of Word2Vec (Word to Vector) model needs huge corpus and high computation, which are the drawback of this method [8,9]. Due to un-availability of mixed script text data, computation power and the parser (for including syntax property), we are not considering distributed representation in this paper. Followed by the distributional representation, similarity measures are computed to carry-on the classification task. Based on the classification result, representation method for the text is fixed to perform the retrieval task. Similarity measures computed are the correlation measure (Pearson correlation coefficient) and distance measure (Jaccard distance, Euclidean distance and Cosine distance) [3].

Considering the above discussed pros and cons, this experiment is carried over to asses the performance of VSM and VSMs based text representation methods in the classification and retrieval task. In submitted system after the fundamental pre-processing steps, questions and tweets are represented as a Document Term Matrix and NMF is applied on it to get the distributional representation. Followed by the representation, correlation measure and distance measures between entropy vector (sum of vectors belongs to the target classes) of each class and vector representation of the question are computed in order to perform the question classification task. Based on the performance in the classification task parameters for the representation is fixed to experiment the retrieval task. In retrieval task, followed by the representation, cosine distance between query and tweets are measured to rank the tweets with respect to the query [14].

2   Text Representation

This section details about the available text representation methods in the lexical and semantic space. This section justifies how the frequency based representation methods have moved towards the semantic representation methods. The objective of this section is, given a set of documents or sentences we need to find its equivalent numerical representation in matrix the format.

$$D = d_1, d_2, d_3, \ldots, d_n \tag{1}$$

Here d represents the sentences or documents, D represents its equivalent matrix format and n is the total number of documents or sentences.

2.1   Vector Space Models

The commonly used methods under VSM are Document-Term Matrix (DTM) and Term Frequency-Inverse Document Frequency Matrix (TF-IDF). These methods are generally called Bag of Word (BOW) methods and it follows bag of word hypothesis. Given a set of texts as in Eq. 1, the function $f()$ converts it into the Document Term Matrix (DTM). The function $f()$ measures the event e, where e is the occurrence of terms in the texts. The term may take words, phrases (n-grams) or both. The above can be represented as,

$$D = f(e) \tag{2}$$

Where D is the DTM with $m \times n$ size. m is the number of documents or sentences and n is the total number of unique words or phrases (types) present in the document set. The DTM fails to handle the nature of human word usage. We generally tend to use more functional words (Determiner, Adverb, Pronouns, etc.) than the content words (Verb, Nouns, etc.). Unfortunately the function words do not contribute much towards the final application and having look-up dictionary for stop word removal is a tedious process.

To solve the above, TF-IDF matrix is introduced. In TF-IDF matrix, the event remains the same but the function is altered such that high weights are given to the rarely occurring words across the documents and low weights are given to the commonly occurring words [4]. To achieve this along with the event e, one more event e' is added that measures term presence across the documents. TF-IDF matrix can be represented as,

$$D = f(e \times e') \tag{3}$$

Here e represents the event measuring term frequency and e' represents the event measuring the inverse document frequency, Mathematically it is represented as,

$$tfidf(t, d, D) = tf(t, d) \times idf(t, D) \tag{4}$$

For e.g.:- a sentence "Arnold Schwarzenegger was a governor of California" needs to be classified into one of the two classes 'cinema' or 'politics'. Here the term "Arnold Schwarzenegger" is mostly present in the 'cinema' documents it gets higher weights under the category 'cinema'. The stop word removal won't remove this content term. The TF-IDF matrix has the capability of giving lower weights to the 'Arnold Schwarzenegger' through inverse document frequency since its tends to appear mostly across the documents.

In the above said two VSM models row vector of the matrix gives the equivalent vector form of the document or sentence and column vector gives the equivalent vector form of the terms in the document or sentence. The problem of VSM is, it does not consider the meaning of the texts. "Raman killed Ravan" and "Ravan killed Raman" both are equivalent with respect to the VSM methods. To solve the above we move towards the VSMs models.

2.2   Vector Space Models of Semantics

VSMs's function f has the capability of re weighting the terms with respect its co-occurrence words. Generally we call it as bag of concepts method. Applying matrix factorization on top of VSM will becomes VSMs. In general matrix factorization is done to get the product of its basis matrices, subject to the reconstruction error as low as possible [5,6].

$$VSMs = Matrix\ Factorization(VSM) \tag{5}$$

To achieve this, generally Singular Value Decomposition (SVD) or Non-Negative Matrix Factorization is applied on DTM or TF-IDF matrix. In SVD,

$$D' = SVD(D) \tag{6}$$

$$D'_{m\times n} = U_{m\times m} \sum_{m\times n} V^T_{n\times n} \tag{7}$$

U comprises the basis vectors (singular vectors) of row space of DD^T, V comprises the basis vectors of column space of $D^T D$ and $\sum$ comprises the singular values in its diagonal in descending order. The selection of values in $\sum$ leads towards the dimensionality reduction (Latent Semantic Analysis). The problem with the SVD is, it forces the basis vectors to be orthogonal to each other. Due to this constraint there are possibilities that we may lose some of the characteristics of the text vectors [10].

NMF is currently evolving and its more suitable for VSMs [6,10]. It does not introduce the constraints like SVD. In NMF the non-negativity constraint is easier in interpreting the results. The NMF decomposes the matrix D into weight matrix W and co-efficient matrix H_T.

$$D' = NMF(D) \tag{8}$$

$$D'_{m\times n} = W_{m\times r} H^T_{r\times n} \tag{9}$$

Where r is the rank, which serves towards the objective of dimensionality reduction. Similar to VSM, here also row vector of the matrix gives the equivalent vector form of document or sentence but column vector gives representation for the concept of document or sentence. By taking these row vectors from VSM and VSMs methods further tasks in the Mixed Script Information Retrieval experimentation is carried over.

3   Experiment and Observations

The data set has been given by the Mixed Script Information Retrieval (MSIR) task organizers [12,13]. The statistics about the data set for the both the tasks are given in Tables 1 and 4.

Table 1. Data-set statistics: classification

Description	Train file	Test file
# Questions	330.0	180.0
Total # Unique Words	407.0	282.0
# Words after Filtering	220.0	133.0
Average # Words per Question	0.67	0.74
# Bi-Grams after Filtering	207.0	118.0
Average # Bi-Grams per Question	0.63	0.66
# Tri-Grams after Filtering	92.0	55.0
Average # Tri-Grams per Question	0.28	0.31
Total # Features	519.0	306.0

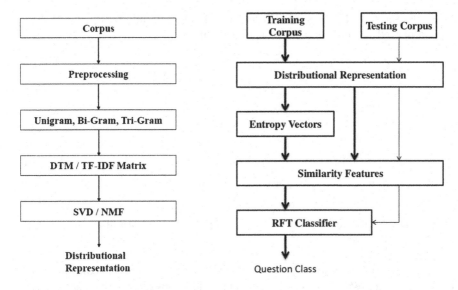

Fig. 1. Representation   **Fig. 2.** Classification

Terms that appears across multiple documents will have a dispute towards the classification as well as retrieval and these terms can be viewed as uninformative features. These terms gets the low weighs in TF-IDF representation. To have the same outcome with TDM, these terms are eliminated if it occurs more than $3/4$ times across the documents. To improve the representation, bi-gram and tri-gram phrases are also considered along with the unigram words.

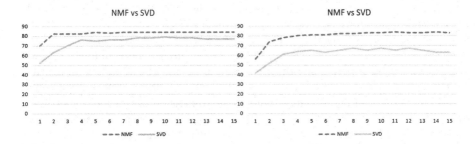

Fig. 3. DTM without filter   **Fig. 4.** TF-IDF without filter

3.1 Question Classification

The objective of this task is to categorize the given question into its corresponding target classes. Let, $Q = q_1, q_2, q_3, \ldots, q_n$ are the questions (q_i represents the ith question), $C = c_1, c_2, \ldots, c_n$ are the classes which the questions falls under and n is the total number of questions in the corpus. The different representation methods of the given training and testing corpus are computed as described in the previous section. The systematic diagram for the remaining approach and the experimented systems are given in Figs. 1 and 2.

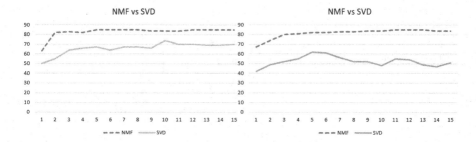

Fig. 5. DTM with filter   **Fig. 6.** TF-IDF with filter

After these representation, the reference vector for each class is computed by summing up the question vectors in that class. This reference vector acts as an entropy vector for its corresponding class. This is mathematically represented as,

$$r_c = \sum_{}^{c} q_i \tag{10}$$

$$s.t. \; q_i \in c$$

$$R_c = r_{c_1}, r_{c_2}, \ldots, r_{c_n} \tag{11}$$

Then the similarity measures between question vector q_i and entropy vectors in R are computed. Similarity measures computed are given in Table 2. These similarity measures that are computed are taken as the attributes for the supervised classification algorithm.

The Random Forest Tree (RFT) with $nC_{\sqrt{n}}$ number of trees are utilized to perform the supervised classification. In order to ensure the performance, 10-fold 10-cross validation is performed during the training and the statistics about the observed results are expressed in Figs. 3, 4, 5 and 6. In these figures x-axis represents the number of components (defines the dimension of the vector) varying from 10 to 150 with constant interval of 10 and y-axis represents the accuracy. It can be observed from the figure that SVD's performance keeps varying abruptly as the filtering and representation method changes but its almost constant with the NMF based representation.

Proposed approach with NMF yields 79.44% as accuracy measure against the test set and statistics about the results are tabulated in Table 3. A total of three runs were submitted to the task committee, which has changes only in the final classification algorithm. So far we have seen about our top rated system among the three runs submitted.

Table 2. Measured similarity features

Measured Feature Functions
Similarity (Dot Product): $P^T * Q$ (12)
Euclidean Distance: $\sqrt{\sum_{i=1}^{d}\|P_i - Q_i\|^2}$
Bray Curtis Dissimilarity: $\dfrac{\sum_{i=0}^{d}\|P_i - Q_i\|}{\sum_{i=0}^{d}(P_i + Q_i)}$
Chebyshev Distance: $imin\|P_i - Q_i\|$
Correlation: $\sum_{i=1}^{d}\dfrac{(P_i - Q_i)^2}{Q_i}$

Table 3. Classification results

Team	Acc	PER	LOC	ORG	NUM	TEMP	MONEY	DIST	OBJ	MISC
AmritaCEN	80.55	0.82	0.81	0.56	0.92	1.00	0.77	0.97	0.57	NA
Ours	**79.44**	**0.80**	**0.89**	**0.60**	**0.85**	**0.97**	**0.72**	**0.95**	**0.58**	**NA**
Anuj	81.11	0.81	0.81	0.55	0.98	0.97	0.96	0.95	0.50	NA
BITS_PILANI	81.11	0.72	0.74	0.74	0.96	0.92	0.94	0.95	0.50	0.20
IINTU	83.33	0.80	0.89	0.65	0.94	1.00	0.81	0.97	0.53	NA
IIT(ISM)D*	80.00	0.77	0.89	0.61	0.89	0.94	0.76	0.95	0.58	NA
NLP-NITMZ	78.88	0.85	0.81	0.70	0.89	0.95	0.74	0.92	0.33	0.20

* This team submitted the runs after the deadline.

3.2 Information Retrieval

The objective of this task is to retrieve the top 20 relevant tweets from the corpus with respect to the input query. The detailed statistics about the data-set is given in Table 4. Primarily queries and corpus are distributionally represented as described in the Sect. 2. The top scored representation method and its parameters from the question classification task has been utilized here to represent the query and the tweets.

$$Q = q_1, q_2, q_3, \ldots, q_n \tag{12}$$

$$T = t_1, t_2, \ldots, t_n \tag{13}$$

Then the cosine distance between the query and the corpus vectors are calculated to retrieve the top 20 tweets with minimum distance. Mathematically it is expressed as,

Table 4. Data-set statistics: information retrieval

Description	Train file	Test file
# Questions	11238.0	5090.0
Total # Words	19654.0	11994.0
# Words after Filtering	13616.0	6756.0
Average # Words per Question	1.21	1.32
# Bi-Grams after Filtering	46673.0	16494.0
Average # Bi-Grams per Question	4.15	3.24
# Tri-Grams after Filtering	56513.0	11961.0
Average # Tri-Grams per Question	5.03	2.35
Total # Features	116802.0	35211.0

$$similarity = \frac{\sum_{i=1}^{n} q_i t_i}{\sqrt{\sum_{i=1}^{n} A_i^2} \sqrt{\sum_{i=1}^{n} B_i^2}} \tag{14}$$

$$distance = \frac{cos^{-1}(similarity)}{\pi} \tag{15}$$

Table 5. Information retrieval results

Team	Mean average precision
UB	0.0217
Anuj	0.0209
Ours	0.0377
NLP-NITMZ	0.0203
NITA_NITMZ	0.0047
CEN@Amrita	0.0315
IIT(ISM)D	0.0083

The proposed distributional representation based approach yields 0.0377 mean average precision against the test queries, which is best amongst the other approaches proposed in this task [13]. The statistics about the obtained results are given in Table 5.

4   Conclusion

The classification task is developed based on the different representation methods of the text. The representation method and parameters from the system with the best result in the classification task has been utilized as it is to represent the query and the tweets in the retrieval task. It is observed that TF-IDF matrix with Non-Negative Matrix Factorization over performs the others representation methods. This experimented approach with TF-IDF and Non-Negative Matrix Factorization outperformed in both the tasks. It attained first place in task 2 and was 3.89% lesser than the top score system in task 1.

Though the distributional representation methods performed well, it suffers from the well known problem 'Curse of Dimensionality' and the mean average precision in task 2 is very low. Hence the future work will be focused on improving the performance of the retrieval system and also to reduce the dimensionality of the basis vectors.

References

1. Salton, G., Anita, W., Chung-Shu, Y.: A vector space model for automatic indexing. Commun. ACM **18**, 613–620 (1975)
2. Manwar, A.B., Mahalle, H.S., Chinchkhede, K.D., Chavan, V.: A vector space model for information retrieval: a matlab approach. Indian J. Comput. Sci. Eng. **3**, 222–229 (2012)
3. Cha, S.-H.: Comprehensive survey on distance/similarity measures between probability density functions. Int. J Math. Models Methods Appl. Sci. **4**(1), 300–307 (2007)
4. Ramos, J.: Using TF-IDF to determine word relevance in document queries. In: Proceedings of the First Instructional Conference on Machine Learning (2003)
5. Reidy, P.: An introduction to latent semantic analysis. Indian J. Comput. Sci. Eng (2017)
6. Xu, W., Liu, X., Gong, Y.: Document clustering based on non-negative matrix factorization. In: Proceedings of the 26th Annual International ACM SIGIR Conference on Research and Development in Information Retrieval, pp. 267–273 (2003)
7. Blacoe, W., Lapata, M.: A comparison of vector-based representations for semantic composition. In: Proceedings of the 2012 Joint Conference on Empirical Methods in Natural Language Processing and Computational Natural Language Learning, pp. 546–556 (2012)
8. Socher, R., Huang, E.H., Pennin, J., Manning, C.D., Ng, A.Y.: Dynamic pooling and unfolding recursive autoencoders for paraphrase detection. In: Advances in Neural Information Processing Systems, pp. 801–809 (2011)
9. Barathi Ganesh, H.B., Anand Kumar, M., Soman, K.P.: Amrita CEN at SemEval-2016 Task 1: semantic relation from word embeddings in higher dimension. In: Proceedings of SemEval-2016, pp. 706–711 (2016)
10. Lee, D.D., Seung, H.S.: Learning the parts of objects by non-negative matrix factorization. Nature **401**(6755), 788–791 (1999)
11. Reshma, U., Barathi Ganesh, H.B., Anand Kumar, M.: Author identification based on word distribution in word space. In: Advances in Computing, Communications and Informatics (ICACCI), pp. 1519–1523 (2015)
12. Banerjee, S., Naskar, S.K., Rosso, P., Bandyopadhyay, S.: The first cross-script code-mixed question answering corpus. In: Modelling, Learning and Mining for Cross/Multilinguality Workshop, pp. 56–65 (2016)

13. Banerjee, S., Naskar, S., Rosso, P., Bandyopadhyay, S., Chakma, K., Das, A., Choudhury, M.: MSIR@FIRE: overview of the mixed script information retrieval. In: Working Notes of FIRE 2016 - Forum for Information Retrieval Evaluation, 7–10 December 2016, Kolkata, India, CEUR Workshop Proceedings (2016)
14. Barathi Ganesh, H.B., Anand Kumar, M., Soman, K.P.: Distributional semantic representation for text classification and information retrieval. In: Working Notes of FIRE 2016 - Forum for Information Retrieval Evaluation, 7–10 December 2016, Kolkata, India, CEUR Workshop Proceedings (2016)
15. Barathi Ganesh, H.B., Anand Kumar, M., Soman, K.P.: Distributional semantic representation in health care text classification. In: Working Notes of FIRE 2016 - Forum for Information Retrieval Evaluation, 7–10 December 2016, Kolkata, India, CEUR Workshop Proceedings (2016)

Algorithms and Corpora for Persian Plagiarism Detection

Overview of PAN at FIRE 2016

Habibollah Asghari[1], Salar Mohtaj[2], Omid Fatemi[1(✉)] [ID],
Heshaam Faili[1], Paolo Rosso[3], and Martin Potthast[4]

[1] School of Electrical and Computer Engineering, College of Engineering,
University of Tehran, Tehran, Iran
`habib.asghari@ictrc.ac.ir`, `omid@fatemi.net`,
`hfaili@ut.ac.ir`
[2] ICT Research Institute, Academic Center for Education,
Culture and Research (ACECR), Tehran, Iran
`salar.mohtaj@ictrc.ac.ir`
[3] PRHLT Research Center, Universitat Politècnica de València, Valencia, Spain
`prosso@dsic.upv.es`
[4] Bauhaus-Universität Weimar, Weimar, Germany
`martin.potthast@uni-weimar.de`

Abstract. The task of plagiarism detection is to find passages of text-reuse in a suspicious document. This task is of increasing relevance, since scholars around the world take advantage of the fact that information about nearly any subject can be found on the World Wide Web by reusing existing text instead of writing their own. We organized the Persian PlagDet shared task at PAN 2016 in an effort to promote the comparative assessment of NLP techniques for plagiarism detection with a special focus on plagiarism that appears in a Persian text corpus. The goal of this shared task is to bring together researchers and practitioners around the exciting topic of plagiarism detection and text-reuse detection. We report on the outcome of the shared task, which divides into two subtasks: text alignment and corpus construction. In the first subtask, nine teams participated, whereas the best result achieved was a PlagDet score of 0.92. For the second subtask of corpus construction, five teams submitted a corpus, which were evaluated using the systems submitted for the first subtask. The results show that significant challenges remain in evaluating newly constructed corpora.

Keywords: Plagiarism detection · Evaluation framework · TIRA platform
Shared task · Persian PlagDet

1 Introduction

In recent years, a lot of research has been carried out concerning text reuse and plagiarism detection for English. But the detection of plagiarism in languages other than English has received comparably little attention. Although there are some language independent approaches for plagiarism detection in different languages, most

© Springer International Publishing AG 2018
P. Majumder et al. (Eds.): FIRE 2016 Workshop, LNCS 10478, pp. 61–79, 2018.
https://doi.org/10.1007/978-3-319-73606-8_5

semantic methods for plagiarism detection are dependent to the target language. In other words, available English plagiarism detection methods are inefficient for plagiarism detection in other languages (e.g. Persian). Although there have been previous developments on tools and algorithms to assist detecting text reuse in Persian, little is known about their detection performance. Therefore, to foster research and development on Persian plagiarism detection, we have organized the first corresponding competition, held in conjunction with the PAN evaluation lab at FIRE 2016.

We overview the detection approaches of nine participating teams and evaluate their respective retrieval performance. Participants were asked to submit their software to the TIRA Evaluation-as-a-Service (EaaS) platform [8] instead of just sending run outputs, rendering the shared task more reproducible. The submitted pieces of software are maintained in executable form so that they can be re-run against new corpora later on. To demonstrate this possibility, we asked participants to also submit evaluation corpora of their own design, which were examined using the detection systems submitted by other participants.

In what follows, Sect. 2 reviews related work with respect to shared tasks on plagiarism detection. Section 3 describes the main steps of tasks. Section 4 describes the evaluation framework, explaining the TIRA evaluation platform as well as the construction of our training and test datasets alongside the performance measures used. In Sect. 5, the evaluation results of both the text alignment and the corpus construction subtasks are reported.

2 Related Work

This section reviews recent competitions and shared tasks on plagiarism detection in English, Arabic and Persian.

PAN. Potthast et al. [16] first pointed out the lack of a controlled evaluation environment and corresponding detection quality measures to evaluate plagiarism detection systems as a major obstacle to evaluating plagiarism detection approaches. To overcome these shortcomings, they organized the first international competition on plagiarism detection in 2009 featuring two subtasks: external plagiarism detection and intrinsic plagiarism detection. An important by-product of this competition was the first evaluation framework for plagiarism detection, which consists of a large-scale plagiarism corpus and a detection quality measure called as PlagDet [16, 17].

The PAN competition was continued in the next years, improving the evaluation corpora with each iteration. As of 2012, the competition was revamped in the form of two new subtasks: source retrieval and text alignment. Moreover, at PAN 2015, for the first time, participants were invited to submit their own text alignment corpora. Here, participants were asked to compile corpora comprising artificial, simulated, or even real plagiarism, formatted according to the data format established for the previous shared tasks [20]. In this corpus submission subtask a total number of 8 corpora were submitted in different languages includes Chinese [26], Persian [10], English [24, 28, 29] and two cross-lingual corpora from Urdu and Persian to English [25, 27].

AraPlagDet. AraPlagDet is the first international competition on detecting plagiarism in Arabic documents. The competition was held as a PAN shared task at FIRE 2015 and included two sub-tasks corresponding to the first shared tasks at PAN: external plagiarism detection and intrinsic plagiarism detection [1]. The competition followed the formats used at PAN. One of the main motivations of organizers for this shared task was to raise awareness in the Arab world on the seriousness of plagiarism, and, to promote the development of plagiarism detection approaches that deal with the peculiarities of the Arabic language, providing for an evaluation corpus that allows for proper performance comparison between Arabic plagiarism detectors.

PlagDet Task at AAIC. The first competition on Persian plagiarism detection was held as the 3rd AmirKabir Artificial Intelligence Competition (AAIC) in 2015. The competition was the first plagiarism detection challenge in Persian language and led to the release of the first plagiarism detection corpus in Persian. Like AraPlagDet, the PAN standard framework on evaluation and corpus annotation has been used in this competition.

3 Task Description

The shared task of Persian plagiarism detection divides into two subtasks: text alignment and corpus construction. Text alignment is based on PAN evaluation framework to assess the detection performance plagiarism detectors: given two documents, the task is to determine all contiguous passages of reused texts between them. Nine teams participated in this subtask.

The corpus construction subtask invited participants to submit evaluation corpora of their own design for text alignment, following the standard corpus format. Five corpora were submitted to the competition. Their evaluation consisted of evaluating the validity of annotations via analyzing corpus statistics, such as the length distribution of the documents, the length distribution of the plagiarized passages, and the ratio of plagiarism per document. Moreover, we report on the performance of the aforementioned nine plagiarism detectors in detecting the plagiarism comprised within the submitted corpora.

4 Evaluation Framework

The text alignment subtask consists of identifying the exact positions of reused text passages in a given pair of suspicious document and source document. This section describes the evaluation platform, corpus, and performance measure that were used in this subtask. Moreover, the submitted detection approaches and their respective evaluation results are presented.

4.1 Evaluation Platform

Establishing an evaluation framework for Persian plagiarism detection was one of the primary goals of our competition, consisting of a large-scale plagiarism detection corpus along with performance measures. The framework may serve as a unified test environment for future activities on Persian plagiarism detection research. Due to the diverse development environments of participants, it is preferable to set up a common platform that satisfies all their requirements. We decided to use the TIRA experimentation platform [8]. TIRA provides for a set of features that facilitate the reproducibility of our shared task while reducing its organizational overhead [6, 7]:

- TIRA provides every participant with a virtual machine that allows for the convenient deployment and execution of sub-mitted software.
- Both Windows and Linux machines are available to participants, whereas deployed software need only be executable from a POSIX command line.
- TIRA offers a convenient web user interface that allows participants to self-evaluate their software by remote-controlling its execution.
- TIRA allows for evaluating submitted software against test datasets hosted at server side. Test datasets are never visible to participants providing for a blind evaluation, and also allowing for sensitive datasets to be used for evaluation that cannot otherwise be shared publicly.
- At the click of a button, the run output of given software is evaluated against the ground truth of a given dataset. Evaluation results are stored and made accessible on TIRA web page as well as for download.

TIRA is widely used as an Evaluation-as-a-Service platform for experimenting information retrieval tasks [9]. In particular, the evaluation platform was used in since the 4th international competition on plagiarism detection at PAN 2012 [18], and now it is a common platform for all of PAN shared tasks [19].

4.2   Construction of Evaluation Corpus

In this section we describe the methodology for compiling the Persian Plagdet evaluation corpus used for our shared task. The corpus comprises cases of simulated, artificial, and real plagiarism. In general, there are a number of reasons why collecting only real plagiarism is not sufficient for evaluating plagiarism detectors. First, collections of real plagiarism that have been detected manually are usually skewed towards ease of detection (i.e. the more difficult a plagiarism case is to be detected, the less likely it will be detected after the fact). Second, collecting real plagiarism is expensive and time consuming. Third, a corpus comprising real plagiarism cases cannot be published due to ethical and legal issues [17]. Because of these reasons, methods to artificially create plagiarism or to simulate plagiarism are often employed to compile plagiarism corpora. These methods aim at emulating humans who try to obfuscate their plagiarism by paraphrasing reused portions of text. An artificial method for compiling plagiarism corpora includes the use of automatic paraphrasing technology to obfuscate plagiarized passages. Simulated passages of plagiarized text are created manually using human resources and crowdsourcing. Simulated methods yield more realistic cases of plagiarism compared to artificial ones, whereas artificial methods are cheaper in terms of both cost and time and hence scalable.

Simulated cases of plagiarism. To create simulated cases of plagiarism, a crowd-sourcing approach has been used. For this purpose, a dedicated crowdsourcing platform has been developed, and a paraphrasing task was designed for crowd workers. Para-phrased passages obtained via crowdsourcing were reviewed by experts to ensure quality. All told, about 10% of the paraphrased fragments were rejected because of poor quality. Table 1 gives an overview of the demographics of the crowd workers recruited.

Artificial cases of plagiarism. In addition to simulated plagiarism based on manual paraphrasing, a large number of artificially created plagiarisms have been constructed for the corpus. As mentioned above, artificial plagiarism is cheaper and faster to compile than simulated plagiarism. To create artificial plagiarism, the previously proposed method of random obfuscation has been used [16]. The method consists of random text operations (i.e. word addition, deletion, shuffling), semantic word varia-tion, and POS-preserving word shuffling. A composition of these operations has been used to create low and high degrees of random obfuscation.

As a result, after the obfuscation of passages extracted from a set of source doc-uments, the simulated and artificial cases of plagiarism were inserted into a selection of suspicious documents. To prevent false positive results because of undesirable cases of plagiarism (near duplicate documents) in raw Wikipedia documents, near duplicate documents have been detected and haven't been chosen as pairs of suspicious and source documents. Some key statistics of the plagiarism cases and the final corpus are shown in the Tables 2 and 3. The final corpus was divided into a train and a test dataset. The training dataset was given to participants for parameters tuning of their algorithms, and the test dataset was used in the final stage for evaluation purpose. The proposed corpus is freely available for research purposes[1].

Table 1. Crowd workers' demographics.

Workers' demographics		
Age	25–30	41%
	30–40	38%
	40–58	21%
Education	College	5%
	BSc.	25%
	MSc.	58%
	PhD	12%
Tasks per worker	Average	19.0
	Std. deviation	14.5
	Minimum	1
	Maximum	54
Gender	Male	74%
	Female	26%

---

[1] http://ictrc.ac.ir/plagdet

Table 2. Plagiarism case statistics

Plagiarism case statistics		
Obfuscation	Number of cases	4118
	None (exact copy)	9%
	Artificial	75%
	Low	40%
	High	41%
	Simulated	16%
Case length	Short (30–50 words)	35%
	Medium (100–200 words)	38%
	Long (200–300 words)	27%

Table 3. Corpus statistics

Corpus Statistics		
Entire corpus	Number of documents	5830
	Number of plagiarism cases	4118
Document purpose	Source documents	48%
	Suspicious documents	52%
Document length	Short (1–500 words)	35%
	Medium (500–2500 words)	59%
	Long (2500–21000 words)	6%
Plagiarism per document	Small (5%–20%)	57%
	Medium (21%–50%)	15%
	Much (50%–80%)	18%
	Entirely (>80%)	10%

4.3 Performance Measures

The PlagDet measure was used to evaluate the submitted software. PlagDet is a weighted F-measure that combines character level precision, recall, and granularity into one metric so that plagiarism detection systems can be ranked [17]. The run output of a given detector lists detected passages of allegedly plagiarized text as character offsets and lengths. Detection precision and recall are then computed as shown in Eqs. 1 and 2 below. In these equations, S is the set of the actual plagiarism cases and R is the set of detected plagiarism cases:

$$prec(S,R) = \frac{1}{|R|} \sum_{r \in R} \frac{\left| \bigcup_{s \in S} (s \sqcap r) \right|}{|r|} \tag{1}$$

$$rec(S,R) = \frac{1}{|S|} \sum_{s \in S} \frac{\left| \bigcup_{r \in R} (s \sqcap r) \right|}{|s|} \tag{2}$$

$$where \quad s \sqcap r = \begin{cases} s \cap r & if\ r\ detects\ s \\ \emptyset & otherwise \end{cases}$$

The granularity measure assesses the capability of a detector to detect a plagiarism case as a whole as opposed to in several pieces. The granularity of a detector is defined as follows:

$$gran(S, R) = \frac{1}{|S_R|} \sum\nolimits_{s \in S_R} |R_S| \tag{3}$$

where S denotes the set of plagiarism cases in the corpus, R denotes the set of detections reported by a plagiarism detector, $S_R \subseteq S$ the cases detected by detections in R, and $R_S \subseteq R$ detections that detect cases in S. Finally, the PlagDet measure is a combination of F1, the equally-weighted harmonic mean of precision and recall, and granularity:

$$plagdet(S, R) = \frac{F_1}{\log_2(1 + gran(S, R))} \tag{4}$$

5 Subtask 1: Text Alignment

This section overviews the submitted software and reports on their evaluation results.

5.1 Survey of Detection Approaches

A collection of 9 teams were registered on TIRA platform and successfully submitted their softwares for the text alignment task. All of the nine participants submitted working notes describing their approaches. In what follows, we survey the approaches.

Talebpour et al. [23] use -trie trees to index the source documents after preprocessing. The preprocessing steps are text tokenization, POS tagging, text cleansing, and text normalization to transform text characters into a unique and normal form, removal of stop words and frequent words, and stemming. Moreover, FarsNet (the Persian WordNet) [22] is used to find words' synonyms and synsets. This may allow for detecting cases of paraphrased plagiarism based on replacing words with their synonyms. After preprocessing both documents, all of the words of a source document and their exact positions are inserted into a -trie. After inserting all source documents into a -trie structure, the suspicious document are iteratively analyzed, checking each word one by one against the -trie to find potential sources.

Minaei and Niknam [14] employ n-grams as seed heuristic to find primary matches between suspicious and source documents. Cases of plagiarism without obfuscation and similar parts of paraphrased text can be found this way. In order to detect cases of plagiarized passages, matches closer than a specified threshold are merged. Finally, to decrease false positive cases, detected cases shorter than a pre-defined threshold are eliminated.

Momtaz et al. [15] use sentence boundaries to split source and suspicious documents. After text normalization and removal of stop words and punctuations, sentences of both documents are turned into graphs, where words represent nodes and an edge is established between each word and its four surrounding words. Such graphs obtained from suspicious and source documents are compared and their similarity computed, whereas sentences of high similarity are labeled as plagiarism. Finally, to improve granularity, sentences close to each other are merged to create contiguous cases of detected plagiarism.

Gillam and Vartapetiance [5] use an approach based on their previous PAN efforts. The task of finding textual matching is undertaken without direct using of the textual content. The proposed approach produces a minimal representation of text by distinguishing content and auxiliary words. Moreover it produces matchable binary patterns directly from these dependent words on the number of classes of interest. Although the approach act similar to hashing functions, but no effort is taken to prevent collision. Contrary, hash collision is encouraged over short distances, by preventing reverse-engineering of the patterns, and uses the number of coincident matches to indicate the extent of similarity.

Mansoorizadeh and Rahgooy [11] and Ehsan and Shakery [2] use sentence boundaries to split source and suspicious documents like the approach in [15]. In both approaches, each sentence is represented under the vector space model, using TF-IDF as weighting scheme. Finally, sentences with cosine similarity greater than a pre-defined threshold between corresponding vectors are considered as cases of plagiarism. In [2] a subsequent match merging stage improves performance with respect to granularity. Moreover, overlapping passages and extremely short passages are removed for the same reason. The lack of such a merging stage in Mansoorizadeh and Rahgooy [11] approach yields high granularity and therefore a poor PlagDet score.

Like most of the submitted software, Esteki and Safi Esfahani [3] split documents into sentences to detect plagiarism cases. After a pre-processing phase, which includes normalization, stemming and stop words removal, a Support Vector Machine (SVM) classifier is used to separate "similar" sentences against non-similar ones. The Levenshtein distance, the Jaccard coefficient, and the Longest Common Subsequence (LCS) are used as features extracted from pairs of sentences. Moreover, synonyms are detected to increase the likelihood of detecting paraphrased sentences.

Gharavi et al. [4] use a deep learning approach to represent sentences of suspicious and source documents as vectors. For this purpose, they use Word2Vec to extract words' vectors and to compute sentence vectors as average word vectors. The most similar sentences between pairs of source document and suspicious document are found using the cosine similarity, the Jaccard coefficient, reporting them as plagiarism cases.

Mashhadirajab and Shamsfard [12] use the vector space model (VSM) with TF-IDF weighting to create sentence vectors from source and suspicious documents. To gain better results, they use an SVM neural net to predict the obfuscation type in order to adjust the required parameters. Moreover, to calculate the semantic similarity between sentences, FarsNet [22] is used to extract synsets of terms. Finally, within extension and filtering steps similar sentences that are close to each other are merged while passages that either overlap or are too short are removed.

5.2 Evaluation Results

Table 4 shows the overall performance and runtimes of the nine submitted text alignment approaches. As can be seen, the approach of Mashhadirajab et al. [12] has achieved the highest PlagDet score on the complete corpus and is hence ranked highest. Regarding runtime, the submission of Gharavi et al. [4] and Minaei and Niknam [14] are outstanding: they process the entire corpus in only 1:03 and 1:33 min, respectively. Table 5 shows the performance of the submitted software dependent on obfuscation types in the corpus. Although, due to the lack of true positives, no performance values can be computed for the sub-corpus without plagiarism, at least false positive detections for this sub-corpus influence the overall performance of participants on the whole corpus [18]. Gharavi et al. [4] is ranked first in detection performance with highest PlagDet for "No obfuscation," and Mashhadirajab and Shamsfard [12] achieves best performance for both "Artificial" and "Simulated" plagiarism. Among all participants, Mashhadirajab achieves best recall across all parts of the corpus, whereas Talebpour et al. [23] and Gharavi et al. [4] outperform it in precision.

6 Subtask 2: Corpus Construction

This section overviews the five submitted text alignment corpora. In the first subsection we will have a survey of submitted corpora and will give a statistical overview of them. In the next subsection the results of validation and evaluation on the submitted corpora will be presented.

The task of corpus evaluation has been examined before in PAN 2015 [20] which consisted of peer review of corpora and also running all of the submitted PD algorithms on them. In this paper, we have used the same method. On the other hand, for validating the submitted corpora, we used the methods presented in [30].

Table 4. Overall detection performance for the nine approaches submitted.

Rank/team	Runtime (h:m:s)	Recall	Precision	Granularity	F-measure	PlagDet
1. Mashhadirajab	02:22:48	**0.9191**	0.9268	1.0014	**0.9230**	**0.9220**
2. Gharavi	**00:01:03**	0.8582	0.9592	1	0.9059	0.9059
3. Momtaz	00:16:08	0.8504	0.8925	1	0.8710	0.8710
4. Minaei	00:01:33	0.7960	0.9203	1.0396	0.8536	0.8301
5. Esteki	00:44:03	0.7012	0.9333	1	0.8008	0.8008
6. Talebpour	02:24:19	0.8361	**0.9638**	1.2275	0.8954	0.7749
7. Ehsan	00:24:08	0.7049	0.7496	1	0.7266	0.7266
8. Gillam	21:08:54	0.4140	0.7548	1.5280	0.5347	0.3996
9. Mansourizadeh	00:02:38	0.8065	0.9000	3.5369	0.8507	0.3899

Table 5. Detection performance of the nine approaches submitted, dependent on obfuscation type

Team	No obfuscation				Artificial obfuscation				Simulated obfuscation			
	Recall	Precision	Granularity	PlagDet	Recall	Precision	Granularity	PlagDet	Recall	Precision	Granularity	PlagDet
Mashhadirajab	**0.993**	0.940	1	0.966	**0.947**	0.941	1.006	**0.944**	**0.804**	0.933	1.004	**0.861**
Gharavi	0.982	0.976	1	**0.979**	0.897	0.964	1	0.930	0.689	**0.968**	1	0.805
Momtaz	0.953	0.896	1	0.924	0.901	0.897	1	0.899	0.653	0.911	1	0.761
Minaei	0.965	0.866	1.011	0.906	0.851	0.932	1.024	0.875	0.561	0.911	1.117	0.642
Esteki	0.978	0.968	1	0.973	0.775	0.947	1	0.853	0.368	0.898	1	0.522
Talebpour	0.975	**0.977**	1	0.976	0.897	**0.967**	1.207	0.814	0.596	0.958	1.411	0.578
Ehsan	0.806	0.733	1	0.768	0.754	0.757	1	0.755	0.515	0.785	1	0.622
Gillam	0.758	0.625	1.485	0.522	0.423	0.774	1.535	0.408	0.256	0.774	1.530	0.287
Mansourizadeh	0.961	0.882	3.774	0.408	0.889	0.912	3.601	0.409	0.494	0.879	3.149	0.308

6.1   Survey of Submitted Corpora

All of the submitted corpora consist of Persian mono-lingual plagiarism for the task of text alignment, except for Mashhadirajab corpus [13] which also contains a set of cross-lingual English-Persian plagiarism cases. All of the corpora are formatted in accordance with the PAN standard annotation format for text alignment corpora. In particular, this includes two sets of documents, namely source documents and suspicious documents, where the latter are to be analyzed for plagiarism from any of the source documents. The annotations of plagiarism cases are stored separately from the text documents within XML documents for each pair of suspicious and source documents. Therein, each plagiarism case is annotated as follows:

- Start position and length of the source passage in the source document
- Start position and length of the suspicious passage in the suspicious document
- Obfuscation type (e.g., indicating to the way that a source passage has been paraphrased before being added as suspicious passage to the suspicious documents)

Dataset Overview

Table 6 shows an overview of the submitted text alignment corpora in terms of the corpus statistics also reported for our corpus. Mashhadirajab corpus [13] is the biggest one in terms of number of documents, whereas Abnar corpus contains the largest number of plagiarism cases. Samim corpus [21] includes larger documents compared to the other corpora, whereas a large volume of small documents have been used for construction of the ICTRC corpus. Samim corpus and the ICTRC corpus comprise the largest and the smallest plagiarism case, respectively. A variety of different obfuscation strategies have been employed. No obfuscation (i.e., exact copy) and artificial obfuscation (random text operations) are two common strategies.

The length distributions of documents and plagiarized passages are depicted in Figs. 1 and 2. Here, the ICTRC corpus contains stands out, containing the smallest documents and plagiarized passages among all submitted corpora. Figure 3 shows the distribution of the plagiarism ratio per suspicious document. The ratio of plagiarism per suspicious documents in Samim corpus is distributed more uniformly compared to the other submitted corpora. In what follows, the documents used to compile the corpora as well as the construction approaches are discussed in detail.

Document Sources

The first step to compile a plagiarism detection corpus is choosing the documents which will be used as the sets of source documents and suspicious documents. Many plagiarism detection corpora intend to simulate plagiarism in technical texts, so that Wikipedia articles and scientific papers are often employed as source and suspicious documents sources in these corpora. This also pertains to the corpora submitted, which mainly employ journal articles and Wikipedia articles. Wikipedia articles have been used as resource to compiling the ICTRC corpus and Niknam corpus. Niknam used 3000 documents larger than 4000 characters, and ICTRC used about 6000 documents larger than 1500 characters. Abnar used texts from a set of novels that were translated to Persian. Despite the genre of books, the documents found in the corpus are not as large as might be expected. Mashhadirajab et al. [13] and Samim [21] used scientific papers to compile their corpora. Mashhadirajab used a combination of Wikipedia articles (40%), articles from the Computer Society of Iran Computer Conference (CSICC) (13%), theses available in online (13%) and Persian open access articles (34%). Samim also collected Persian open access papers from peer reviewed journals to compile their text alignment corpus. The papers used include papers from the humanities (57%), science (25%), veterinary science (10%) and other related subjects (8%).

Obfuscation Synthesis

The second step in compiling a plagiarism detection corpus is to obfuscate passages selected from source documents and then insert them into suspicious documents. Obfuscating text passages aims at emulating plagiarism cases whose authors try to conceal the fact their plagiarized, making it more difficult for human reviewers and plagiarism detection systems alike to identify the plagiarized passages afterwards. As discussed above, creating obfuscated plagiarism manually is laborious and expensive, so that most participants resorted to automatic obfuscation methods. It is remarkable that two of the corpora (the ones of Mashhadirajab and ICTRC) comprise plagiarism that has been manually created. Otherwise, a variety of different approaches have been employed for obfuscation (see Table 6, rows "Obfuscation type"). All of the submitted corpora also contain a portion of plagiarized passages without any obfuscation to simulate verbatim copying.

Niknam employed a set of text operations consisting of addition, deletion and shuffling of words, replacing words with their synonyms and POS-preserving word replacement. Similar obfuscation strategies have been used to compile Samim's corpus. It contains "Random Text Operations" and "Semantic Word Variation" in addition to "No obfuscation." In addition to these obfuscation types, the authors of the ICTRC corpus used a crowdsourcing platform for paraphrasing test passages. About 30 people of various ages, both genders, and different levels of education have participated in the paraphrasing process. Abnar's corpus comprises obfuscation approaches such as replacing words with synonyms, shuffling sentences, circular translation, and a combination of the aforementioned ones. The circular translation approach includes translating the text to an intermediate language and then translating it back to the original one, hoping that the resulting text will significantly differ from the original one while maintaining its meaning. From a diversity point of view, Mashhadirajab's corpus

Table 6. Corpus statistics for the submitted corpora

		Niknam	Samim	Mashhadirajab	ICTRC	Abnar
Entire corpus	Number of documents	3218	4707	11089	5755	2470
	Number of plagiarism cases	2308	5862	11603	3745	12061
Document purpose	Source documents	52%	50%	48%	49%	20%
	Suspicious documents	48%	50%	52%	51%	80%
Document length	Short (1–10000 words)	35%	2%	53%	91%	51%
	Medium (10000–30000 words)	56%	48%	32%	8%	48%
	Long (>30000 words)	9%	50%	15%	1%	1%
Plagiarism per document	Hardly (<20%)	71%	29%	39%	57%	29%
	Medium (20%–50%)	28%	25%	14%	37%	60%
	Much (50%–80%)	1%	31%	20%	6%	10%
	Entirely (>80%)	–	15%	27%	–	1%
Case length	Short (1–500 words)	21%	15%	6%	51%	45%
	Medium (500–1500 words)	76%	22%	52%	46%	54%
	Long (>1500 words)	3%	63%	42%	3%	1%
Obfuscation types	No obfuscation (exact copy)	25%	40%	17%	10%	22%
	Artificial (word replacement)	27%	–	–	–	–
	Artificial (synonym replacement)	25%	–	–	–	–
	Artificial (POS-preserving shuffling)	23%	–	–	–	–
	Random	–	40%	–	81%	–
	Semantic	–	20%	–	–	15%
	Near copy	–	–	28%	–	–
	Summarizing	–	–	33%	–	–
	Paraphrasing	–	–	6%	–	–
	Modified copy	–	–	4%	–	–
	Circle translation	–	–	3%	–	21%
	Semantic-based meaning	–	–	1%	–	–
	Auto translation	–	–	2%	–	–
	Translation	–	–	6%	–	–
	Simulated	–	–	–	9%	–
	Shuffle sentences	–	–	–	–	21%
	Combination	–	–	–	–	21%

contains the most variety in terms of obfuscation. In addition to artificial and simulated cases, they used summarizing cyclic translation and text manipulation approaches to create cases of plagiarism. Moreover, the corpus comprises also cross-lingual plagiarism where source documents have been translated to Persian using manual and automatic translation.

6.2 Corpus Validation

In order to validate the submitted corpora, we analyzed them quantitatively and qualitatively. For the latter, samples have been drawn from each corpus and obfuscation type for manual review. The review involved of validating the plagiarism annotations, such as offsets and lengths of annotated plagiarism in both source and suspicious documents. Moreover, the suspicious passage and its corresponding source have been checked manually to observe the impact of different obfuscation strategies as well as the level of obfuscation. Altogether, no important issues have been found among the studied samples during peer-review.

In addition to manual review, we also analyzed the corpora quantitatively: Figs. 1 and 2 depict the length distributions of the documents and the plagiarism cases in the corpora. Both Abnar's corpus and the ICTRC corpus have clear expected values, whereas the other corpora are more evenly distributed. Figure 3 depicts the ratio of plagiarism per document, showing that the ratios are quite unevenly distributed across corpora; Niknam's corpus and the ICTRC corpus comprise mostly suspicious documents with a small ratio of plagiarism. Figures 4 and 5 show the distribution of plagiarized passages in terms of where they start within suspicious documents (i.e., their character offset), and where they start within source documents. The distributions of start offsets within suspicious documents are similar across all corpora with a negative bias against offsets at the beginning of a suspicious document (see Fig. 4). The distributions are also similar for the start offsets within source documents with one notable exception: the source passages of Samim's corpus have almost always been chosen from the same offsets of source documents which is a clear bias and may allow for trivial detection.

Finally, we analyzed the plagiarized passages in the submitted corpora with regard to their similarity between source passage and suspicious passage. The experiment consists of comparing source passages with suspicious passages using 10 retrieval models. Each model is an n-gram vector space model (VSM), where n ranges from 1 to 10 words, employing stop word removal, TF-weighting and the cosine similarity [17]. For high-quality corpora, a pattern similar to that of PAN corpora is expected.

Since there are many obfuscate types to choose from, we only compare a selection: the simulated plagiarism cases of Mashhadirajab and ICTRC are compared to the PAN corpora (Fig. 6). Moreover, the artificial parts of all corpora are compared to each other (Fig. 7). Abnar's corpus is omitted since it lacks artificial obfuscation. Almost all of the corpora show same patterns of similarity for different ranges of n, except the Mashhadirajab's corpus which has a higher range of similarity in comparison to others.

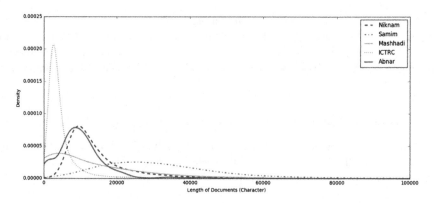

Fig. 1. Length distribution of documents

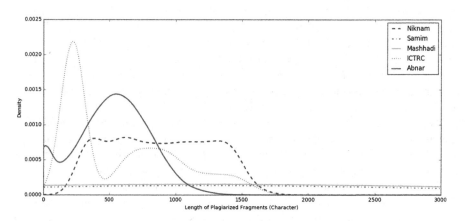

Fig. 2. Length distribution of fragments

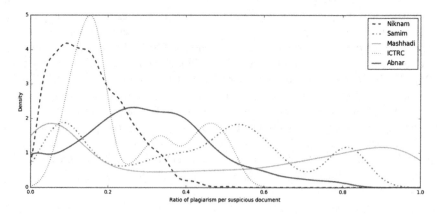

Fig. 3. Ratio of plagiarism per document

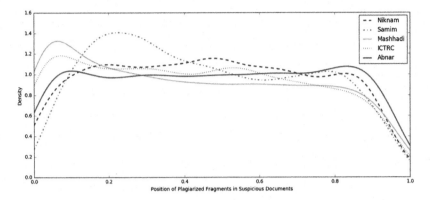

Fig. 4. Start position of plagiarized fragments in suspicious documents

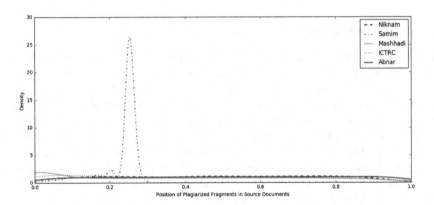

Fig. 5. Start position of plagiarized fragments in source documents

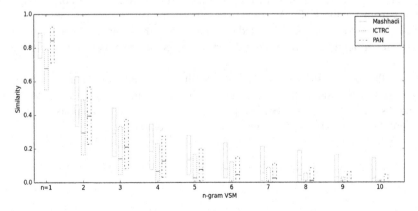

Fig. 6. Comparison of simulated part of Mashhadirajab and ICTRC corpora

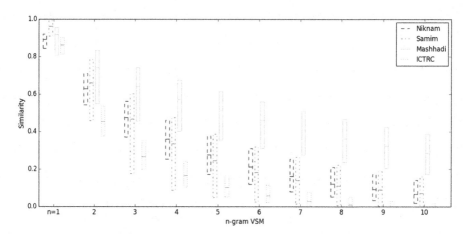

Fig. 7. Comparison of artificial part of Niknam, Samim, Mashhadirajab and ICTRC corpora

6.3 Corpus Evaluation

Exploiting the virtues of TIRA, our final experiment was to run the nine submitted detection approaches on the five submitted corpora, providing for a first impression on how difficult it is to detect plagiarism within these corpora. Table 7 overviews the results of this experiment. Unfortunately, not all submitted approaches succeeded in processing all corpora. One reason was scalability issues: since some of the submitted corpora are significantly larger than our evaluation corpus, it seems participants did not pay a lot of attention to scalability. The approaches of Talebpour and Gillam failed to process the corpora in time. The approaches of Momtaz and Esteki failed to process some of the corpora at first, the results of the former are only partially reliable to date, whereas the latter of which could be fixed in time. This shows that submitting datasets to shared tasks presents its own challenges. Participants will be invited to fix their software to make it work on all corpora, so that further results may become available after publication of this paper, e.g., on TIRA's web page. Considering the detection performance, it can be seen that the PlagDet scores are generally lower compared to our corpus, except for the ICTRC corpus, where the same performance scores have been reached. This shows that the submitted corpora present their own challenges, rendering them more difficult, and presenting future researchers with new opportunities for contributions.

Given the results from all our experiments, the submitted corpora are of reasonable quality. Although some of them are too easy to be solved and comprise a biased sample of plagiarism cases, the diversity of corpora ensures that future evaluations can be done with confidence as long as all available datasets are employed.

Table 7. PlagDet performance of some submitted approaches on the submitted corpora

Team	Niknam	Samim	Mashhadirajab	ICTRC	Abnar
Gharavi	0.8657	0.7386	**0.5784**	0.9253	0.3927
Momtaz	0.8161	–	–	0.8924	–
Minaei	**0.9042**	0.6585	0.3877	0.8633	0.7218
Esteki	0.5758	–	–	0.8455	0.3830
Ehsan	0.7196	0.5367	0.4014	0.7104	0.5890
Mansourizadeh	0.2984	0.1594	0.1286	0.3889	0.2687
Mashhadirajab	0.8747	**0.7416**	0.4744	**0.9325**	**0.8366**

7   Conclusion

In conclusion, our shared task has attracted considerable attention from the community of scientists working on plagiarism detection. The shared task has served as a means to establish a new state of the art in performance evaluation for Persian plagiarism detection. Altogether six new evaluation corpora are available now, and nine detection approaches have been evaluated on them. The results show that Persian plagiarism detection is far from being a solved problem. In addition, our contributions broaden the scope of the text alignment task which has been studied mostly for English until now. This may allow future work on plagiarism detection approaches that work on both languages simultaneously.

Acknowledgments. This work has been funded by ICT Research Institute, ACECR, under the partial support of Vice Presidency for Science and Technology of Iran - Grant No. 1164331. The work of Paolo Rosso has been partially funded by the SomEMBED MINECO TIN2015-71147-C2-1-P research project and by the Generalitat Valenciana under the grant ALMAMATER (PrometeoII/2014/030). We would like to thank the participants of the competition for their dedicated work. Our special thanks go to the renowned experts who served on the organizing committee for their contributions and devoted work to make this shared task possible. We would like to thank Javad Rafiei and Khadijeh Khoshnava for their help in construction of evaluation corpus. We are also immensely grateful to Vahid Zarrabi for his comments and valuable help along the way which greatly assisted this challenging shared task.

References

1. Bensalem, I., Boukhalfa, I., Rosso, P., Abouenour, L., Darwish, K., Chikhi, S.: Overview of the AraPlagDet PAN@ FIRE2015 Shared Task on Arabic Plagiarism Detection, vol. 1587, pp. 111–122. CEUR-WS.org (2015)
2. Ehsan, N., Shakery, A.: A pairwise document analysis approach for monolingual plagiarism detection. In: Working Notes of FIRE 2016 - Forum for Information Retrieval Evaluation, Kolkata, India, 7–10 December 2016, CEUR Workshop Proceedings. CEUR-WS.org (2016)
3. Esteki, F., Safi Esfahani, F.: A plagiarism detection approach based on SVM for Persian texts. In: Working Notes of FIRE 2016 - Forum for Information Retrieval Evaluation, Kolkata, India, 7–10 December 2016, CEUR Workshop Proceedings. CEUR-WS.org (2016)

4. Gharavi, E., Bijari, K., Zahirnia, K., Veisi, H.: A deep learning approach to Persian plagiarism detection. In: Working Notes of FIRE 2016 - Forum for Information Retrieval Evaluation, Kolkata, India, 7–10 December 2016, CEUR Workshop Proceedings. CEUR-WS.org (2016)

5. Gillam, L., Vartapetiance, A.: From English to Persian: conversion of text alignment for plagiarism detection. In: Working Notes of FIRE 2016 - Forum for Information Retrieval Evaluation, Kolkata, India, 7–10 December 2016, CEUR Workshop Proceedings. CEUR-WS.org (2016)

6. Gollub, T., Burrows, S., Stein, B.: First experiences with TIRA for reproducible evaluation in information retrieval. In: SIGIR, vol. 12, pp. 52–55, August 2012

7. Gollub, T., Stein, B., Burrows, S.: Ousting ivory tower research: towards a web framework for providing experiments as a service. In: Proceedings of the 35th International ACM SIGIR Conference on Research and Development in Information Retrieval, pp. 1125–1126. ACM, August 2012

8. Gollub, T., Stein, B., Burrows, S., Hoppe, D.: TIRA: configuring, executing, and disseminating information retrieval experiments. In: 2012 23rd International Workshop on Database and Expert Systems Applications, pp. 151–155. IEEE, September 2012

9. Hopfgartner, F., Hanbury, A., Müller, H., Kando, N., Mercer, S., Kalpathy-Cramer, J., Potthast, M., Gollub, T., Krithara, A., Lin, J., Balog, K.: Report on the Evaluation-as-a-Service (EaaS) expert workshop. In: ACM SIGIR Forum, vol. 49, no. 1, pp. 57–65. ACM, June 2015

10. Khoshnavataher, K., Zarrabi, V., Mohtaj, S., Asghari, H.: Developing monolingual Persian corpus for extrinsic plagiarism detection using artificial obfuscation. Notebook for PAN at CLEF 2015. In: CLEF (Working Notes) (2015)

11. Mansoorizadeh, M., Rahgooy, T.: Persian plagiarism detection using sentence correlations. In: Working Notes of FIRE 2016 - Forum for Information Retrieval Evaluation, Kolkata, India, 7–10 December 2016, CEUR Workshop Proceedings. CEUR-WS.org (2016)

12. Mashhadirajab, F., Shamsfard, M.: A text alignment algorithm based on prediction of obfuscation types using SVM neural network. In: Working Notes of FIRE 2016 - Forum for Information Retrieval Evaluation, Kolkata, India, 7–10 December 2016, CEUR Workshop Proceedings. CEUR-WS.org (2016)

13. Mashhadirajab, F., Shamsfard, M., Adelkhah, R., Shafiee, F., Saedi, S.: A text alignment corpus for Persian plagiarism detection. In: Working Notes of FIRE 2016 - Forum for Information Retrieval Evaluation, Kolkata, India, 7–10 December 2016, CEUR Workshop Proceedings. CEUR-WS.org (2016)

14. Minaei, B., Niknam, M.: An n-gram based method for nearly copy detection in plagiarism systems. In: Working Notes of FIRE 2016 - Forum for Information Retrieval Evaluation, Kolkata, India, 7–10 December 2016, CEUR Workshop Proceedings. CEUR-WS.org (2016)

15. Momtaz, M., Bijari, K., Salehi, M., Veisi, H.: Graph-based approach to text alignment for plagiarism detection in Persian documents. In: Working Notes of FIRE 2016 - Forum for Information Retrieval Evaluation, Kolkata, India, 7–10 December 2016, CEUR Workshop Proceedings. CEUR-WS.org (2016)

16. Potthast, M., Stein, B., Eiselt, A., Barrón-Cedeño, A., Rosso, P.: Overview of the 1st international competition on plagiarism detection. In: 3rd PAN Workshop. Uncovering Plagiarism, Authorship and Social Software Misuse (2009)

17. Potthast, M., Stein, B., Barrón-Cedeño, A., Rosso, P.: An evaluation framework for plagiarism detection. In: Proceedings of the 23rd International Conference on Computational Linguistics: Posters, pp. 997–1005. Association for Computational Linguistics, August 2010

18. Potthast, M., Gollub, T., Hagen, M., Graßegger, J., Kiesel, J., Michel, M., Oberländer, A., Tippmann, M., Barrón-Cedeño, A., Gupta, P., Rosso, P., Stein, B.: Overview of the 4th international competition on plagiarism detection. In: CLEF (Online Working Notes/Labs/Workshop) (2012)

19. Potthast, M., Gollub, T., Rangel, F., Rosso, P., Stamatatos, E., Stein, B.: Improving the reproducibility of PAN's shared tasks. In: Kanoulas, E., Lupu, M., Clough, P., Sanderson, M., Hall, M., Hanbury, A., Toms, E. (eds.) CLEF 2014. LNCS, vol. 8685, pp. 268–299. Springer, Cham (2014). https://doi.org/10.1007/978-3-319-11382-1_22

20. Potthast, M., Hagen, M., Göring, S., Rosso, P., Stein, B.: Towards data submissions for shared tasks: first experiences for the task of text alignment. In: Working Notes Papers of the CLEF, pp. 1613–0073 (2015)

21. Rezaei Sharifabadi, M., Eftekhari, S.A.: Mahak Samim: a corpus of Persian academic texts for evaluating plagiarism detection systems. In: Working notes of FIRE 2016 - Forum for Information Retrieval Evaluation, Kolkata, India, 7–10 December 2016, CEUR Workshop Proceedings. CEUR-WS.org (2016)

22. Shamsfard, M.: Developing FarsNet: a lexical ontology for Persian. In: Proceedings of the 4th Global WordNet Conference (2008)

23. Talebpour, A., Shirzadi, M., Aminolroaya, Z.: Plagiarism detection based on a novel trie-based approach. In: Working Notes of FIRE 2016 - Forum for Information Retrieval Evaluation, Kolkata, India, 7–10 December 2016, CEUR Workshop Proceedings. CEUR-WS.org (2016)

24. Mohtaj, S., Asghari, H., Zarrabi, V.: Developing monolingual English Corpus for Plagiarism Detection using Human Annotated Paraphrase Corpus—Notebook for PAN at CLEF 2015 (2015)

25. Asghari, H., Khoshnavataher, K., Fatemi, O., Faili, H.: Developing Bilingual Plagiarism Detection Corpus Using Sentence Aligned Parallel Corpus—Notebook for PAN at CLEF 2015 (2015)

26. Kong, L., Lu, Z., Han, Y., Qi, H., Han, Z., Wang, Q., Hao, Z., Zhang, J.: Source Retrieval and Text Alignment Corpus Construction for Plagiarism Detection—Notebook for PAN at CLEF 2015 (2015)

27. Hanif, I., Nawab, A., Arbab, A., Jamshed, H., Riaz, S., Munir, E.: Cross-Language Urdu-English (CLUE) Text Alignment Corpus—Notebook for PAN at CLEF 2015 (2015)

28. Alvi, F., Stevenson, M., Clough, P.: The Short Stories Corpus—Notebook for PAN at CLEF 2015 (2015)

29. Cheema, W., Najib, F., Ahmed, S., Bukhari, S., Sittar, A., Nawab, R.: A Corpus for Analyzing Text Reuse by People of Different Groups—Notebook for PAN at CLEF 2015 (2015)

30. Zarrabi, V., Rafiei, J., Khoshnava, K., Asghari, H., Mohtaj, S.: Evaluation of Text Reuse Corpora for Text Alignment Task of Plagiarism Detection—Notebook for PAN at CLEF 2015 (2015)

Predicting Type of Obfuscation to Enhance Text Alignment Algorithms

Fatemeh Mashhadirajab[(✉)] and Mehrnoush Shamsfard

NLP Research Lab, Faculty of Computer Science and Engineering,
Shahid Beheshti University, Tehran, Iran
f.mashhadirajab@mail.sbu.ac.ir, m-shams@sbu.ac.ir

Abstract. Plagiarism detection can be divided into source retrieval and text alignment subtasks. The text alignment subtask extracts all plagiarized passages from a given a pair of documents. The challenge is to identify passages of text that have been obfuscated. A given pair of documents could contain different types of obfuscation. Information about the type of obfuscation in a document pair could be useful for text alignment algorithms in plagiarism detection systems when choosing the most suitable algorithm for each type. The current paper describes a proposed approach to improve text alignment algorithms. The SVM neural network is used for classification of documents according to the type of obfuscation strategy used in the document pair. The parameter values in the proposed text alignment algorithm are set based on the type of obfuscation detected. The results of the proposed algorithm for Persian Plagdet corpus 2016 are shown. The proposed algorithm ranked first in the Persian Plagdet 2016 competition from among nine participant teams.

Keywords: Plagiarism detection · Text alignment · SVM neural network

1 Introduction

Because human beings use varied and sometimes sophisticated methods to conceal plagiarism, systems with highly-varied algorithms have been designed for automatic discovery of plagiarism types. Many plagiarism detection systems have been developed [1–3] and plagiarism detection has become a task in the PAN competition[1] held every year since 2009. At the PAN competition, the plagiarism detection task is divided into source retrieval and text alignment subtasks. The source retrieval task is to retrieve documents similar to the suspicious document from a set of source documents and the text alignment task is to extract all plagiarized passages from a given source-suspicious document pair [4]. Figure 1 shows different parts of a plagiarism detection system. At the PAN competition, the text alignment algorithms are assessed by evaluation corpora that contain different types of obfuscation. In the PAN 2013–2014 competitions, for example, the evaluation corpus consisted of the None, Random, Translation and Summary obfuscation types [5]. The Persian Plagdet 2016 evaluation corpus included the None (exact copy) and Artificial (random) types created by automatic paraphrasing

---

[1] http://pan.webis.de/.

© Springer International Publishing AG 2018
P. Majumder et al. (Eds.): FIRE 2016 Workshop, LNCS 10478, pp. 80–93, 2018.
https://doi.org/10.1007/978-3-319-73606-8_6

technology for word addition, deletion and shuffling, semantic word variation and Simulated obfuscation created by crowdsourcing [6]. PAN corpus 2010 contained None, Artificial and Simulated obfuscation [7]. Different methods could be used to detect the type of obfuscation to in plagiarized passages and or different sets of values could be defined for each parameter set to improve performance of the text alignment algorithm. In PAN text alignment corpora, it is assumed that just one type of obfuscation is employed in each document pair [7]; thus, most participants try to predict the type of obfuscation strategy used in a document pair and detect similarities based on the predicted type [8–10].

The current paper describes the proposed algorithm, which was submitted to the Persian Plagdet 2016 competition[2]. Persian Plagdet 2016 is a subtask of the PAN Fire 2016 competition[3] that is held for the Persian language and the text alignment algorithms were evaluated on a Persian corpus [6]. The proposed approach includes four stages: preprocessing, seeding, extension and filtering. After preprocessing, a neural network is used to detect the type of obfuscation in each document pair. The parameters in the text alignment algorithm are set based on the detected type of obfuscation. In the seeding stage, similar sentence pairs are extracted from the given document pair. In extension, the seeds are extended to detect the longest similar passages from the suspicious and source documents. Small or overlapping passages are removed in the filtering stage. The rest of the paper is organized as follows. Section 2 reviews published work related to the text alignment task. Section 3 explains the proposed algorithm with a focus on the obfuscation type detection module. Section 4 describes the evaluation framework, training and test datasets and the performance measures used for evaluation. The experimental results are discussed in Sect. 4 and the conclusion and future work are reported in Sect. 5.

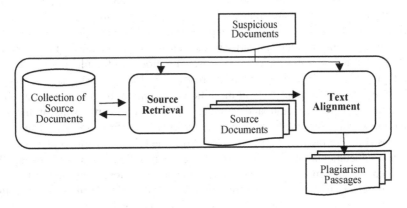

Fig. 1. Plagiarism detection systems.

[2] http://ictrc.ac.ir/plagdet/.

[3] http://fire.irsi.res.in/fire/2016/home.

2 Related Work

The text alignment task is to extract all plagiarized passages from a given a pair of documents. The challenge with this task is to identify passages of text that have been obfuscated. Text alignment algorithms usually consist of three phases: seeding, extension and filtering [5]. Before seeding, some algorithms contain a preprocessing stage. In preprocessing, non-alphanumeric characters and stop words are removed and words are stemmed. The task of seeding is to extract small fragments from a source document and a suspicious document that are similar. At the end of this stage, a large collection of similar fragments will be constructed that are called "seeds". The small fragments could be character [11], word [8, 12] or skip word [13] n-grams or a combination of n-grams [11, 14]. Some algorithms use sentences as small fragments [15–19]. To extract similar fragments, some algorithms use exact matching [8, 11, 13, 14, 18]. Alvi et al. [11] used the Rabin-Karp algorithm and Sanchez-Perez et al. [15, 16] used cosine similarity and the Dice coefficient in a vector space model (VSM) for matching. In the extension phase, the set of seeds is extended to larger fragments that are reported as plagiarism cases. Plagiarism cases are fragments in the given source-suspicious document pair that are similar. Many algorithms have been applied in the extension stage. For example, for the text alignment task in the PAN competition, the extension algorithms were either rule-based, dynamic programming or clustering-based approaches [5]. Alvi et al. [11] used rule-based approaches to merge matching pairs. They divided matching pairs into four categories based on their proximity to one another. Two mapping pairs could be merged if they belong to a specific category. Glinos et al. [8] applied the Smith-Waterman [10] dynamic programming algorithm to find maximal length passages. Ehsan et al. [20] also used the dynamic algorithms to detect alignments between n-grams. Abnar et al. [21] and Gross et al. [13] applied clustering algorithms to detect maximally-aligned sequences of document pairs. The extension phase in the Miguel algorithm [15, 16] consisted of clustering and validation parts. In this approach, the seeds were clustered based on a distance *maxgap* and then the similarity in each cluster was computed. If the similarity in a cluster fell below a threshold value, it was discarded. In the filtering phase, some short [8, 11, 13, 15, 16, 19, 21] or overlapping [15, 16, 19] passages are removed. The PAN evaluation corpora contain the following: none obfuscation, random obfuscation, translation obfuscation and summary obfuscation. Participants at the PAN competition use various methods to predict the type of obfuscation and detect similarities based on the predicted type. At PAN 2014, the Glinos algorithm [8] divided all plagiarism documents into order-based and non-order based categories. The order-based plagiarism detects none and random obfuscations. The non-order-based plagiarism detects translation and summary obfuscation. The Smith-Waterman algorithm [10] is used to detect aligned sequences of document pairs and order-based plagiarism cases. If no aligned sequences are found, the document pairs are given to the clustering component to detect non-order-based plagiarism cases. Sanchez-Perez et al. [15, 16] categorized the document pairs of PAN 2014 corpus into verbatim, summary and other plagiarism categories and set the parameters based on these categories. They used the longest common substring algorithm to find every single common sequence of word (th-verbatim). If at least one verbatim case has been found, the document pair is considered to be verbatim plagiarism. If no verbatim cases are found and the length of plagiarism fragment in the suspicious document is much smaller than the length of the source fragments, the document pair is considered to be summary plagiarism; otherwise the document pair is considered to be another plagiarism case. Palkovskii and Belov [9] used a graphical clustering algorithm to detect the type of plagiarism in a document pair. They classified the document pairs of the PAN 2014 text alignment corpus into verbatim, random, summary type and undefined plagiarism. They then set the parameters based on the detected type of plagiarism. Persian plagdet 2016 corpus has three types of obfuscation: none, random and simulated. In the proposed approach, the document pairs of the Persian plagdet 2016 corpus are classified into verbatim and simulated plagiarism categories. The SVM neural network was used to detect the type of plagiarism in the proposed algorithm and was trained by type of obfuscation in the Persian Plagdet 2016 training corpus. The parameters were then set based on the detected type of plagiarism. The proposed algorithm was entered into the Persian Plagdet 2016 competition and was evaluated using their evaluation corpus. Table 1 summarizes the other approaches used by participants in the Persian Plagdet 2016 competition using the four stages mentioned above.

Table 1. The summarizing of some submitted approaches at Persian Plagdet corpus 2016

			Our approach	Talebpour et al. [22]	Minaei and Niknam [12]	Ehsan and Shakery [19]	Momtaz et al. [23]	Esteki and Esfahani [24]	Gharavi et al. [25]	Mansoori and Rahgooy [26]	Gillam and Vartapetiance [27]
Pre-processing	Stop_words removal		✓	✓		✓	✓	✓	✓		
	Stemming		✓	✓				✓			
	POS tagging			✓							
	Special character removal		✓	✓			✓	✓			
	Tokenizing		✓	✓			✓				
	FarsNet		✓	✓				✓			
Seeding	Small fragment	Character-ngram									
		Word-ngram		✓	✓	✓	✓				✓
		Sentence	✓			✓	✓	✓	✓	✓	
		Bag of words							✓	✓	
	Matching method	W2V, cosin							✓		
		VSM, cosin	✓							✓	
		levenshtein						✓			
		Jaccard						✓	✓		
		Dice						✓			
		LCS						✓			
		SVM						✓			
		Graph matching		✓			✓				
Extension	Rule based		✓	✓	✓	✓	✓				✓
	Dynamic programming					✓					
	Clustering		✓					✓			
Filtering	Small passage removal		✓		✓	✓					✓
	Overlapping removal		✓		✓	✓	✓				

3 The Proposed Approach

The proposed text alignment algorithm, like many other text alignment algorithms [5], includes preprocessing, seeding, extension and filtering stages. Each stages is explained below. Figure 2 is an overall scheme of the proposed text alignment algorithm that shows these four stages.

3.1 Preprocessing

In the preprocessing stage, the text is first segmented into sentences and then tokenized using STeP_1 [28]. The stop words [29] are removed and inflectional and derivational stems of the tokens are extracted and restored by STeP_1. Preprocessing is done for a suspicious document and a source document. These sentences will be given in the seeding stage.

3.2 Seeding

The seeding stage extracts similar seed sentence pairs from source and suspicious documents. The proposed method was initially based on the method introduced by Sanchez-Perez et al. [15]. The method was then expanded using the SVM neural net to predict the obfuscation type and adjust the parameters to gain better results. Based on the VSM method, first the *tf-idf* vector is calculated for all sentences of the suspicious and source documents in which *tf* is the term frequency in the corresponding sentence and *idf* is the inverse sentence frequency. The similarity of each sentence pair in the suspicious and source documents is calculated using the cosine measure and Dice coefficient as in Eqs. (1), (2) and (3):

$$cosine(susp_i, src_j) = \frac{susp_i.src_j}{|susp_i||src_j|} \tag{1}$$

$$Dice(susp_i, src_j) = \frac{2|\delta(susp_i).\delta(src_j)|}{|\delta(susp_i)|^2 + |\delta(src_j)|^2} \tag{2}$$

$$\delta(x) = \begin{cases} 1 & if\ x \neq \emptyset \\ 0 & otherwise \end{cases} \tag{3}$$

where $susp_i$ is the vector of the ith sentence from the suspicious document, src_j is the vector from the jth sentence of the source and $|.|$ is the Euclidean length.

The cosine measure and Dice coefficient are calculated for all pairs of sentences and if the similarity of $susp_i$ and src_j is greater than the threshold of 0.3 (chosen based on Sanchez-Perez et al. [15]), this pair of sentences are considered to be a seed. For pairs of sentences having a similarity of more than 0.1 and less than 0.3 (based on experimentation), the semantic similarity is computed. The SVM neural network[4] is used to

---

[4] http://www.csie.ntu.edu.tw/~cjlin/libsvm/.

predict the type of obfuscation strategy used in the document pairs. To create a SVM input vector, the cosine similarity measure between all sentence pairs was computed for the given suspicious and source documents and then all values were divided into 8 clusters. Values between 0.2 and 0.3 are placed in the first cluster[5], values between 0.3 and 0.4 are placed in the second cluster and so on. An 8-bit vector is considered for each document pair. Each bit of the vector is set as follows:

$$v_i = \begin{cases} 0 & if\ cluster_i = \varnothing \\ 1 & otherwise \end{cases} \tag{4}$$

Where v_i is the ith bit of the input vector and $cluster_i$ is the ith cluster that contains values between $\frac{i+1}{10}$ and $\frac{i+2}{10}$. For example, for $i = 1$, if no cosine similarity value exists between 0.2 and 0.3 in all sentence pairs of a document pair, then $v_1 = 0$; otherwise, $v_1 = 1$. These vectors were created for all document pairs in the Persian Plagdet training dataset 2016 and then SVM neural network was trained by these vectors.

The threshold is set for semantic similarity based on the type of obfuscation. If the SVM predicts that the type of obfuscation is simulated, then the threshold will be equal 0.2; otherwise it will be equal to 0.3. To calculate the semantic similarity, FarsNet [30] is used to extract synsets of each term and STeP_1 is used to extract inflectional and derivational stems of each term. For each term, a set of words called $\varphi(\omega)$ is considered as shown in Fig. 3. For each w_i in vector $susp_i$, if $\varphi(w_i)$ overlaps $\varphi(\acute{w}_j)$ of vector src_j, w_i of vector $susp_i$ is replaced by $\acute{w}_j$ of vector src_j. The similarity of the cosine and Dice coefficients are calculated for the resulting vectors and the similarities are averaged between the results at this stage and the results of the cosine and Dice coefficients in the previous stage; if the average is greater than the threshold (0.2 for simulated and 0.3 for artificial and noun), the pair of $susp_i$ and src_j are considered to be seeds. The set of seeds obtained in this stage then enter the extension stage.

3.3   Extension

The purpose of the extension stage is the extraction of the longest similar passages from the suspicious and source documents. Figure 2 shows that the extension consists of clustering and validation parts. In the clustering stage, the seeds are clustered into passages that are not separated by more than a *maxgap* number of sentences. The *maxgap* is 4 in the proposed implementation. In the validation stage, those pairs of passages created in the clustering stage that are not similar are removed. The thresholds of all stages are shown in Table 2. For the extension stage, the method proposed by Sanchez-Perez et al. [15] was extended and enhanced. In the validation stage, the semantic similarity measure was used instead of the cosine measure to determine the similarity between pairs of passages.

---

[5] In clustering, the values between 0 and 0.1 are removed because almost all documents pairs contain at least one value between 0 and 0.1.

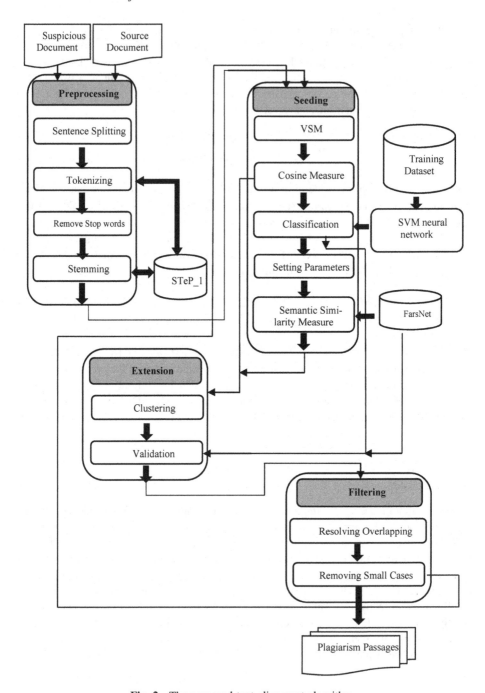

Fig. 2. The proposed text alignment algorithm.

3.4   Filtering

The filtering stage removes passages that either overlap or are too short. To remove overlapping passages the method proposed by Sanchez-Perez et al. [15] is used. To remove passages that are too short, a recursive algorithm is used. If the length of a passage

Table 2. Parameters settings

Parameter		Value
Threshold-cosine similarity		0.3
Threshold-dice similarity		0.3
MaxGap		4
Min PlagPassage length		100
Simulated	Threshold-semantic similarity	0.2
	Threshold-validation	0.2
Artificial and noun	Threshold-semantic similarity	0.3
	Threshold-validation	0.3
Conditions to calculate the semantic similarity of two sentences		$0.1 <$ cosine similarity < 0.3

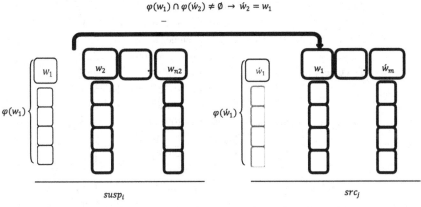

$$\varphi(w_1) \cap \varphi(\acute{w}_2) \neq \emptyset \rightarrow \acute{w}_2 = w_1$$

$susp_i$

src_j

n = the number of terms in $susp_i$ m = the number of terms in src_j

$$for \ (w_i = 1 \ to \ n \ in \ susp_{terms})$$
$$for \ (\acute{w}_j = 1 \ to \ m \ in \ src_{terms})$$
$$if \ (\varphi(w_i) \cap \varphi(\acute{w}_j)) \neq \emptyset$$
$$\acute{w}_j = w_i$$
$$Where \ \varphi(\omega) = the \ set \ of \ inflectional \ and$$
$$derivational \ stems \ and \ Synsets \ of \ \omega.$$

Fig. 3. New vectors for semantic similarity.

is less than a 100 characters, it is first assumed that other seeds exist in the passage, but have not been identified. The semantic similarity threshold is thus reduced to −0.06 and goes back to the seeding stage. The new seeds are then extracted based on the new threshold (old threshold - 0.06); and all stages are repeated to remove passages that are too short. If the passage is less than 100 characters again, this passage will be removed.

4   Experiments

4.1   Dataset

The Persian Plagdet evaluation corpus 2016 includes the none (exact copy), artificial (random) and simulated obfuscation categories. Artificial obfuscation consists of word additions, deletions and shuffling, semantic word variation and POS-preserving word shuffling. A crowdsourcing approach was used to create simulated obfuscation [6]. This dataset contains 5830 documents organized by the ICT Research Institute, ACECR, under the partial support of Vice Presidency for Science and Technology of Iran. Table 3 shows some of the statistics of this corpus.

Table 3. Corpus statistics [6]

Corpus statistics		
Entire corpus	Number of documents	5830
	Number of plagiarism cases	4118
Document purpose	Source documents	48%
	Suspicious documents	52%
Document length	Short (1–500 words)	35%
	Medium (500–2500 words)	59%
	Long (2500–21000 words)	6%
Plagiarism per document	Small (5%–20%)	57%
	Medium (21%–50%)	15%
	Much (51%–80%)	18%
	Entirely (>80%)	10%
Obfuscation	Number of cases	1628
	None	11%
	Artificial	81%
	Simulated	8%

4.2   Performance Measures

The evaluation measures used in this competition are the recall, precision, granularity and plagdet scores [5]. These criteria are defined in accordance with the following equations:

$$prec(S, R) = \frac{1}{|R|} \sum_{r \in R} \frac{|\cup_{s \in S}(s \prod r)|}{|r|} \qquad (5)$$

$$rec(S, R) = \frac{1}{|S|} \sum_{s \in S} \frac{|\cup_{r \in R}(s \prod r)|}{|s|} \qquad (6)$$

$$\text{Where} \quad s \prod r = \begin{cases} s \cap r & \text{if } r \text{ detects } s, \\ \varnothing & \text{otherwise.} \end{cases} \qquad (7)$$

Where S is the set of plagiarism cases in the corpus and R is the set of cases of plagiarism detected by the algorithm. Each plagiarism case is defined by $s = s_{plg}, d_{plg}, s_{src}, d_{src}$, where $s \in S$, d_{plg} is the suspicious document, d_{src} is the source document, s_{plg} is the plagiarized segment, s_{src} is the source segment and $r \in R$ is the discovered plagiarism case.

Granularity addresses overlapping or multiple detection for one plagiarism case and is defined as:

$$gran(S, R) = \frac{1}{|S_R|} \sum_{s \in S_R} |R_s| \qquad (8)$$

Where $S_R = \{s | s \in S \wedge \exists r \in R : r \text{ detects } s\}$ and $R_s = \{r | r \in R \wedge r \text{ detects } s\}$. These measures combine into a single plagdet score as:

$$plagdet(S, R) = \frac{F_1}{\log_2(1 + grand(S, R))} \qquad (9)$$

Where F1 is the average harmonic weight of precision and recall [5].

All these metrics are computed at character level. The plagdet measure used to evaluate the software submitted to Persian Plagdet 2016 is a combination of character level precision, recall and granularity. The plagiarism detection systems were ranked according to their character level performance. Detection performance could be also measure at the case and document levels. Potthast et al. [5] measured detection performance at the case level and the document level. The case level fixes the minimum precision and recall with which a plagiarism case must be detected. The document level

Table 4. The proposed algorithm performance at case level and document level in Persian Plagdet training dataset 2016

	Parameter	Value
Case_level	Recall	0.9769
	Precision	0.9574
	F-measure	0.9671
Document_level	Recall	0.9801
	Precision	0.9705
	F-measure	0.9753

disregards whether or not all plagiarism cases in a document have been detected as long as a significant portion of one has been detected. Table 4 shows the results of the proposed algorithm for the training Persian plagdet corpus at the case and document levels.

4.3   Results

The proposed algorithm was submitted to the Persian Plagdet 2016 competition and compared with other participants approaches on Persian PlagDet corpus 2016 [6] based on the PAN evaluation setup [7, 31, 32]. Table 5 shows the overall performance and runtimes of the nine submitted text alignment approaches. As seen, the proposed approach achieved the highest PlagDet score for the complete corpus and ranked first. Gharavi et al. [25] completed the entire corpus in only 00:01:03 min and the proposed approach required 02:22:48. Table 6 shows the results of the proposed algorithm on all obfuscation strategies in the training dataset. Table 6 column P_1 shows the results of the proposed algorithm for type of obfuscation in the training dataset where semantic similarity measure is not used. The P_2 column shows the algorithm results using the semantic similarity measure. Column P_3 shows the results of the proposed algorithm after adding the criterion of semantic similarity and adjusting the parameters based on detected type of obfuscation using a neural network. As seen in column P_2, adding the semantic similarity criteria improved the recall for the types of obfuscation in training corpus, but the precision declined in some cases. In column P_3, adding a neural network to the system for the diagnosis of type of obfuscation and parameter settings based on the type of obfuscation improved precision and recall dramatically for all types of obfuscation.

Table 7 shows the results of the submitted algorithms on obfuscation types in the test corpus. Gharavi et al. [25] ranked first for no obfuscation and the proposed approach ranked first for both artificial and simulated plagiarism. The proposed approach ranked first for best recall across all parts of the corpus.

Table 5. The text alignment algorithms performance on Persian Plagdet corpus 2016 [6]

Rank/team	Runtime (h:m:s)	Recall	Precision	Granularity	F-measure	PlagDet
1 Mashhadirajab	02:22:48	**0.9191**	0.9268	1.0014	**0.9230**	**0.9220**
2 Gharavi	**00:01:03**	0.8582	0.9592	1	0.9059	0.9059
3 Momtaz	00:16:08	0.8504	0.8925	1	0.8710	0.8710
4 Minaei	00:01:33	0.7960	0.9203	1.0396	0.8536	0.8301
5 Esteki	00:44:03	0.7012	0.9333	1	0.8008	0.8008
6 Talebpour	02:24:19	0.8361	**0.9638**	1.2275	0.8954	0.7749
7 Ehsan	00:24:08	0.7049	0.7496	1	0.7266	0.7266
8 Gillam	21:08:54	0.4140	0.7548	1.5280	0.5347	0.3996
9 Mansourizadeh	00:02:38	0.8065	0.9000	3.5369	0.8507	0.3899

Table 6. The proposed algorithm on types of obfuscation in Plagdet training dataset 2016

Obfuscation	Parameter	P_1	P_2	P_3
None	Plagdet	0.94	0.96	0.97
	Recall	0.96	0.98	0.99
	Precision	0.92	0.95	0.94
	Granularity	1	1	1
Artificial	Plagdet	0.81	0.84	0.94
	Recall	0.78	0.84	0.93
	Precision	0.85	0.84	0.94
	Granularity	1	1	1
Simulated	Plagdet	0.55	0.69	0.86
	Recall	0.41	0.61	0.83
	Precision	0.84	0.80	0.91
	Granularity	1	1	1

Table 7. The algorithm submitted based on types of obfuscation in Persian Plagdet test dataset 2016 [6]

Team	No obfuscation				Artificial obfuscation				Simulated obfuscation			
	Recall	Precision	Granularity	PlagDet	Recall	Precision	Granularity	PlagDet	Recall	Precision	Granularity	PlagDet
Mashhadirajab	**0.9939**	0.9403	1	0.9663	**0.9473**	0.9416	1.0006	**0.9440**	**0.8045**	0.9336	1.0047	**0.8613**
Gharavi	0.9825	0.9762	1	**0.9793**	0.8979	0.9647	1	0.9301	0.6895	**0.9682**	1	0.8054
Momtaz	0.9532	0.8965	1	0.9240	0.9019	0.8979	1	0.8999	0.6534	0.9119	1	0.7613
Minaei	0.9659	0.8663	1.0113	0.9060	0.8514	0.9324	1.0240	0.8750	0.5618	0.9110	1.1173	0.6422
Esteki	0.9781	0.9689	1	0.9735	0.7758	0.9473	1	0.8530	0.3683	0.8982	1	0.5224
Talebpour	0.9755	**0.9775**	1	0.9765	0.8971	**0.9674**	1.2074	0.8149	0.5961	0.9582	1.4111	0.5788
Ehsan	0.8065	0.7333	1	0.7682	0.7542	0.7573	1	0.7557	0.5154	0.7858	1	0.6225
Gillam	0.7588	0.6257	1.4857	0.5221	0.4236	0.7744	1.5351	0.4080	0.2564	0.7748	1.5308	0.2876
Mansourizadeh	0.9615	0.8821	3.7740	0.4080	0.8891	0.9129	3.6011	0.4091	0.4944	0.8791	3.1494	0.3082

5 Conclusions and Future Work

The current work described the proposed text alignment approach and compared it to the eight other approaches submitted to the Persian Plagdet 2016 competition. The detection performance for all nine approaches has been provided. The proposed method consists of four stages used to aligned the passages of a given document pair. The SVM neural network was used to identify the type of obfuscation and set the parameters on the basis of obfuscation. The results showed that this was effective for improving precision and recall. Although the proposed approach ranked first for performance compared with other participants, the runtime should be decreased to make it much shorter than two hours. Future study will focus on improving the runtime and the semantic similarity measure in the seeding stage. The most of runtime is spent on the preprocessing and seeding stages to detect similar sentences. So, in order to improve runtime, we intend to use deep learning techniques instead of using multiple tools to discover similarities.

References

1. Fiedler, R., Kaner, C.: Plagiarism detection services: how well do they actually perform. IEEE Technol. Soc. Mag. **29**, 37–43 (2010)
2. Alzahrani, M., Salim, N., Abraham, A.: Understanding plagiarism linguistic patterns, textual features, and detection methods. IEEE Trans. Syst. Man Cybern.—Part C Appl. Rev. **42**(2), 133–149 (2012)
3. Ali, A.M.E.T., Abdulla, H.M.D., Snasel, V.: Survey of plagiarism detection methods. In: IEEE Fifth Asia Modelling Symposium (AMS), pp. 39–42 (2011)
4. Potthast, M., Göring, S.: Towards data submissions for shared tasks: first experiences for the task of text alignment. In: Working Notes Papers of the CLEF 2015 Evaluation Labs, CEUR Workshop Proceedings (2015). ISSN 1613-0073
5. Potthast, M., Hagen, M., Beyer, A., Busse, M., et al.: Overview of the 6th international competition on plagiarism detection. In: Working Notes for CLEF 2014 Conference, Sheffield, UK, 15–18 September, CEUR Workshop Proceedings, vol. 1180, pp. 845–876 (2014). CEUR-WS.org
6. Asghari, H., Mohtaj, S., Fatemi, O., Faili, H., et al.: Overview of the PAN@FIRE2016 shared task on persian plagiarism detection and text alignment corpus construction. In: Notebook Papers of FIRE 2016, FIRE-2016 (2016). CEUR-WS.org
7. Potthast, M., Stein, B., Barrón-Cedeño, A., Rosso, P.: An evaluation framework for plagiarism detection. In: 23rd International Conference on Computational Linguistics (COLING 2010), pp. 997–1005 (2010)
8. Glinos, D.: A hybrid architecture for plagiarism detection. In: Notebook for PAN at CLEF 2014. CLEF 2014 Evaluation Labs and Workshop – Working Notes Papers, Sheffield, UK, 15–18 September (2014). CEUR-WS.org. ISSN 1613-0073
9. Palkovskii, Y., Belov, A.: Developing high-resolution universal multi-type n-gram plagiarism detector. In: Notebook for PAN at CLEF 2014. CLEF 2014 Evaluation Labs and Workshop – Working Notes Papers, Sheffield, UK, 15–18 September (2014). CEUR-WS.org. ISSN 1613-0073
10. Smith, T., Waterman, M.: Identification of common molecular subsequences. J. Mol. Biol. **147**(1), 195–197 (1981)
11. Alvi, F., Stevenson, M., Clough, P.: Hashing and merging heuristics for text reuse detection. In: Notebook for PAN at CLEF (2014)
12. Minaei, B., Niknam, M.: An n-gram based method for nearly copy detection in plagiarism systems. In: Working notes of FIRE 2016 - Forum for Information Retrieval Evaluation, Kolkata, India, 7–10 December 2016, CEUR Workshop Proceedings (2016). CEUR-WS.org
13. Gross, P., Modaresi, P.: Plagiarism alignment detection by merging context seeds. In: Notebook for PAN at CLEF (2014)
14. Torrejón, D.A.R., Ramos, J.M.M.: CoReMo 2.3 plagiarism detector text alignment module. In: Notebook for PAN at CLEF (2014)
15. Sanchez-Perez, M.A., Gelbukh, A.F., Sidorov, G.: Dynamically adjustable approach through obfuscation type recognition. In: Working Notes of CLEF 2015 - Conference and Labs of the Evaluation forum, Toulouse, France, 8–11 September 2015, CEUR Workshop Proceedings, vol. 1391 (2015). CEUR-WS.org
16. Sanchez-Perez, M., Sidorov, G., Gelbukh, A.: The winning approach to text alignment for text reuse detection at PAN 2014. In: Notebook for PAN at CLEF 2014, Sheffield, UK, 15–18 September, CEUR Workshop Proceedings, vol. 1180, pp. 1004–1011 (2014). CEUR-WS.org. ISSN 1613-0073

17. Kong, L., Han, Y., Han, Z., Yu, H., Wang, Q., Zhang, T., Qi, H.: Source retrieval based on learning to rank and text alignment based on plagiarism type recognition for plagiarism detection. In: Notebook for PAN at CLEF (2014)

18. Shrestha, P., Maharjan, S., Solorio, T.: Machine translation evaluation metric for text alignment. In: Notebook for PAN at CLEF (2014)

19. Ehsan, N., Shakery, A.: A pairwise document analysis approach for monolingual plagiarism detection. In: Working Notes of FIRE 2016 - Forum for Information Retrieval Evaluation, Kolkata, India, 7–10 December 2016, CEUR Workshop Proceedings (2014). CEUR-WS.org

20. Ehsan, N., Tompa, F.W., Shakery, A.: Using a dictionary and n-gram alignment to improve fine-grained cross-language plagiarism detection. In: Proceedings of the 2016 ACM Symposium on Document Engineering, pp. 59–68. ACM (2016)

21. Abnar, S., Dehghani, M., Zamani, H., Shakery, A.: Expanded n-grams for semantic text alignment. In: Notebook for PAN at CLEF (2014)

22. Talebpour, A., Shirzadi, M., Aminolroaya, Z.: Plagiarism detection based on a novel trie-based approach. In: Working Notes of FIRE 2016 - Forum for Information Retrieval Evaluation, Kolkata, India, 7–10 December 2016, CEUR Workshop Proceedings (2016). CEUR-WS.org

23. Momtaz, M., Bijari, K., Salehi, M., Veisi, H.: Graph-based approach to text alignment for plagiarism detection in Persian documents. In: Working Notes of FIRE 2016 - Forum for Information Retrieval Evaluation, Kolkata, India, 7–10 December 2016, CEUR Workshop Proceedings (2016). CEUR-WS.org

24. Esteki, F., Esfahani, F.S.: A plagiarism detection approach based on SVM for Persian texts. In: Working Notes of FIRE 2016 - Forum for Information Retrieval Evaluation, Kolkata, India, 7–10 December 2016, CEUR Workshop Proceedings (2016). CEUR-WS.org

25. Gharavi, E., Bijari, K., Zahirnia, K., Veisi, H.: A deep learning approach to Persian plagiarism detection. In: Working Notes of FIRE 2016 - Forum for Information Retrieval Evaluation, Kolkata, India, 7–10 December 2016, CEUR Workshop Proceedings (2016). CEUR-WS.org

26. Mansoorizadeh, M., Rahgooy, T.: Persian plagiarism detection using sentence correlations. In: Working Notes of FIRE 2016 - Forum for Information Retrieval Evaluation, Kolkata, India, 7–10 December 2016, CEUR Workshop Proceedings (2016). CEUR-WS.org

27. Gillam, L., Vartapetiance, A.: From English to Persian: conversion of text alignment for plagiarism detection. In: Working Notes of FIRE 2016 - Forum for Information Retrieval Evaluation, Kolkata, India, 7–10 December 2016, CEUR Workshop Proceedings (2016). CEUR-WS.org

28. Shamsfard, M., Jafari, H.S., Ilbeygi, M.: STeP-1: a set of fundamental tools for Persian text processing. In: LREC 2010, Malta (2010)

29. Davarpanah, M.R., Sanji, M., Aramideh, M.: Farsi lexical analysis and stop word list. Libr. Hi Tech **27**, 435–449 (2009)

30. Shamsfard, M., Hesabi, A., Fadaei H., et al.: Semi automatic development of FarsNet; the Persian WordNet. In: Proceedings of 5th Global WordNet Conference (2010)

31. Gollub, T., Stein. B., Burrows, S.: Ousting Ivory tower research: towards a web framework for providing experiments as a service. In: 35th International ACM Conference on Research and Development in Information Retrieval (SIGIR 2012), pp. 1125–1126. ACM (2012). ISBN 978-1-4503-1472-5

32. Potthast, M., Gollub, T., Rangel, F., Rosso, P., Stamatatos, E., Stein, B.: Improving the reproducibility of PAN's shared tasks: plagiarism detection, author identification, and author profiling. In: Kanoulas, E., Lupu, M., Clough, P., Sanderson, M., Hall, M., Hanbury, A., Toms, E. (eds.) CLEF 2014. LNCS, vol. 8685, pp. 268–299. Springer, Cham (2014). https://doi.org/10.1007/978-3-319-11382-1_22

A Fast Multi-level Plagiarism Detection Method Based on Document Embedding Representation

Erfaneh Gharavi, Hadi Veisi$^{(\boxtimes)}$ (ID), Kayvan Bijari, and Kiarash Zahirnia

Faculty of New Sciences and Technologies, University of Tehran, Tehran, Iran
{e.gharavi,h.veisi,kayvan.bijari,zahirnia.kia}@ut.ac.ir

Abstract. Nowadays, global networks facilitate access to vast amount of textual information and enhance the feasibility of plagiarism as a consequence. Given the amount of text material produced everyday, the need for an automated fast plagiarism detection system is more crucial than ever. Plagiarism detection is defined as identification of reused text materials. In this regard, different algorithms have been proposed to perform the task of plagiarism detection in text documents. Due to limitation in semantic representation and computational inefficiency of traditional algorithms for plagiarism detection, in this paper, we proposed an embedding based document representation to detect plagiarism in documents using a two-level decision making approach. The method is language-independent and works properly on various languages as well. In the proposed method, words are represented as multi-dimensional vectors, and simple aggregation methods are used to combine the word vectors in order to represent sentences. By comparing representations of source and suspicious sentences, sentence pairs with the highest similarity score are considered as the candidates of the plagiarism cases. The final decision whether or not the pairs are plagiarized is taken using another level of similarity calculation using Jaccard metric by comparing the word sets of two sentences. Our method has been used in PAN2016 Persian plagiarism detection contest and results in 85.8% recall, 95.9% precision and 90.6% plagdet which is a combination of the these two measures with the measure of how concretely we retrieve plagiarism cases, on the provided data sets in a short amount of time. This method achieved the second place regarding plagdet and the first rank based on runtime.

Keywords: Text embedding · Word vector representation
Multi-level plagiarism detection · Persian

1 Introduction

Due to the growth and expansion of the global networks and the increasing volume of unstructured data by both human and machine, an automated intelligent processing and knowledge extraction system is required. The primary goal of language processing methods is to achieve direct human computer interaction as the main purpose of artificial intelligence [1]. Natural language processing

© Springer International Publishing AG 2018
P. Majumder et al. (Eds.): FIRE 2016 Workshop, LNCS 10478, pp. 94–108, 2018.
https://doi.org/10.1007/978-3-319-73606-8_7

(NLP) encompasses wide variety of tasks and applications including: part of speech tagging (POS), text classification, machine translation, text similarity detection, and etc. One well-known application of text similarity detection is to identify plagiarism especially for scientific documents. Plagiarism is defined as the act of taking someone else's works or ideas and presenting them as one's own without explicitly acknowledging the original source which is considered immoral and illegal [2]. Plagiarism is being done at various ways and in various levels (such as simple copy-paste, translation plagiarism and theft ideas), and often it is difficult to prove whether a text is plagiarized or not. Previously, the plagiarism was detected only manually and based on the reviewer's knowledge. But nowadays, due to the difference between human cognition and vast amount of information, the process of plagiarism detection is very challenging to be performed manually. Therefore, automated plagiarism detection gets wide attention in the recent years [2,3].

In 2000, only 5 systems have been developed for the purpose of plagiarism detection, four of which was used to detect plagiarism in text and one system was used to detect copied programming codes [4]. This number increased to 47 in 2010 which indicates an increase in demand of such systems as well as the need to improve speed and performance efficiencies. It should be noted that previous approaches often benefit from string matching scheme in order to detect copied texts. The inadequacy of existing systems leads the research direction to new approaches for plagiarism detection. The main drawback in this area is system's inability to recognize the syntactic and semantic changes in the text data. Although it seems very simple for human beings, but the computer is facing many difficulties in this detection, especially when the detection is dependent on exact text matching. Plagiarism detection steps is outlined in the below algorithm.

1. Data pre-processing: preparation of the input data including original and plagiarized text.
2. Similarity comparison: in this step, texts from original and plagiarized source are compared based on a similarity measure.
3. Filtering: based on a predefined threshold, the generated rates in the previous step are used to identify candidate pairs.
4. Further processing: at this step, pairs are evaluated based on other similarity measures.
5. Classification: The final step is to assign a label indicating whether the texts are plagiarized or not. This can be done using the calculated rate resulted from the 4-th step.

Scientific plagiarized text comprises of word sequences including N-grams which are exactly the same or paraphrased form of the original text. This sequence of words can be in different lengths to include whole or a part of the original documents. Examples of rules that show how the plagiarism in scientific fields has occurred, are provided in the following [5].

- Inadequate referencing
- Direct copy from one or more sources of text
- Displacement of words in a sentence
- Paraphrase and rewrite the texts, present other's ideas with different words
- Translation, expression of an idea in one language into another one

Plagiarism can include changes in the vocabulary, syntactic or semantic representation of the text. These types will be discussed further in the following:

- **Vocabulary changes:** Including the addition, deletion or replacement of words in a given text. Such changes would be indistinguishable by string matching approach.
- **Synthetic changes:** Changes in the structure includes rearranging words and expressions, and turning sentences from active to passive and vice versa.
- **Semantic changes:** This kind of plagiarism is more fundamental and usually includes paraphrase as well as semantic and vocabulary changes. Detecting such changes requires semantic analysis of the information in the text data to see whether or not the texts imply the same sense.

Plagiarism detection can also be divided into two main categories: external plagiarism detection, and intrinsic plagiarism detection. External plagiarism detection tries to extract plagiarism in a text by checking all given source documents. Intrinsic plagiarism detection analyzes the given suspicious document, and tries to discover parts of the input document which are not written by the same author. In this study, we propose a new method to detect external plagiarism for Persian documents using embedded document representation [6] which consider all of the three mentioned changes implicitly.

In order to be processed in natural language processing algorithms, textual data should be numerically described. In traditional approaches, lists of the words are considered as distinct features for the textual data. In such methods, the similarity between the synonym words is not taken into account. Furthermore, due to the sparseness of new feature space and time complexity of feature extraction, these approaches are not computationally efficient [7]. To overcome deficiencies of the traditional feature extraction methods, recently deep learning techniques are used which have resulted in promising performance in many applications specially in NLP [8]. The essential goal of deep learning is to improve the processing, and pre-processing methods of NLP in an automatic, efficient, and fast way [9]. In text mining applications, deep learning methods represent words as a vector of numerical values [2]. This new representation contains a major part of synthetic as well as semantic rules of the text data. This vectorized representation of words is core of many applications in information retrieval [10–13]. In applications such as similarity detection and text classification, much larger units such as phrases, sentences and documents should be described as a vector. For this purpose, there are a number of methods ranging from simple mathematical approaches [14] to more complicated ones such as neural networks-based combination functions [15], or paragraph vector models [16]. Vectorized representation of text data makes it easy to compare words and sentences as well as minimizing the need to use lexicons.

In this paper, an approach based on text embedding used for plagiarism detection in a two-level decision making and evaluate our method in Persian PAN plagiarism detection contest. This method results in 90.6% plagdet, 85.8% recall, 95.9% precision on the PAN provided data sets. The main contributions of our proposed method are: first we used embedding representation of words and simple vector composition functions in order to represent sentences, as a result, it makes sentence comparison much faster and reliable. Furthermore, the two-level comparison is applied to take both semantic and lexical similarities into account, this strategy leads to better performance and accuracy.

Rest of this paper is organized as follows: in Sect. 2 we described plagiarism and the act of plagiarism detection, followed by presenting related works in Sect. 2. Section 3 is devoted to illustrate deep learning feature and the approaches of using it in NLP applications. Section 4 introduces our proposed method and Sect. 5 demonstrates the experimental results. Finally, we provide a summary and explain benefits of our methods in Sect. 6.

2   Related Works

In this section some plagiarism detection methods are reviewed. These methods are categorized based on features that are used to determine the similarity between two documents which address different kind of plagiarism:

- Lexical methods: These methods consider text as a sequence of characters or terms. The assumption is that the more terms both documents have in common, the more similar they are. Methods that use features such as longest common subsequence, and N-grams are included in this kind of methods. These methods usually end up with a satisfactory outcome when the words are not changed by their synonyms [6, 17–23].
- Syntactical methods: Some methods use text's syntactical units for comparing the similarity between documents. This is a realization of the intuition that similar documents would have similar syntactical structure. This methods make use of characteristics such as POS tag to compare the similarity between different documents [24, 25].
- Semantic methods: These methods use semantic similarity for comparing documents. Methods that use synonyms, antonyms, hypernyms, and hyponyms are placed in this category [17, 26].

To the best of our knowledge, due to lack of Persian corpus (Persian tagged data) [27], there exist only few studies on Persian plagiarism detection. Mahdavi et al., [24] introduce Persian plagiarism detector based on bag of word model. Their approach has two steps: at first, most relevant source documents are retrieved by using cosine similarity, then, using the overlap coefficient and tri-gram model, plagiarism is identified. Mahmoodi et al., [25] use different combination of N-grams, Clough metric [2] and Jaccard similarity coefficient for automatic Persian plagiarism detection. Most of conducted studies in Persian plagiarism detection are lexical in nature. As it is mentioned earlier, this kind of methods does not acts well when the words are changed and rewritten. Applying semantic similarity in Persian language has some limitations due to the constraints of the Persian WordNets.

Persian PlagDet shared task at PAN 2016 is one of the most recent efforts which targets plagiarism detection. As reported in [28], nine teams participated in this task which some of the most successful attended methods are reviewed in the following. Support Vector Machine (SVM) is used in Mashhhadirajab's method to predict obfuscation type. Their method used Term-Frequency Inverse Document Frequency (TF-IDF) to create vector space model and benefits FarsNet [29] to extract synsets of a term. Momtaz used a graph based method to transform documents into graph and then adopts graph similarity schemes to reveal plagiarism in textual data. The N-gram based scheme is used as a heuristic to discover plagiarism in Minaei's approach. Esteki used the Levenshtein distance, the Jaccard coefficient, and the Longest Common Subsequence (LCS) as extracted features to classifying sentences to similar and non-similar sentences using SVM. Talebpour used trie tree to index preprocessed source documents. Preprocessing step involves POS tagging, stemming, and finding word synonyms by employing FarsNet, and WordNet. In their design, based on an iterative manner, each suspicious document is analyzed against the trie to determine its potential sources [28].

Regarding deep approaches, Socher et al. proposed a deep method for paraphrase detection based on recursive auto-encoder networks [30]. In this article word embedding feature approach is introduced which uses semantic and lexical features to detect plagiarism in Persian documents. To the best of our knowledge there is no reported study that uses word embedding for Persian plagiarism detection.

3   Word Embedding

Deep learning is a branch of machine learning which tries to find more abstract features using deep multiple layer graph. Each layer has linear or non-linear function to transform data into more abstract ones [31]. One of the reasons that the deep learning helps to improve NLP is the hierarchical nature of concepts. Concepts exist in natural world are generally hierarchical. For example a cat is a domestic animal which itself is a branch of animals. In most, not all, cases the word "cat" can be replaced by "dog" in any sentence with no change in resulting sentence. So abstract concepts in higher level are less sensitive to changes [32].

Recently, three factors contributed to the better performance of deep architecture: large datasets, faster computers and parallel processing in addition to the increasing number of machine learning methods for normalization and improvement of algorithms [33].

Due to the large amount of textual data and mentioned problems for natural language processing tasks, using automatic methods like deep learning seem mandatory. Advantages of using deep methods for NLP task are listed below:

– No hand crafted feature engineering is required
– Fewer number of features
– No labeled data is required

Multi-layer networks in deep learning, called deep belief network, can also lead to analogous set of features for all natural language processing tasks [34]. Using these representations reduces the number of features and the text can be described by far fewer features through combination functions.

3.1   Word Vector Representation

Most of language processing algorithms consider words as single symbols. This kind of representation suffers from sparsity since the length of vector corresponds to the size of word glossary. This vector has zero in all elements except one. This approach, called One-hot, is unable to distinguish similarity between two synonyms. To address this challenge, an idea of representing a word by its neighbors was introduced by Firth [35].

In application of deep learning in natural language processing, each word is described by the surrounding context. The vector generated automatically by a deep neural networks and contain semantic and syntactic information about the word. Distributed word representation, generally known as word-embedding, is used to solve the aforementioned problems of high dimensionality and sparsity in language model. Here similar words have similar vectors [15].

Distributed representation learning introduced by Hinton for the first time [36] and developed in language modeling concept by Bengio [37]. Collobert [8] shows that distributed representation of words with almost no engineered features can be shared by several NLP tasks resulting the equal or more accuracy than the state of the art methods. Finally, authors in [38] indicate that this kind of presentation not only encompass a huge part of syntactic and semantic rules, but also the relationship between words can be modeled by vectors offset. This offset can also presents the plurality, syntactic label (noun, verb, etc.), semantic feature (pet, animal, car, etc.) of a word. This representation is used in all NLP tasks like Name-Entity-Recognition (NER), word-sense-disambiguation, parsing, and machine translation [34].

There are two approaches to learning word vector representation: (1) General matrix decomposition methods such as Latent Semantic Analysis (LSA) and (2) context-based methods such as skip-grams, continuous bag of words [39, 40].

Skip-grams and continuous bag of words, which are employed by this study, are two-layer neural networks that are trained for language modeling task. Skip-gram uses one-on representation of words in a limited window size as an input and tries to predict the middle word of the context. Another version of this network, continuous bag of words, is used to predict the context considering a middle word. The resulted vectors, which are the weights of the neural network, are the same for semantically similar words.

3.2 Text Document Vector Representation

There are a variety of composition functions for combining word vectors to generate a representation for text document.

Paragraph vector is an unsupervised algorithm that learns representation for variable-length pieces of texts, such as sentences, paragraphs, and documents. The algorithm used the idea of word vector training and considered a matrix for each piece of text. This matrix also updated during language modeling task. Paragraph vector outperforms other methods such as bag-of-words models for many applications [41].

Socher [15] introduce Recursive Deep Learning methods which are variations and extensions of unsupervised and supervised recursive neural networks (RNNs). This method uses the idea of hierarchical structure of the text and encodes two word vectors into one vector by auto-encoder networks. Socher also presents many variation of these deep combination functions such as Recurrent Neural Network (RNN) and Matrix-Vector Recursive Neural Networks (MV-RNN).

There are also some simple mathematical methods which applied as a composition function generally used as benchmarks [14].

4 Proposed Method

In this paper, in order to detect plagiarism, a sentence by sentence comparison approach is carried out in two levels. Word vectors are extracted by word2vec algorithm [39], and Persian stop words were removed while text pre-processing. A vector representation is required for comparing two sentences. A variety of composition functions for calculating sentences vector of word vectors like simple mathematical methods, recursive auto-encoder, convolutional neural networks, etc. are available. One of the simplest method is averaging which reduces time and space complexities. For each sentence an average of all word vectors is calculated as in Eq. (1).

$$S_i = \frac{\Sigma_{j=1}^n W_j}{n} \tag{1}$$

Where S_i is the vector representation for the i-th sentences and W_j is the word vector for $j - th$ word of the sentences and n is the number of words in that sentence.

After feature extraction, in the first level, each sentence in a suspicious document is compared with all the sentences in the source documents. Cosine similarity is used as a comparison metric, which is described in Eq. (2).

$$CosineSimilarity = \frac{S1 \cdot S2}{\|S1\| \times \|S2\|} = \frac{\Sigma_{i=1}^K (S1_i \times S2_i)}{\sqrt{\Sigma_{i=1}^K S1_i^2} \times \sqrt{\Sigma_{i=1}^K S2_i^2}} \tag{2}$$

Where $S1$ is the sentence vector of the sentence from suspicious documents and $S2$ is the sentence vector of the sentence from source documents and K denoted the dimension of the document vectors.

This level helps us to find the most semantically similar sentences in a real time processing. The output of this level is a set of sentences from the source documents that are candidates of being a plagiarized sentence.

After retrieving the candidate with semantic similarity, in the second level, lexical similarity of two sentences is assessed by the Jaccard similarity measur as in Eq. (3). This similarity is calculated for pairs of sentences that their similarity in the first level are higher than a threshold, i.e., α.

$$JaccardSimilarity = \frac{S1_w \cap S2_w}{S1_w \cup S2_w} \qquad (3)$$

Where $S1_w$ is the set of unique words in the first sentence and $S2_w$ is the set of unique words in the second sentence.

The suspicions sentence is decided as the plagiarism sentence, its similarity to the candidates sentences passes Jaccard similarity threshold. We used training corpus to fine-tune the both thresholds (i.e., first and second levels). The pseudocode of our method is represented in Algorithm 1. The function receive a pair of source-suspicious documents as an input and split them up to obtain the sentences. The similarity of each suspicious sentence is calculated to all source sentences and the sentence with highest cosine similarity, higher than threshold is opted for the next step. The subscription of two sentences are then computed by Jaccard similarity metrics. Two sentences is considered as plagiarism if they share more common words to pass the Jaccard threshold.

5   Experiments

In this section, we provide the evaluation results of our method in comparison with the other methods presented in Persian PAN2016. In this section, first the dataset an evaluation metrics are given, afterward results are presented.

5.1   Dataset

To train Persian word embedding we have used ISNA corpus which consists 500,000,000 words. The quality of vectors is evaluated by finding synonym words and calculating minimum distances between vectors. We trained our learning parameters on Persian PAN2016 dataset [28]. This corpus consists of pairs of documents, one of which may contain passages of text reused from the other, with or without obfuscation, or no plagiarism at all. A short statistics of the plagiarism cases are shown in the Table 1.

5.2   Parameter Definition

In our work, there are two parameters to be optimized. The task is to answer the following questions.

– What is the minimum of cosine similarity measure to consider two sentences similar semantically?
– What is the minimum of Jaccard similarity measure to consider two sentences similar lexically?

Algorithm 1. The proposed two-level embedding representation plagiarism detection method

---

Input: Source Document, Suspicious Document, Cosine Similarity Threshold, Jaccard Similarity Threshold
Output: *plagiarized_cases*
 1: *Initialization Phase*:
 2: *src_doc* ← Source Document
 3: *susp_doc* ← Suspicious Document
 4: α ← Cosine Similarity Threshold
 5: β ← Jaccard Similarity Threshold
 6:
 7: **for all** *susp_sentence* in *susp_doc* **do**
 8:     **for all** *src_sentence* in *src_doc* **do**
 9:         *susp_sentence_vector* ← *SentenceVector(susp_sentence)*   ▷ vectorization
10:         *src_sentence_vector* ← *SentenceVector(src_sentence)*   ▷ vectorization
11:         *cs* ← *CosineSim(susp_sentence, src_sentence)* based on Eq. (2)
12:         **if** $cs > \alpha$ **then**
13:             *js* ← *JaccardSim(susp_sentence, src_sentence)* based on Eq. (3)
14:             **if** $js > \beta$ **then**
15:                 add *susp_sentence* to *plagiarized_cases*
16:             **end if**
17:         **end if**
18:     **end for**
19: **end for**
20: **return** *plagiarized_cases*

Table 1. Corpus statistics

Statistics		
Entire corpus	Number of documents	5830
	Number of plagiarism cases	4118
Document purpose	Source documents	48%
	Suspicious documents	52%
Document length	Short (1–500 words)	35%
	Medium (500–2500 words)	59%
	Long (2500–21000 words)	6%
Plagiarism per document	Small (5%–20%)	57%
	Medium (21%–50%)	15%
	Much (50%–80%)	18%
	Entirely (>80%)	10%

Two sentences are considered as plagiarized if they pass the cosine similarity threshold (α). The second threshold (β) filters the selected sentences to assure lexical similarity. These thresholds were fine-tuned by several trials on the training corpus. Figure 1 shows plagdet, Recall and Precision fluctuation by these two parameters plus merging character threshold. The results achieved when $\alpha = 0.3$ and $\beta = 0.3$. We used the same value to run the algorithm on the test corpus.

5.3   Evaluation Metrics

Evaluation measures on the context of text alignment and plagiarism detection task are defined as Precision (4), Recall (5), and Granularity (6), which are combined together and define the Plagdet (7) score [42].

$$Precision(S, R) = \frac{1}{R} \sum_{r \in R} \frac{\left| \bigcup_{s \in S}(S \sqcap r) \right|}{|r|} \tag{4}$$

$$Recall(S, R) = \frac{1}{S} \sum_{s \in S} \frac{\left| \bigcup_{r \in R}(S \sqcap r) \right|}{|s|} \tag{5}$$

In Eqs. (4) and (5), $S \sqcap r$ is defined as $S \sqcap r = \begin{cases} s \cap r & \text{if } r \text{ detects } s, \\ \emptyset & \text{otherwise.} \end{cases}$ in

which s is a plagiarism case in the set of plagiarism cases S in the corpus, and r is a detected case in the set of detected plagiarism cases R.

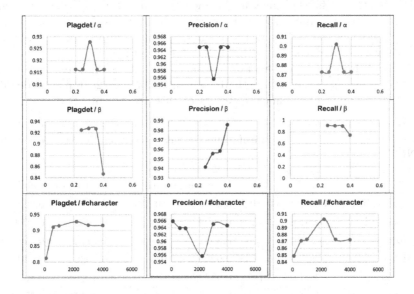

Fig. 1. Sensitivity analysis of the proposed algorithm to its parameters

Granularity is defined to address overlapping or multiple detection for one plagiarism case and is defined as Eq. (6).

$$Granularity(S, R) = \frac{1}{S_R} \sum_{s \in S_R} |R_S| \tag{6}$$

All these measure combined into a single score, palgdet, as follows:

$$Plagdet(S, R) = \frac{F_1}{\log_2(1 + gran(S, R))} \tag{7}$$

Where F_1 is the harmonic mean of precision and recall.

5.4   Results

The results of applying this method to Persian PAN2016 corpus is presented in Table 2, row 2, which is also reported in [28]. Persian plagiarism detection contest, PAN2016, was hosted on Tira [43,44], a framework for shared tasks, and evaluated based on evaluation framework presented in [42].

As it is clearly shown in Table 2, the proposed method processed the entire corpus in only 63 s and hence ranked first from the point of view of runtime. It should also be noted that the proposed method detects the plagiarism cases more accurately compared to the other novel plagiarism detection methods. The details of different plagiarism detection algorithms reported in [28] indicates that our method is ranked first in detecting plagiarism with highest plagdet for "no obfuscation" type of plagiarism. The reason is that the vectorized representation of two equivalent texts is exactly the same. Our proposed method have also ideally detected artificial changes in text including adding, omitting, or replacing words owing to the similarity of the representing vectors. Furthermore, since the proposed algorithm detects the plagiarism cases entirely as a whole, it's granularity score remains perfect in all sorts of plagiarism.

We have also evaluated Two-Level, cosine similarity among text embedding vectors and Jaccard similarity methods, separately on PAN2016 provided training data set. Table 3 presents the results of this assessment. Text embedding

Table 2. Results of text alignment software submissions in PersianPlagDet-2016 (PAN16)

Rank/team	Runtime	Recall	Precision	Granularity	F-measure	PlagDet
1 Mashhadirajab	02:22:48	0.9191	0.9268	1.0014	0.9230	0.9220
2 Gharavi	00:01:03	0.8582	0.9592	1	0.9059	0.9059
3 Momtaz	00:16:08	0.8504	0.8925	1	0.8710	0.8710
4 Minaei	00:01:33	0.7960	0.9203	1.0396	0.8536	0.8301
5 Esteki	00:44:03	0.7012	0.9333	1	0.8008	0.8008
6 Talebpour	02:24:19	0.8361	0.9638	1.2275	0.8954	0.7749

method detected more plagiarism cases and also achieved higher plagdet score than what the Jaccard method achieved. The Jaccard based method was more accurate in detecting the plagiarized cases in such a way that outperforms text embedding method in case of precision. As it can be seen the Proposed Two-Level model detects a majority of the plagiarized cases more precisely. In the Two-Level plagiarism detection model, first we apply text embedding method and decrease the threshold gradually so that more plagiarized cases pass this step. Then, the Jaccard similarity refines the detected cases by its threshold. The hybrid method resulted in 93% plagdet on PAN 2016 training corpus.

Table 3. Assesment of the text embedding, jaccard, and proposed two-leve methods separately on PAN 2016 train data

Method	Precision	Recall	PlagDet
Proposed two-level method	0.96	0.90	0.93
Text embedding method	0.87	0.77	0.82
Jaccard method	0.92	0.72	0.81

6 Conclusion

In this paper, we used embedded representation of words for plagiarism detection task. Sentence-by-sentence comparison is applied to find text similarities. Advantages of this method among others are its simplicity and its runtime. This methods has resulted in 90.6% plagdet, 85.8% recall, 95.9% precision on the PAN2016 provided data sets.

Since our comparison transformed from word-by-word or N-gram-by-N-gram representation of text to numerical one, the calculation of similarity is executed in a much faster and easier way. Our method can easily and immediately address plagiarism with no obfuscation since the average of two sentences' word vectors are exactly the same. The proposed method also detects artificial obfuscation plagiarism with synthetic changes, include changes in the word's order, two synthetically changed sentences have the same average vectors. Vocabulary changes include adding or omitting words, which is indistinguishable for string matching approaches, can be identified by the proposed method efficiently and expeditiously. The reason is that the average vector is insensitive to few number of changes in a sentence vocabulary. In simulated obfuscation cases including semantic changes, which is our main privilege in this task among other N-gram based methods, plagiarism could easily be detected due to the similarity of synonym word vectors which make no or little changes on final sentence representation. Therefore, it makes time consuming synonym word retrieval from lexicon inessential.

Furthermore, given its admirable runtime, our proposed method is scalable and is applicable for large number of documents and can be used for practical purpose. As a future work, we are going to apply other composition functions and also try word-by-word vector comparison in order to eliminate drawbacks of current method.

Acknowledgments. The authors would like to thank the reviewers for providing helpful comments and recommendations which improve the paper significantly.

References

1. Manning, C.D., Schütze, H.: Foundations of Statistical Natural Language Processing, vol. 999. MIT Press, Cambridge (1999)
2. Clough, P.: Old and new challenges in automatic plagiarism detection. National Plagiarism Advisory Service, p. 14, February 2003
3. Chong, M.Y.M.: A study on plagiarism detection and plagiarism direction identification using natural language processing techniques (2013)
4. Lathrop, A., Foss, K.: Student Cheating and Plagiarism in the Internet Era. A Wake-Up Call. Libraries Unlimited Inc., Englewood (2000)
5. Maurer, H., Zaka, B.: Plagiarism-a problem and how to fight it. In: Proceedings of Ed-Media, pp. 4451–4458 (2007)
6. Hoad, T.C., Zobel, J.: Methods for identifying versioned and plagiarized documents. J. Am. Soc. Inf. Sci. Technol. **54**(3), 203–215 (2003)
7. Bengio, Y., Ducharme, R., Vincent, P., Jauvin, C.: A neural probabilistic language model. J. Mach. Learn. Res. **3**(Feb), 1137–1155 (2003)
8. Collobert, R., Weston, J., Bottou, L., Karlen, M., Kavukcuoglu, K., Kuksa, P.: Natural language processing (almost) from scratch. J. Mach. Learn. Res. **12**, 2493–2537 (2011)
9. Hinton, G.E., Osindero, S., Teh, Y.-W.: A fast learning algorithm for deep belief nets. Neural Comput. **18**(7), 1527–1554 (2006)
10. Roy, D., Ganguly, D., Mitra, M., Jones, G.J.: Representing documents and queries as sets of word embedded vectors for information retrieval arXiv preprint arXiv:1606.07869 (2016)
11. Roy, D., Ganguly, D., Mitra, M., Jones, G.J.: Word vector compositionality based relevance feedback using kernel density estimation. In: Proceedings of the 25th ACM International on Conference on Information and Knowledge Management, pp. 1281–1290. ACM (2016)
12. Guo, J., Fan, Y., Ai, Q., Croft, W.B.: A deep relevance matching model for ad-hoc retrieval. In: Proceedings of the 25th ACM International on Conference on Information and Knowledge Management, pp. 55–64. ACM (2016)
13. Ganguly, D., Roy, D., Mitra, M., Jones, G.J.: Word embedding based generalized language model for information retrieval. In: Proceedings of the 38th International ACM SIGIR Conference on Research and Development in Information Retrieval, pp. 795–798. ACM (2015)
14. Mitchell, J., Lapata, M.: Composition in distributional models of semantics. Cogn. Sci. **34**(8), 1388–1429 (2010)
15. Socher, R.: Recursive deep learning for natural language processing and computer vision. Ph.D. thesis, Citeseer (2014)
16. Ai, Q., Yang, L., Guo, J., Croft, W.B.: Analysis of the paragraph vector model for information retrieval. In: Proceedings of the 2016 ACM on International Conference on the Theory of Information Retrieval, pp. 133–142. ACM (2016)

17. Chen, C.-Y., Yeh, J.-Y., Ke, H.-R.: Plagiarism detection using ROUGE and Word-Net. J. Comput. **2**(3), 34–44 (2010)
18. Elhadi, M., Al-Tobi, A.: Use of text syntactical structures in detection of document duplicates. In: 3rd International Conference on Digital Information Management, ICDIM 2008, pp. 520–525 (2008)
19. Elhadi, M., Al-Tobi, A.: Duplicate detection in documents and WebPages using improved longest common subsequence and documents syntactical structures. In: Fourth International Conference on Computer Sciences and Convergence Information Technology, ICCIT 2009, pp. 679–684. IEEE (2009)
20. Glinos, D.S.: A hybrid architecture for plagiarism detection. In: CLEF (Working Notes), pp. 958–965 (2014)
21. Nahnsen, T., Uzuner, O., Katz, B.: Lexical chains and sliding locality windows in content-based text similarity detection (2005)
22. Suchomel, S., Kasprzak, J., Brandejs, M., et al.: Three way search engine queries with multi-feature document comparison for plagiarism detection. In: CLEF (Online Working Notes/Labs/Workshop), pp. 1–8. Citeseer (2012)
23. Zini, M., Fabbri, M., Moneglia, M., Panunzi, A.: Plagiarism detection through multilevel text comparison. In: 2006 Second International Conference on Automated Production of Cross Media Content for Multi-Channel Distribution (AXMEDIS 2006), pp. 181–185. IEEE (2006)
24. Mahdavi, P., Siadati, Z., Yaghmaee, F.: Automatic external Persian plagiarism detection using vector space model. In: 2014 4th International eConference on Computer and Knowledge Engineering (ICCKE), pp. 697–702. IEEE (2014)
25. Mahmoodi, M., Varnamkhasti, M.M.: Design a Persian automated plagiarism detector (AMZPPD). arXiv preprint arXiv:1403.1618 (2014)
26. Torres, S., Gelbukh, A.: Comparing similarity measures for original wsd lesk algorithm. Res. Comput. Sci. **43**, 155–166 (2009)
27. Franco-Salvador, M., Bensalem, I., Flores, E., Gupta, P., Rosso, P.: Pan 2015 shared task on plagiarism detection: evaluation of corpora for text alignment. In: Volume 1391 of CEUR workshop proceedings, CLEF and CEUR-WS.org (2015)
28. Asghari, H., Mohtaj, S., Fatemi, O., Faili, H., Rosso, P., Potthast, M.: Algorithms and corpora for Persian plagiarism detection: overview of pan at fire 2016. In: Working notes of FIRE 2016-Forum for Information Retrieval Evaluation, pp. 7–10 (2016)
29. Shamsfard, M., Hesabi, A., Fadaei, H., Mansoory, N., Famian, A., Bagherbeigi, S., Fekri, E., Monshizadeh, M., Assi, S.M.: Semi automatic development of FarsNet; the Persian Wordnet. In: Proceedings of 5th Global WordNet Conference, Mumbai, India, vol. 29 (2010)
30. Socher, R., Huang, E.H., Pennin, J., Manning, C.D., Ng, A.Y.: Dynamic pooling and unfolding recursive autoencoders for paraphrase detection. In: Advances in Neural Information Processing Systems, pp. 801–809 (2011)
31. Bengio, Y.: Learning deep architectures for AI. Foundations and trends® Mach. Learn. **2**(1), 1–127 (2009)
32. Bengio, Y., Courville, A., Vincent, P.: Representation learning: a review and new perspectives. IEEE Trans. Pattern Anal. Mach. Intell. **35**(8), 1798–1828 (2013)
33. Dahl, G., Ranzato, M., Mohamed, A.-R., Hinton, G.: Phone recognition with the mean-covariance restricted Boltzmann machine. In: Advances in Neural Information, pp. 469–477 (2010)
34. Collobert, R., Weston, J.: A unified architecture for natural language processing: deep neural networks with multitask learning. In: International Conference on Machine Learning, vol. 20, p. 160–167 (2008)

35. Firth, J.R.: A synopsis of linguistic theory 1930–55. Studies in Linguistic Analysis (special volume of the Philological Society), vol. 1952-1959, pp. 1–32 (1957)

36. Hinton, G.E.: Learning distributed representations of concepts. In: Proceedings of the Eighth Annual Conference of the Cognitive Science Society, Amherst, MA, vol. 1, p. 12 (1986)

37. Bengio, Y., Schwenk, H., Sencal, J.S., Morin, F., Gauvain, J.L.: Neural probabilistic language models. Stud. Fuzziness Soft Comput. **194**, 137–186 (2006)

38. Mikolov, T., Yih, W.-T., Zweig, G.: Linguistic regularities in continuous space word representations. HLT-NAACL **13**, 746–751 (2013)

39. Mikolov, T., Chen, K., Corrado, G., Dean, J.: Efficient estimation of word representations in vector space. arXiv preprint arXiv:1301.3781 (2013)

40. Pennington, J., Socher, R., Manning, C.D.: Glove: global vectors for word representation. EMNLP **14**, 1532–43 (2014)

41. Le, Q.V., Mikolov, T.: Distributed representations of sentences and documents. ICML **14**, 1188–1196 (2014)

42. Potthast, M., Stein, B., Barrón-Cedeño, A., Rosso, P.: An evaluation framework for plagiarism detection. In: Proceedings of the 23rd International Conference on Computational Linguistics: Posters, pp. 997–1005. Association for Computational Linguistics (2010)

43. Gollub, T., Stein, B., Burrows, S.: Ousting ivory tower research: towards a web framework for providing experiments as a service. In: Proceedings of the 35th International ACM SIGIR Conference on Research and Development in Information Retrieval, pp. 1125–1126. ACM (2012)

44. Potthast, M., Gollub, T., Rangel, F., Rosso, P., Stamatatos, E., Stein, B.: Improving the reproducibility of PAN's shared tasks: In: Kanoulas, E., Lupu, M., Clough, P., Sanderson, M., Hall, M., Hanbury, A., Toms, E. (eds.) CLEF 2014. LNCS, vol. 8685, pp. 268–299. Springer, Cham (2014). https://doi.org/10.1007/978-3-319-11382-1_22

Plagiarism Detection Based on a Novel Trie-Based Approach

Alireza Talebpour(ID), Mohammad Shirzadi Laskoukelayeh(ID),
and Zahra Aminolroaya(✉)(ID)

CyberSpace Research Institute, Shahid Beheshti University, Tehran, Iran
Talebpour@sbu.ac.ir, m.shirzadi@email.kntu.ac.ir,
z.aminolroaya@Mail.sbu.ac.ir

Abstract. Nowadays, plagiarism detection becomes as one of the major problems in the text mining field. New coming technologies have made plagiarisation easy and more feasible. Therefore, it is vital to develop a system which can automatically detect plagiarisation in different contents.

In this paper, we propose a Trie to compare source and suspicious text documents. We use PersianPlagDet text documents as a case study. Both character-based and knowledge-based techniques for detection purposes have improved our method. Besides, our fast algorithm for insertion and retrieval has made possible to compare long documents with high-speed.

Keywords: Plagiarism detection · Trie-based method · Text mining

1 Introduction

Plagiarism means trying to pass off somebody else's words as your own [1]. Plagiarism detection is the process of locating text reuse within a suspicious document [2]. Nowadays, with the advent of technologies like the internet and the growth of digital content creation, plagiarism, especially in the format of text from existed contents, becomes a growing problem and one of the major problems in the text mining field. For example, plagiarism as a way to release the pressure to publish papers pushes down the quality of scientific papers. In [3], Lesk declares that, in some countries, 15% of submissions to arXiv contain duplicated materials and are plagiarized. Due to these problems, it is urgent to provide a system to automatically detect plagiarism and validate them.

There have been many approaches proposed based on lexical and semantic methods. On the one hand, the plagiarisation problem could be reduced to the problem of finding exactly matched phrases, and, on the other hand, it could be as hard as finding restated phrases. Due to what a problem asked, different knowledge-based or character-based techniques could be applied. One of the lexical database for the knowledge-based approach is the wordnet database. In this database, different words are grouped together based on their cognitive synonyms

P. Majumder et al. (Eds.): FIRE 2016 Workshop, LNCS 10478, pp. 109–117, 2018.
https://doi.org/10.1007/978-3-319-73606-8_8

[4]. This database could be used to find restated phrases. Words in different locations in sentences may have different applications, so knowing syntactic category (POS) of the words *i.e.* noun, verb, etc. could simplify the problem of plagiarism detection.

Plagiarized documents can be in any languages which need different policies to be detected due to different semantics and grammars. In this paper, we have proposed a novel approach for the PAN FIRE Shared Task of Persian plagiarism detection in the international contest PersianPlagDet 2016. We have used a hybrid method considering both character-based and knowledge-based approaches. A Persian wordnet database, Farsnet, is considered as our knowledge database [5]. Besides, we have applied POS tagging by using HAZM package [6]. By finding nouns and their synsets from the Farsnet, we could more precisely save and retrieve source and suspicious words from our proposed tree structure. In our plagiarism detection methodology, we have applied a novel extended prefix tree *i.e.* Trie to store and retrieve documents.

1.1   Related Works

There are many studies to find solutions for plagiarism detection problems and document matching. In the Nineties, studies on copy detection mechanisms in digitalized documents have led to computerized detecting plagiarism [7]. By the growth of generated data, the speed of plagiarism detectors has become an important criterion. In [8], a parameterized backward Trie matching is considered as a fast method for the problem of source and suspicious documents alignment.

The plagiarism detection problem is also studied in different languages. For Persian language plagiarism detection, In [9], after the preprocessing phase for source and suspicious documents, different similarity measurements like "Jaccard similarity coefficient", "Clough & Stevenson metric" and "LCS" are used for similarity comparison. Also, by applying FarsNet, Rakian *et.al* propose an approach, "Persian Fuzzy Plagiarism Detection (PFPD)", to detect plagiarized cases [10].

Our fast trie-based approach is proposed for the problem of the Persian language plagiarisation detection. We describe the problem data and data preprocessing applied to documents in Sect. 2. Then, in Sect. 3, the novel approach for plagiarism detection is described, and, in Sect. 4, algorithm evaluation measurement is described, and our approach will be evaluated. Finally, the results are concluded in Sect. 5.

2   Data

The data is a set of suspicious and source text documents released by PersianPlagDet competition [11]. In PersianPlagDet data, the document plagiarisms could happen in different ways: parts of a source text document could exactly be copied into a suspicious text, parts of a source text document with some random changes could be copied into a suspicious text, and parts of a restated source text document could be seen in a suspicious text.

2.1 Data Preparation

Before applying plagiarism detection method, the source and suspicious text documents should be prepared. We explain the necessary processes needed before plagiarism detection step by step:

Text Cleansing and Normalization. First, we normalize text documents. Normalization is the task of transforming text characters into a unique and normal form of a language. For example, we convert all Arabic "ي" and "ك" to Persian "ی" and "ک" for preprocessing Persian text documents and unify all numbers with different Persian and English characters. Punctuations are also removed from text documents.

Text Tokenization and POS Tagging. We tokenize text documents into words. Tokenization is the procedure of splitting a text into words, phrases, or other meaningful parts, namely tokens [12]. In addition to tokenization process, the exact position of tokens *i.e.* word offsets are stored. A token offset represents the token character-based distance from the beginning of the document. By applying the Hazm POS tagger, we also specify part-of-speech of each word. The nouns help to compare phrases for plagiarism detection purpose. Thus, nouns are flagged for the next stages of processing.

Removing Stop Words and Frequent Words. Stop words are also removed from text data. Stop words are words which are moved out from text data in processing steps because they do not contain significant information. First, a group of stop words has been selected which an expert has proposed. Then, frequent words are also chosen and removed with considering a frequency threshold value.

Stemming Words. The next step is to specify words stems. There are many kinds of words inflections and derivations. The suffices "ها" , "ان" , "ات" , "یان" , "ین" and sometimes "گان" could make a single word plural. Noun suffices have been removed. Also, Arabic broken plurals are the most challenging kinds of noun pluralization which cannot be distinguished by removing some suffices. An expert has provided the words stems by the help of Dehkhoda and Moein dictionaries which could help us to convert Arabic broken plural nouns to singular ones.

Acquiring Words Synsets. After defining words part-of-speech, we search through the Farsnet to find the nouns cognitive synonyms, synsets. We find synsets because words may be used instead of their synonyms in different positions. For example, "computers" may be used as "estimators" or "data processors". Synsets information is also stored.

3 Methodology

After the preprocessing of source and suspicious documents, we use a method to find similar fragments and their exact offsets in both suspicious and source files.

Before source and suspicious documents being compared, documents are saved to and retrieved from a Trie data structure. In the next subsections, there would be a brief survey of Trie trees and an explanation of our new proposed Trie.

3.1   Brief Survey of Trie Trees

A tokenized document is a set of words which can be stored in a dictionary. A Trie data structure can be used to insert and find words in a dictionary in $O(n)$ in which n represents a single word length. The word "Trie" actually comes from the "retrieval" which is its usage. In the Trie tree, the prefix tree, each node is a word or a prefix. All prefix characters of a word are inserted as a node, and the last letter is flagged as the word end in Trie. The Fig. 1 shows an example of a Trie structure used in this paper. Gray-colored nodes are words which are specified based on Dehkhoda and Moein dictionaries. Words with similar prefixes may have similar subpaths like the words "رای" and "رایانه" in the Fig. 1. Also, Satellite data like word and their front word offsets exist as word nodes payloads in the proposed Trie explained in the following.

3.2   Proposed Trie Trees

In this paper, we use Trie data structure to insert and retrieve documents words due to Trie properties like fast insertion and searching and its high adjustment to our problem solving like defining the offsets of plagiarized strings. Our method for plagiarism detection is divided into two different processes:

Inserting Documents to Data Structures. After preprocessing both source and suspicious documents, all the words with their exact positions in the source document are inserted into Trie, and the suspicious words are added into an ordered list based on their position in the document. Each Trie node is a part of preprocessed words. In the insertion phase, a source document is added to the Trie. Each word has a "source offset list" which includes the word occurrence positions in the source document. A word node also includes a "front node offset list" which is the word front node offset in the source document. Knowing "source front node offset lists" helps to keep the contiguity of words in the source document. Notice that words may have occurred in different positions in the document, but they are only inserted once in the Trie. Also, noun words synsets are also added to the Trie which their source offset lists and front node offset lists are as same as the noun words offset lists in the source document. In the Fig. 1, an example of a source sentence, "کامپیوتر اینجا است.", is inserted into a Trie. The sentence includes two nouns "کامپیوتر" and "اینجا" and a verb "است". Only a synset of "کامپیوتر" which is "رایانه" is shown in the Figure for the simplicity. Both source offset lists and front node offset lists of "کامپیوتر" and "رایانه" are the same which would help to find synsets in the retrieval phase.

Due to enhancing searching speed, It is better to save the longer document in the Trie, however, we always save the source document in the Trie for simplicity.

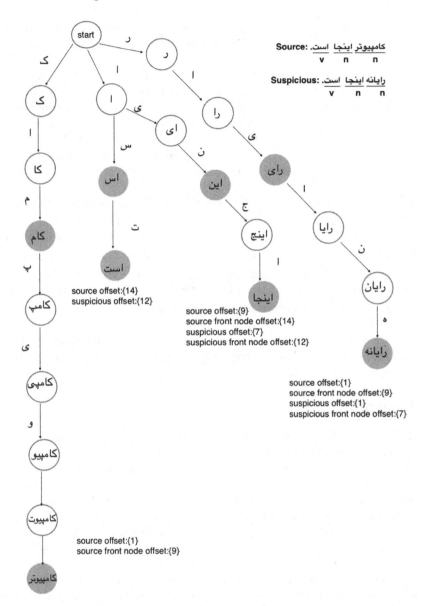

Fig. 1. An example of Trie data structure.

Finding the Longest Plagiarized Fragments. To report plagiarized sections, it is important to find similar words based on their sequential occurrences in the source and suspicious documents. For the source documents, the words offsets and front words offsets added in the Trie will help us to find the order of words in the source plagiarized sections.

Now, we iterate over the suspicious document words one by one and find the corresponding words in source Trie. After matched words found by traversing both source and suspicious documents, the detected plagiarized positions of the suspicious document and their front word offset are added to the corresponding word "suspicious offset" and "suspicious front node offset" lists in the Trie. These matched offset data of suspicious help to find matched fragments in the next step. After constructing documents data structure, the longest plagiarized fragments should be found in both source and suspicious documents. The "sentence list" includes the first words of plagiarized sections. By looking at words in the sentence list and finding them in the Trie, all the plagiarized fragments could be found.

In Fig. 1, the sentence "کامپیوتر اینجا است." is a source sentence inserted in the Trie, and the sentence "رایانه اینجا است." is a suspicious sentence kept in an ordered list. These two sentences are traversed, and they are matched. The word "کامپیوتر" from the source sentence and the word "رایانه" from suspicious sentence are synsets. In the "رایانه" node existed in the Trie, the "رایانه" offset is added to suspicious offset list, and its front word "اینجا" offset is inserted to suspicious front node offset list. This process applied for other matched words. The "رایانه" is also added to the "sentence list".

After the source offsets information and matched words information of suspicious added to Trie word nodes, the longest fragments could be found with the help of these satellite data.

4   Evaluation

The TIRA as an Evaluation-as-a-Service platform was used for experimenting information retrieval tasks in the Persian Plagdet contest [13]. The contest evaluation corpus consists of simulated, artificial, and real plagiarism cases. Real copied passages were gathered in the case of real plagiarism. In artificial case, an automatic paraphrasing technology was used for obfuscation. Also, Some human resources manually created simulated passages.

In the contest, macro-averaged precision, recall, granularity measurements, and the plagdet score described was used for evaluation. The precision and recall measurements evaluate the performance of detection in character level, while granularity considers the contiguity of text plagiarised phrases detected in source and suspicious documents. The granularity of detections R under true plagiarisms S is described as below [14];

$$gran(S, R) = \frac{1}{|S_R|} \sum_{s \in S_R} |R_S| \tag{1}$$

Where $S_R \subseteq S$ are the cases which are detected by detections and $R_S \subseteq R$ are the detections by considering s:

$$S_R = \{s|s \in S \land \exists r \in R : r \quad detects \quad s\},$$
$$R_S = \{r|r \in R \land r \quad detects \quad s\}.$$

Plagdet score is an overall score which considers the other mentioned measurements. The Plagdet score overall score is as follows [14];

$$plagdet(S, R) = \frac{F_\alpha}{\log_2(1 + gran(S, R))} \tag{2}$$

In which S and R are detections and true cases of a plagiarism and F_α is $F_\alpha -$ *Measure*, the weighted harmonic mean of precision and recall which can be defined as below;

$$F_\alpha = (1 + \alpha^2).\frac{precision.recall}{(\alpha^2.precision) + recall} \tag{3}$$

If α is not predefined, we consider $\alpha = 1$.

Table 1. The overall evaluation [13].

Measure	Plagdet	Granularity	Precision	Recall
Value	0.775	1.228	0.964	0.837

Table 2. Detection performance based on obfuscation type [13].

	Recall	Precision	Granularity	PlagDet
No obfuscation	0.98	0.98	1.00	0.98
Artificial obfuscation	0.90	0.97	1.21	0.81
Simulated obfuscation	0.60	0.96	1.41	0.58

Table 1 shows the overall evaluation of our approach on the test data released by PersianPlagDet 2016 competition which is based on TIRA and the PAN evaluation setup [15–17]. Our approach high precision, recall and acceptable granularity values contribute to the admissible plagdet score. Our algorithm had the highest precision amongst all approaches. Also, Table 2 shows the performance of our algorithm based on obfuscation types in the corpus. The algorithm had the high precision in all cases. However, the results of exact copy and artificial obfuscation are better than the simulated one.

5   Conclusions

The advents of digitalization and technology have simplified the act of plagiarizing. Thus, it is crucial to develop automatic systems to detect plagiarisation in different contents.

We took part in the international PersianPlagDet 2016 contest. We made the released data ready by preprocessing, tokenization and Morphological analysis (e.g. POS tagging) before documents comparison. In this paper, we have proposed a novel Trie-based approach to save and retrieve source and suspicious documents for solving the plagiarism detection problem. Fast inserting and retrieval of long sentences were our reasons to exploit Trie trees structures for the detection problem. We saved noun words and their synsets to our extended Trie which have helped us to improve our text comparison. The nodes satellite data like source, suspicious and front node offset lists helped us to find matched fragments in source and suspicious documents. After completing the Trie, longest matched fragments were extracted from the Trie.

To evaluate our algorithm, we used macro-averaged precision, recall, granularity measurements, and the plagdet score which were proposed by the PersianPlagDet competition. High precision, recall and acceptable granularity made the overall plagdet score for our algorithm admissible. The algorithm performed well in the cases of exact copy and artificial obfuscation. Although the precision is high in the case of simulated obfuscation, some highly paraphrased were not detected in the case of simulated obfuscation via crowdsourcing.

In the next study, we will work on the contiguity of plagiarised phrase for better granularity results. Besides, we will consider other part-of-speech synsets like verb synsets to improve our algorithm performance especially in the case of simulated obfuscation.

References

1. Lea, M.R., Street, B.: Understanding textual practices in higher education. Writ.: Texts Process. Pract. 62 (2014)
2. Asghari, H., Khoshnava, K., Fatemi, O., Faili, H.: Developing bilingual plagiarism detection corpus using sentence aligned parallel corpus. In: Notebook for PAN at CLEF (2015)
3. Lesk, M.: How many scientific papers are not original? Proc. Nat. Acad. Sci. **112**(1), 6–7 (2015)
4. Miller, G.A.: WordNet: a lexical database for English. Commun. ACM **38**(11), 39–41 (1995)
5. Shamsfard, M., Hesabi, A., Fadaei, H., Mansoory, N., Famian, A., Bagherbeigi, S., Fekri, E., Monshizadeh, M., Assi, S.M.: Semi automatic development of FarsNet; the Persian WordNet. In: Proceedings of 5th Global WordNet Conference, Mumbai, India, vol. 29 (2010)
6. Hazm (2013). https://github.com/sobhe/hazm
7. Brin, S., Davis, J., Garcia-Molina, H.: Copy detection mechanisms for digital documents. In: ACM SIGMOD Record, vol. 24, pp. 398–409. ACM (1995)
8. Mozgovoy, M.: Enhancing Computer-Aided Plagiarism Detection. University of Joensuu, Joensuu (2007)
9. Mahmoodi, M., Varnamkhasti, M.M.: Design a Persian automated plagiarism detector (AMZPPD). arXiv preprint arXiv:1403.1618 (2014)
10. Rakian, S., Esfahani, F.S., Rastegari, H.: A Persian fuzzy plagiarism detection approach. J. Inf. Syst. Telecommun. (JIST) **3**(3), 182–190 (2015)

11. Persianplagdet 2016. http://www.ictrc.ac.ir/plagdet (2016)
12. Uysal, A.K., Gunal, S.: The impact of preprocessing on text classification. Inf. Process. Manag. **50**(1), 104–112 (2014)
13. Asghari, H., Mohtaj, S., Fatemi, O., Faili, H., Rosso, P., Potthast, M.: Algorithms and corpora for Persian plagiarism detection: overview of PAN at FIRE 2016. In: Working Notes of FIRE 2016 - Forum for Information Retrieval Evaluation, CEUR Workshop Proceedings (2016). CEUR-WS.org
14. Potthast, M., Stein, B., Barrón-Cedeño, A., Rosso, P.: An evaluation framework for plagiarism detection. In: Proceedings of the 23rd International Conference on Computational Linguistics: Posters, pp. 997–1005. Association for Computational Linguistics (2010)
15. Potthast, M., Stein, B., Barrón-Cedeño, A., Rosso, P.: An evaluation framework for plagiarism detection. In: Huang, C.R., Jurafsky, D. (eds.) 23rd International Conference on Computational Linguistics (COLING 2010), pp. 997–1005. Association for Computational Linguistics, Stroudsburg, Pennsylvania, August 2010
16. Gollub, T., Stein, B., Burrows, S.: Ousting Ivory tower research: towards a web framework for providing experiments as a service. In: Hersh, B., Callan, J., Maarek, Y., Sanderson, M. (eds.) 35th International ACM Conference on Research and Development in Information Retrieval (SIGIR 2012), pp. 1125–1126. ACM, August 2012
17. Potthast, M., Gollub, T., Rangel, F., Rosso, P., Stamatatos, E., Stein, B.: Improving the reproducibility of PAN's shared tasks: plagiarism detection, author identification, and author profiling. In: Kanoulas, E., Lupu, M., Clough, P., Sanderson, M., Hall, M., Hanbury, A., Toms, E. (eds.) CLEF 2014. LNCS, vol. 8685, pp. 268–299. Springer, Cham (2014). https://doi.org/10.1007/978-3-319-11382-1_22

Using Local Text Similarity in Pairwise Document Analysis for Monolingual Plagiarism Detection

Nava Ehsan[(⊠)] and Azadeh Shakery

School of Electrical and Computer Engineering, College of Engineering,
University of Tehran, Tehran, Iran
{n.ehsan,shakery}@ut.ac.ir

Abstract. Rapid growth of documents and the increased accessibility of electronic documents lead to the need to develop effective tools for detecting plagiarised texts. The task of plagiarism detection entails two main subtasks, suspicious candidate retrieval and pairwise document similarity analysis also called detailed analysis. In this paper we focus on the second subtask. We will report our monolingual plagiarism detection system which is used to process the Persian plagiarism corpus for the task of pairwise document similarity. To retrieve plagiarised passages this paper presents a pairwise plagiarism detection algorithm based on a vector space model considering the proximity of the terms. The proposed framework is applicable in any language and it could also adapted for cross language domain. We evaluate the performance in terms of precision, recall, granularity and *Plagdet* metrics.

1 Introduction

The task of plagiarism detection comprises two main subtasks: candidate document retrieval and pairwise document detection or detailed analysis. Some researchers also included a third step, called post-processing, where the extracted passage pairs are cleaned, filtered, and possibly visualized for later presentation [23]. Detailed analysis of plagiarism detection task is retrieving passages of text which have originated from another document. This process is comparing source and suspicious pairs and retrieving plagiarized fragments.

In this paper we introduce a vector space model for this task. The algorithm tries to detect local similarity between the texts. The proximity of words are considered by dividing the text into passages and also using n-gram alignment. In the first step of the algorithm, after creating the passages we didn't take into account the order of the words in each passage. Thus, this approach is insensitive to punctuations, extra white spaces and permutation of the document context in the passages. The approach is followed by precise similarity analysis based on a dynamic text alignment algorithm. We also didn't use any language specific feature. Thus, our approach is applicable in any language. The result we obtained on the training data was about 0.82 with respect to *Plagdet* score. In addition,

© Springer International Publishing AG 2018
P. Majumder et al. (Eds.): FIRE 2016 Workshop, LNCS 10478, pp. 118–127, 2018.
https://doi.org/10.1007/978-3-319-73606-8_9

by taking advantage of any translation resource this framework could be used for cross language domain [14]. A preliminary version of our work is presented in [13]. We extend our work by (1) using a keyword based approach, and (2) adding more analysis along with results and examples.

The rest of the paper is organized as follows: Sect. 2 outlines related works in monolingual plagiarism detection. Section 3 describes the pairwise document similarity approach. Finally experimental results are discussed in Sect. 4. Conclusion and future work are reported in Sect. 5.

2   Related Work

Plagiarism detection could be classified into two classes, intrinsic and external also called without reference or with reference, respectively. Intrinsic evaluation is referred to those methods, which use style analysis to detect parts of the text that are inconsistent in terms of writing style [19, 20]. The aim of external plagiarism detection is not only finding the suspicious text but also finding the reference of the suspicious text. In monolingual plagiarism detection, the suspicious text could be an exact copy or a modified copy [22] and it should be large enough to be more than just a coincidence.

One method for monolingual plagiarism detection is comparing fragments of suspicious and source documents using fingerprint indexing. Winnowing approach [28], which is used in the widely used plagiarism detection tool, MOSS, is based on fingerprint indexing.

There are different approaches for detection monolingual plagiarism detection. Some of these approaches could be classified into fingerprinting [18,28], string matching [11,15], using stopwords [30], vector space models [7,17], probability models [4], classification [1,21], semantic models [8,9] and structural models [10,29]. According to monolingual experiments in [5] paraphrasing could make plagiarism detection more difficult. There have been some works for detecting paraphrased sentences in monolingual texts [2].

In recent years PAN competition offers evaluation environment to evaluate plagiarism detection algorithms. This competition also offers evaluation corpora. AraPlagDet was a competition on detecting plagiarism in Arabic documents. The competition was held as a PAN shared task at FIRE2015. The overview of this task is presented in [6]. PAN@FIRE Persian Plagdet 2016 competition [3] prepares a set of suspicious and source documents written in Persian and the task is to find all plagiarized sections in the suspicious documents and, if available, the corresponding source sections. This external plagiarism detection task provides a situation to evaluate Persian plagiarism detection systems. An overview of Persian plagiarism detection methods participated in PAN@FIRE Persian Plagdet 2016 is presented in [3].

3   Pairwise Document Similarity Analysis

In this section we deal with pairwise document similarity analysis and we will introduce a method based on a vector space model to detect plagiarized fragments of specified set of suspicious and source document pairs. In other words, we will describe a system that makes a pairwise document comparison for plagiarism detection. We assume that the source and suspicious pairs are pre-defined for the system. According to PAN competition this process is called, detailed analysis stage. The problem of pairwise document analysis is defined as follows: let S' be a suspicious document and S be a source document that is likely to contain similar passages to some passages in S'. S and S' are compared section-wise using a language retrieval model. A plagiarism is considered, if for a pair of sections (S_f and $S'_{f'}$) a similarity above a threshold is detected.

According to [23] the detection approaches of this subtask includes three building blocks named (1) seeding, (2) match merging, and (3) extraction filtering. In the following subsections, we describe them in detail.

3.1 Seeding

Given a suspicious document and a source document, matches between the two documents are identified using some seeds [23]. In our approach, first, preprocessing phase is performed. Given a document, a preprocessing phase is performed. We substitute Arabic ي and ك with Persian ی and ک . The reason is that the mentioned two letters have different character encodings. Then, stopwords, punctuations and extra white spaces are removed and tokens are extracted.

Since plagiarism usually happens in parts of the text, a plagiarism detection method should be able to detect local similarities where only a short passage may be in common in both documents. Thus, there is a requirement to segment the texts into fragments. We consider sentences as the basic units for plagiarism detection, thus, a fragment is a sequence of contiguous sentences. For each document pair, we split the texts into sentences by using ".", "?" and "!" marks. We choose an amount of consecutive sentences as the smallest unit of plagiarism. Documents are divided into some fragments each containing n sentences with one sentence overlap. The sensitivity of the algorithm with respect to parameter n is shown in Sect. 4.

After sentence splitting, a vector space model is created. The terms of the source document are considered as the vocabulary. We used two different approaches for extracting the vocabulary. (1) All the words (excluding stopwords) of the source document are considered as the vocabulary; and (2) the keywords of the source document are extracted to construct the domain of our vocabulary. In the second approach the terms are weighted using $tf.idf$ weights, and the terms whose weights are above a threshold are considered as a keyword. After extracting our vocabulary a binary weighting scheme is used by setting the ith index 1 if the ith term occurs in the fragment and 0 otherwise.

We consider reference fragment S_f and suspicious fragment $S'_{f'}$ as pairs of plagiarism candidate fragments whose cosine similarity is greater than a threshold t_1, and at least three terms of the source text are found in the suspicious fragment. The last criterion is added to avoid retrieving fragments with coincidental similarity. S_f will be considered as a plagiarism source of suspicious fragment $S'_{f'}$ if it has maximum cosine similarity among all source fragments with similarity above the threshold.

The vector creation approach is similar to Eurovoc-based model proposed in [26] except that we use it for monolingual texts rather than cross-lingual texts. Thus, this approach could be easily adapted to cross language plagiarism detection.

3.2   Match Merging

Finding seed matches between a suspicious and a source document, they are merged into aligned passages of maximal length which are then reported as plagiarism detections [23].

To improve performance with respect to the granularity metric, we merge adjacent suspicious and source fragments to report a single plagiarism case. In this step, the match merging rule is applied on fragments obtained in the first step of the algorithm. If the number of characters between two detected fragments of source and suspicious documents are below a threshold t_2 those fragments are considered as adjacent fragments and they are merged to report a single plagiarism case.

3.3   Extraction Filtering

Given a set of aligned passages, a passage filter removes all aligned passages that do not meet certain criteria. For example, dealing with overlapping passages or extremely short passages [23].

After retrieving potential plagiarized fragments in previous steps, the sentences within a fragment are partitioned into non-overlapping n-grams. This stage of alignment aims at pairing corresponding segments and it takes into account situations in which a plagiarized text might merge or split segments in the suspicious document. For extraction filtering step we applied a method similar to result filtering approach proposed in [14] for excluding false positive detections and improving precision. We used the dynamic algorithm to find the alignments between the n-grams of the source and suspicious texts and then the null alignments are excluded from the start and end of the reported fragments.

4   Results

The results of Persian detailed analysis subtask on PAN@FIRE Persian Plagdet 2016 are reported and analysed in [3]. The corpus used for evaluating this shared task comprises Persian plagiarised cases including exact copy (11%), aritificial cases (81%), and simulated cases (8%) [3]. In this section we will go through our approach step by step to analyse our proposed algorithm. The results of Persian detailed analysis subtask on PAN@FIRE Persian Plagdet 2016 [3] using the training data is summarized in Tables 1, 2 and 3. The experimentation platform TIRA is used for our evaluations [16,24].

Compared to the character level measures reported in Table 1, the case level measures, reported in Table 2, relaxes the fine-grained measurement of plagiarism detection quality by allowing a detection algorithm to detect about 50% of a plagiarism case while about 50% of a plagiarism detection is a true detection, and the document level measures, reported in Table 3, further relax the requirements to detecting a pair of documents, disregarding whether it finds all plagiarism cases contained [25].

Parameters t_1 and n are respectively the similarity threshold and number of consecutive sentences described in Sect. 3.1. The adjacency threshold t_2, described in Sect. 3.2, is set to 1500 characters. The n value for n-gram creation described in Sect. 3.3 for each sentence is chosen to be 9, except for the final partition of the sentence that may include fewer or more than 9 terms.

The evaluation metrics are described in [27]. The evaluation is based on macro-average precision and recall. Also, the granularity measure characterizes the power of a detection algorithm. It shows whether a plagiarism case is detected as a whole or in several pieces. The *Plagdet* score is the combination of the three metrics, precision, recall and granularity defined as follows for plagiarism cases S and plagiarism detections R [27]:

$$plagdet(S,\ R)\ =\ \frac{F_1}{\log(1\ +\ granularity(S,\ R))} \tag{1}$$

4.1   Seeding: Using All Words

As we described in Sect. 3.1 we used two different approaches for the seeding step of the algorithm. In the first approach we extract all the terms except stopwords of the source document. In this case, the results of the Table 1 show that the *Plagdet* score improves by decreasing the amount of the sentences in a fragment. The reason could be that there are more short plagiarized texts than long ones in the dataset. According to dataset statistics, 73% of plagiarised cases were short and medium length cases, containing between 30 to 200 words [3]. The increase in precision comparing different number of sentences in a fragment using 0.3 for the value t_1, could show that decreasing the amount of sentences in a fragment may have higher impact on decreasing rather than increasing the false positive detections.

We also analysed the effect of the first step of the algorithm individually. Figure 1 shows a sample of matched pair of fragments obtained from the first step of the algorithm (candidate sentence selection) for a pair of documents. The bold words are the common words which are the indication that these two pieces of text might be a plagiarized case.

We realized that without applying the extraction filtering part of the approach, the precision of the first phase for $(t_1 = 0.3,\ n = 3)$ was 0.6026 and the *Plagdet* score was 0.7087. This shows that the extraction filtering step improved the *Plagdet* score about 14%. Figure 2 is a sample of alignments obtained from this step of the algorithm, which shows the result of applying dynamic algorithm to the fragments shown in Fig. 1. In this example the first two sentences of the suspicious case will be dropped from the reported case.

We used 0.3 for t_1 and 5 sentences for parameter n (number of consecutive sentences) for the test set of the Persian Plagdet shared task. The results on the test set are shown in Table 4. The runtime of the algorithm was about 24 min. More results of Persian detailed analysis subtask on PAN@FIRE Persian Plagdet 2016 are reported and analysed in [3].

4.2 Seeding: Using Keywords

In order to decrease detections with coincidental similarities between the texts, we used the keywords of the source document to construct the vocabulary domain. For this reason, the terms are weighted using $tf.idf$ weights, and the terms whose weights are above 0.1 of the weight of the second maximum weight in each document are considered as the keywords (The second maximum is used to decrease the chance of noise in the document). The results, using Persian Plagdet training data set are represented in Table 5. We could see that by using keywords as the signal of plagiarism the results improved about 2.5%. The running time for $t_1 = 0.3$, $n = 3$ and using all the words was about 15 min. By using the keywords the running time of the algorithm is decreased to 10 min.

Detected source text:

ولی این حرکت که به قیام افسران خراسان شهرت یافت و به سرعت سرکوب شد، حساسیت فراوانی برانگیخت. عده‌ای از افسران مبارز به فرمان ستاد ارتش به کرمان تبعید شدند. طرح دستگیری روزبه نیز ریخته شد اما روزبه که در مرخصی یک‌ماهه به سر می‌برد، به جای بازگشت به خدمت، مخفی شد و از بازداشت نجات یافت

Detected suspicious text:

شهرتش بیشتر به سبب شاعری و سرودن حمله حیدری است

باذل با ناصر علی سرهندی (متوفی ۱۱۰۸)، شاعر نامدار آن روزگار، مصاحبت داشت.تبعید افسران مبارز به فرمان ستاد ماهی‌گیر ارتش سر کرمان رقم . مرخصی دستگیری روزبه نیز ریخته_ شد اما روزبه و به طرح یک‌ماهه به سر می‌برد ، به جای بازگشت وظیفه ، مخفی شد که از بازداشت رهایی یافت .. اما سرهندی او را در مجلس خود استهزا کرد

Fig. 1. Step 1: Identifying potentially plagiarized fragments

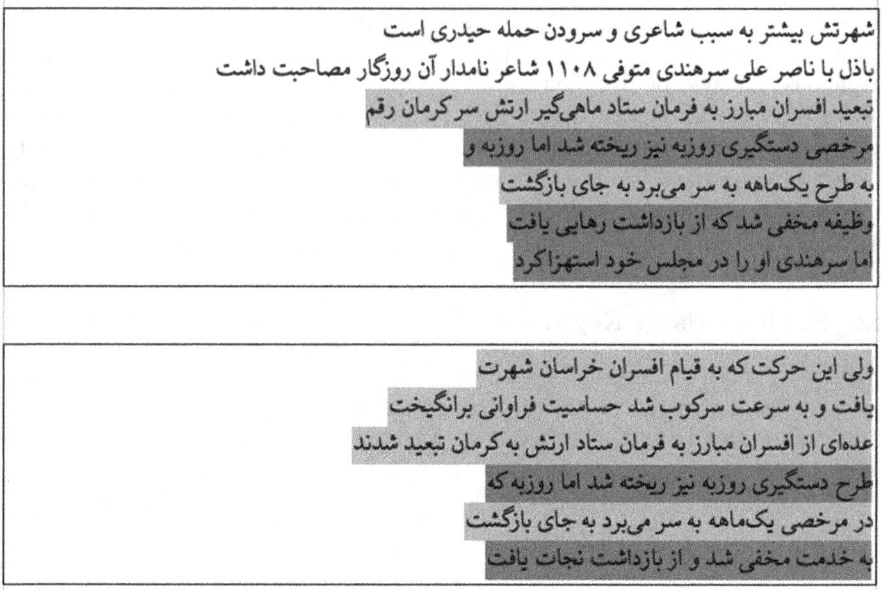

شهرتش بیشتر به سبب شاعری و سرودن حمله حیدری است

باذل با ناصر علی سرهندی متوفی ۱۱۰۸ شاعر نامدار آن روزگار مصاحبت داشت

تبعید افسران مبارز به فرمان ستاد ماهی‌گیر ارتش سرکرمان رقم

مرخصی دستگیری روزیه نیز ریخته شد اما روزیه و

به طرح یک‌ماهه به سر می‌برد به جای بازگشت

وظیفه مخفی شد که از بازداشت رهایی یافت

اما سرهندی او را در مجلس خود استهزاء کرد

ولی این حرکت که به قیام افسران خراسان شهرت

یافت و به سرعت سرکوب شد حساسیت فراوانی برانگیخت

عده‌ای از افسران مبارز به فرمان ستاد ارتش به کرمان تبعید شدند

طرح دستگیری روزیه نیز ریخته شد اما روزیه که

در مرخصی یک‌ماهه به سر می‌برد به جای بازگشت

به خدمت مخفی شد و از بازداشت نجات یافت

Fig. 2. Step 2: aligned n-grams of the fragments in Fig. 1

Table 1. Results of detailed analysis subtask using macro-averaged precision, recall, granularity, and the *Plagdet* score

	Precision	Recall	Granularity	Plagdet
$(t_1 = 0.2, n = 5)$	0.4004	0.8151	1	0.5370
$(t_1 = 0.3, n = 5)$	0.7630	0.7486	1	0.7557
$(t_1 = 0.4, n = 5)$	0.8532	0.5357	1	0.6582
$(t_1 = 0.3, n = 3)$	0.7867	0.8304	1	**0.8080**
$(t_1 = 0.4, n = 3)$	0.8604	0.6567	1	0.7449

Table 2. Results of detailed analysis subtask in case-level

	Precision	Recall	F_1
$(t_1 = 0.2, n = 5)$	0.4379	0.8292	0.5731
$(t_1 = 0.3, n = 5)$	0.8484	0.7631	0.8035
$(t_1 = 0.4, n = 5)$	0.9434	0.5478	0.6931
$(t_1 = 0.3, n = 3)$	0.8931	0.8518	0.8720
$(t_1 = 0.4, n = 3)$	0.9474	0.6775	0.7900

Table 3. Results of detailed analysis subtask in document-level

	Precision	Recall	F_1
$(t_1 = 0.2,\ n = 5)$	0.6266	0.8342	0.7156
$(t_1 = 0.3,\ n = 5)$	0.8798	0.7701	0.8213
$(t_1 = 0.4,\ n = 5)$	0.9457	0.5534	0.6982
$(t_1 = 0.3,\ n = 3)$	0.9312	0.8555	0.8918
$(t_1 = 0.4,\ n = 3)$	0.9498	0.6831	0.7947

Table 4. Results of detailed analysis subtask on the test set

	Precision	Recall	Granularity	Plagdet
$(t_1 = 0.3,\ n = 5)$	0.7496	0.7050	1	0.7266

Table 5. Results of detailed analysis subtask with keyword extraction using macro-averaged precision, recall, granularity, and the *Plagdet* score

	Precision	Recall	Granularity	Plagdet
$(t_1 = 0.3,\ n = 3)$	0.5118	0.8858	1	0.6487
$(t_1 = 0.4,\ n = 3)$	0.6431	0.8928	1	0.7476
$(t_1 = 0.5,\ n = 3)$	0.7475	0.8862	1	0.8110
$(t_1 = 0.6,\ n = 3)$	0.8117	0.8459	1	**0.8282**
$(t_1 = 0.7,\ n = 3)$	0.8522	0.7531	1	0.7996

5   Conclusion and Future Work

The task of plagiarism detection entails two subtasks, suspicious candidate retrieval and pairwise document similarity. We introduce a pairwise document analysis approach for Persian language. An approach based on a vector space model is described for computing pairwise document similarity. The principle of this approach is that sentences containing more common words are likely to be a source of plagiarism. Also, the proximity of words are considered by dividing the text into passages and also using n-gram alignments. The results are improved by using keywords instead of all the words, and detecting fragments containing more common keywords. The method contains three building blocks named seeding, match merging and extraction filtering. The proposed approach could be applied in any language. Our work is tested on a Persian corpora which offers evaluation environment to evaluate plagiarism detection algorithms.

Detailed analysis subtask will be improved by expanding the representative words of the document to find appropriate substitutes for a word in the context in order to capture intelligent plagiarisms. For this reason, there is requirement to minimize the risk of noises that word expansion may cause. A complete plagiarism detection system could be developed by adding a candidate selection [12] step before pairwise document analysis.

References

1. Abnar, S., Dehghani, M., Shakery, A.: Meta text aligner: text alignment based on predicted plagiarism relation. In: International Conference of the Cross-Language Evaluation Forum for European Languages, pp. 193–199 (2015)
2. Androutsopoulos, I., Malakasiotis, P.: A survey of paraphrasing and textual entailment methods. J. Artif. Intell. Res. **38**, 135–187 (2009)
3. Asghari, H., Mohtaj, S., Fatemi, O., Faili, H., Rosso, P., Potthast, M.: Algorithms and corpora for persian plagiarism detection: overview of pan at fire 2016. In: Working notes of FIRE 2016 - Forum for Information Retrieval Evaluation. CEUR Workshop Proceedings, CEUR-WS.org (2016)
4. Barrón-Cedeño, A., Rosso, P., Benedí, J.-M.: Reducing the plagiarism detection search space on the basis of the kullback-leibler distance. In: Gelbukh, A. (ed.) CICLing 2009. LNCS, vol. 5449, pp. 523–534. Springer, Heidelberg (2009). https://doi.org/10.1007/978-3-642-00382-0_42
5. Barrón-Cedeno, A., Vila, M., Martí, M.A., Rosso, P.: Plagiarism meets paraphrasing: insights for the next generation in automatic plagiarism detection. Comput. Linguist. **39**(4), 917–947 (2013)
6. Bensalem, I., Boukhalfa, I., Rosso, P., Abouenour, L., Darwish, K., Chikhi, S.: Overview of the araplagdet pan@ fire2015 shared task on arabic plagiarism detection, pp. 111–122 (2015)
7. Brin, S., Davis, J., Garcia-Molina, H.: Copy detection mechanisms for digital documents. In: ACM SIGMOD Record, vol. 24, pp. 398–409. ACM (1995)
8. Chen, C.Y., Yeh, J.Y., Ke, H.R.: Plagiarism detection using rouge and wordNet. J. Comput. **2**(3), 34–44 (2010)
9. Chong, M., Specia, L.: Lexical generalisation for word-level matching in plagiarism detection. In: RANLP, pp. 704–709 (2011)
10. Chow, T.W., Rahman, M.: Multilayer SOM with tree-structured data for efficient document retrieval and plagiarism detection. IEEE Trans. Neural Netw. **20**(9), 1385–1402 (2009)
11. Clough, P., Stevenson, M.: Developing a corpus of plagiarised short answers. Lang. Resour. Eval. **45**(1), 5–24 (2011)
12. Ehsan, N., Shakery, A.: Candidate document retrieval for cross-lingual plagiarism detection using two-level proximity information. Inf. Process. Manage. **52**(6), 1004–1017 (2016)
13. Ehsan, N., Shakery, A.: A pairwise document analysis approach for monolingual plagiarism detection. In: Working Notes of FIRE 2016-Forum for Information Retrieval Evaluation, pp. 7–10 (2016)
14. Ehsan, N., Tompa, F.W., Shakery, A.: Using a dictionary and n-gram alignment to improve fine-grained cross-language plagiarism detection. In: Proceedings of the 2016 ACM Symposium on Document Engineering, pp. 59–68. ACM (2016)
15. Errami, M., Sun, Z., George, A.C., Long, T.C., Skinner, M.A., Wren, J.D., Garner, H.R.: Identifying duplicate content using statistically improbable phrases. Bioinformatics **26**(11), 1453–1457 (2010)
16. Gollub, T., Stein, B., Burrows, S.: Ousting ivory tower research: towards a web framework for providing experiments as a service. In: Hersh, B., Callan, J., Maarek, Y., Sanderson, M. (eds.) 35th International ACM Conference on Research and Development in Information Retrieval (SIGIR 2012), pp. 1125–1126. ACM (August 2012)

17. Grozea, C., Gehl, C., Popescu, M.: Encoplot: pairwise sequence matching in linear time applied to plagiarism detection. In: 3rd PAN Workshop. Uncovering Plagiarism, Authorship and Social Software Misuse, pp. 10–18 (2009)
18. Manku, G.S., Jain, A., Das Sarma, A.: Detecting near-duplicates for web crawling. In: Proceedings of the 16th International Conference on World Wide Web, pp. 141–150. ACM (2007)
19. Meyer zu Eissen, S., Stein, B.: Intrinsic plagiarism detection. In: Lalmas, M., Mac-Farlane, A., Rüger, S., Tombros, A., Tsikrika, T., Yavlinsky, A. (eds.) ECIR 2006. LNCS, vol. 3936, pp. 565–569. Springer, Heidelberg (2006). https://doi.org/10.1007/11735106_66
20. Oberreuter, G., Velásquez, J.D.: Text mining applied to plagiarism detection: the use of words for detecting deviations in the writing style. Expert Syst. Appl. **40**(9), 3756–3763 (2013)
21. Pereira, R.C., Moreira, V.P., Galante, R.: A new approach for cross-language plagiarism analysis. Multiling. Multimodal Inf. Access Eval. **6360**, 15–26 (2010)
22. Potthast, M., Barrón-Cedeño, A., Stein, B., Rosso, P.: Cross-language plagiarism detection. Lang. Resour. Eval. **45**(1), 45–62 (2011)
23. Potthast, M., Gollub, T., Hagen, M., Kiesel, J., Michel, M., Oberländer, A., Tippmann, M., Barrón-Cedeño, A., Gupta, P., Rosso, P., et al.: Overview of the 4th international competition on plagiarism detection. In: CLEF (Online Working Notes/Labs/Workshop) (2012)
24. Potthast, M., Gollub, T., Rangel, F., Rosso, P., Stamatatos, E., Stein, B.: Improving the reproducibility of PAN's shared tasks: plagiarism detection, author identification, and author profiling. In: Kanoulas, E., Lupu, M., Clough, P., Sanderson, M., Hall, M., Hanbury, A., Toms, E. (eds.) CLEF 2014. LNCS, vol. 8685, pp. 268–299. Springer, Cham (2014). https://doi.org/10.1007/978-3-319-11382-1_22
25. Potthast, M., Hagen, M., Beyer, A., Busse, M., Tippmann, M., Rosso, P., Stein, B.: Overview of the 6th international competition on plagiarism detection. In: CLEF (Online Working Notes/Labs/Workshop) (2014)
26. Potthast, M., Stein, B., Anderka, M.: A wikipedia-based multilingual retrieval model. In: Macdonald, C., Ounis, I., Plachouras, V., Ruthven, I., White, R.W. (eds.) ECIR 2008. LNCS, vol. 4956, pp. 522–530. Springer, Heidelberg (2008). https://doi.org/10.1007/978-3-540-78646-7_51
27. Potthast, M., Stein, B., Barrón-Cedeño, A., Rosso, P.: An evaluation framework for plagiarism detection. In: Proceedings of the 23rd International Conference on Computational Linguistics: Posters, pp. 997–1005. Association for Computational Linguistics (2010)
28. Schleimer, S., Wilkerson, D.S., Aiken, A.: Winnowing: local algorithms for document fingerprinting. In: Proceedings of the 2003 ACM SIGMOD International Conference on Management of Data, pp. 76–85. ACM (2003)
29. Si, A., Leong, H.V., Lau, R.W.: Check: a document plagiarism detection system. In: Proceedings of the 1997 ACM Symposium on Applied Computing, pp. 70–77. ACM (1997)
30. Stamatatos, E.: Plagiarism detection using stopword n-grams. J. Am. Soc. Inform. Sci. Technol. **62**(12), 2512–2527 (2011)

Shared Task on Detecting Paraphrases in Indian Languages (DPIL): An Overview

M. Anand Kumar$^{(\boxtimes)}$ ⓘ, Shivkaran Singh, B. Kavirajan,
and K. P. Soman

Centre for Computational Engineering and Networking (CEN),
Amrita School of Engineering, Amrita Vishwa Vidyapeetham,
Coimbatore, India
m_anandkumar@cb.amrita.edu

Abstract. This paper explains the overview of the shared task on "Detecting Paraphrases in Indian Languages" (DPIL) conducted at FIRE 2016. Given a pair of sentences in the same language, participants were asked to detect the semantic equivalence between sentences. This shared task was proposed for four Indian languages, namely Tamil, Malayalam, Hindi, and Punjabi. There were two subtasks given under the shared task on Detecting Paraphrase in Indian Languages. Given a pair of sentences, the subtask-1 was to classify them as paraphrases or not paraphrases. The subtask-2 was to identify whether they are paraphrases or semi-paraphrases or not paraphrases. The dataset created for the shared task has been made available online, and it is the first open-source paraphrase detection corpora for Indian languages. In this overview paper, we describe both subtasks, datasets, evaluation methods and system descriptions as well as performances of the submitted runs.

Keywords: Paraphrase detection · Semantic analysis · Indian languages
DPIL corpora

1 Introduction

A paraphrase is a linguistic phenomenon. It has many applications in the field of language teaching as well as computational linguistics. Linguistically, paraphrases are defined in terms of meaning. According to Meaning-Text Theory [11], if one or more syntactic construction retains semantic evenness, those are addressed as paraphrases. The exchangeability of semantic alikeness between the source text and the paraphrased version marks the range of semantic alikeness between them. A paraphrase is a very fine mechanism to shape various language models. Different linguistic units like synonyms, semi-synonyms, figurative meaning, and metaphors are considered as the basic elements for paraphrasing. Paraphrasing is not only found in lexical-level but also found in another linguistic level such as phrasal and sentential. Different levels of paraphrasing disclose the diversified forms of paraphrases and the semantic relationship to its source text. In paraphrase typologies, Lexical paraphrasing is the most popular forms of paraphrasing found in the literature. For example: If a source text is, *"The two ships were acquired by the navy after the war"*, then possible paraphrased versions are:

© Springer International Publishing AG 2018
P. Majumder et al. (Eds.): FIRE 2016 Workshop, LNCS 10478, pp. 128–140, 2018.
https://doi.org/10.1007/978-3-319-73606-8_10

"The two ships were conquered by the navy after the war" and *"The two ships were won by the Navy after the war"*. There are even more paraphrases possible for the given sentence. Here the source verb 'acquire' is paraphrased with its exact synonyms. The source and paraphrases show the same syntactic structural phenomena. These types of paraphrase are the best examples of accurate paraphrases. Some of the other common paraphrase typologies are; approximate paraphrases, sentential level paraphrases, adding extra linguistic units, changing the order, etc.

A paraphrase can be defined as "the same meaning of a sentence is expressed in another sentence using different words". Paraphrases can be identified, generated or extracted. The proposed task is focused on sentence-level paraphrase identification for Indian languages (Tamil, Malayalam, Hindi, and Punjabi). Identifying paraphrases in Indian languages is a difficult task because estimating the semantic similarity of the underlying content and understanding the morphological variations of the language are more critical. Paraphrase identification is strongly connected with the generation and extraction of paraphrases. Paraphrase identification systems improve the performance of a paraphrase generation in terms of choosing the best paraphrase candidate from the list of candidates generated by the paraphrase generation system. Paraphrase identification is also used in validating the paraphrase extraction system and the machine translation system. In the question answering system, paraphrase identification plays a vital role in matching the questions asked by the user to the existing questions for choosing the best answer. Automatic short answers grading is another interesting application which needs semantic similarity for providing grades to the short answers. Plagiarism detection is a well-known task which needs the paraphrase identification technique to detect the sentence is a paraphrase of another sentence.

One of the most commonly used corpora for paraphrase detection is the MSRP corpus [1], which contains 5801 English sentence pairs from news articles manually labeled with 67% paraphrases and 33% non-paraphrases. Since there is no annotated corpora or automated semantic interpretation systems available for Indian languages till date, creating benchmark data for paraphrases and utilizing that data in openly shared task competitions will motivate the research community for further research in Indian languages.

Dataset can be downloaded from the website[1] after submitting the registration form. Related works and shared task regarding the paraphrases are given in the Sect. 2. The descriptions of the subtasks and evaluation metrics are discussed in Sect. 3, Paraphrase corpus creation and statistics are explored in Sect. 4, system descriptions of participants and result analyses are done in Sect. 5. Findings and the results are discussed in Sect. 6.

2   Related Works and Existing Paraphrase Corpora

In SemEval-2015[2], a shared task on Paraphrase and Semantic Similarity In Twitter (PIT) [2] was conducted with the English Twitter Paraphrase Corpus [3]. The task has two sentence-level sub-tasks: a paraphrase identification task and a semantic textual

---

[1] http://nlp.amrita.edu/dpil_cen/

[2] http://alt.qcri.org/semeval2015/

similarity task. The same dataset was used for both sub-tasks but it differs in annotation and evaluation. A freely available manually annotated corpus of Russian sentence pairs is ParaPhraser [4], which is used in the recently organized shared task on Paraphrase detection for the Russian language. There were two subtasks, the first one is three-class classification: given a pair of sentences, to predict, whether they are precise paraphrases, near paraphrases or non-paraphrases. Second is a binary classification task: given a pair of sentences to predict whether they are paraphrases or non-paraphrases. The PAN plagiarism corpus 2010 (Paraphrase for Plagiarism-P4P) is used for the evaluation of automatic plagiarism detection algorithms. The corpus [5] is manually annotated with the paraphrase phenomena they contain. It is composed of 847 source-plagiarism pairs in English. The complete summary of an existing paraphrase corpora and the linguistic phenomenon for paraphrases are discussed in [6]. In [7], an issue of text plagiarism for Hindi language using English documents was addressed. For Tamil languages, paraphrase detection using deep learning techniques was applied in [8]. For Malayalam, paraphrase identification using fingerprinting [9] and statistical similarity [10] has been performed.

3   The Challenges in Paraphrase Detection

This section explains the challenges present in the automatic paraphrase detection system.

- *Morphology Variations*: Handling the morphological variations and finding the morphologically related words in given sentences is a challenging task especially for languages like Tamil and Malayalam.
- *Ambiguity*: Every language has its own ambiguity and so it differs from language to language. The proportion of ambiguity is always depends upon the language. So this ambiguity issue causes the system to struggle for analyzing the words and sentences during the similarity detection process.
- *Synonyms:* The paraphrase detection system should identify the synonym relationship between the words. Understanding the words and its synonym is not an easy task.
- *Numeric data*: Apart from natural language characters, the given input sentence can also contain numeric data in one sentence and the corresponding words for that numeric data in another sentence, which give the exact meanings. So the system should understand the mapping between the numeric and words.

4   Detecting Paraphrases in Indian Languages Shared Task

This section mainly focused on the shared task descriptions and the evaluation metrics used in evaluating the participant's output.

4.1   Task Description

There were two subtasks given under shared task on Detecting Paraphrase in Indian Languages (DPIL). The description of the subtask is given below.

Subtask 1: Given a pair of sentences from newspaper domain, the task is to classify them as paraphrases (P) or not paraphrases (NP).

Subtask 2: Given a pair of sentences from newspaper domain, the task is to identify whether they are paraphrases (P) or semi-paraphrases (SP) or not paraphrases (NP).

The subtask 2 was similar to the subtask 1 except the 3-point scale tag in paraphrases. This makes the shared task even more challenging. The example of four languages is depicted in Tables 1 and 2.

Table 1. Examples of Hindi and Tamil paraphrases

Hindi	मृतका निशा तीन भाई-बहनों में सबसे बड़ी थी। *[The deceased Nisha was eldest of three siblings]* तीन भाई-बहनों में सबसे बड़ी थी मृतका निशा। *[Out of three siblings, deceased Nisha was the eldest]*	P
	उपमंत्री की बेसिक सैलरी 10 हजार से बढ़कर 35 हजार हो गई है। *[The basic salary of the deputy minister is increased from 10k to 35k]* उपमंत्री की बेसिक सैलरी 35 हजार हो गई है। *[The basic salary of the deputy minister is 35k]*	SP
	जिमनास्टिक में दीपा 4th पोजिशन पर रही थीं। *[Deepa came at 4th position in gymnastics]* 11 भारतीय पुरुष जिमनास्ट आजादी के बाद से ओलिंपिक में जा चुके हैं। *[Since independence 11 male athletes have been to Olympics]*	NP
Tamil	புதுச்சேரியில் 84 சதவீத வாக்குப்பதிவு *[84 percent voting in Puducherry]* புதுச்சேரி சட்டசபை தேர்தலில் 84 சதவீத ஓட்டுப்பதிவானது *[Puducherry assembly elections recorded 84 percent of the vote]*	P
	அப்துல்கலாம் கனவை நிறைவேற்றும் வகையில் மாதம் ஒரு செயற்கைகோள் அனுப்ப திட்டம் *[In order to fulfill Abdul Kalam's dream, planning is to send a satellite per month]* ஒரு செயற்கைகோளை அனுப்ப வேண்டும் என்பது அப்துல்கலாமின் கனவு *[Abdul Kalam's dream was to send a satellite]*	SP
	அறைகளில் இருந்தும் சிலைகள், ஓவியங்கள் கிடைத்தன *[Statues and paintings were found from the rooms]* மூன்று நாட்கள் நடத்தப்பட்ட சோதனையில் மொத்தம் 71 கற்சிலைகள் மீட்கப்பட்டுள்ளன *[A total of 71 stone statues have been recovered in a three day raid]*	NP

Table 2. Examples of Malayalam and Punjabi paraphrases

Malayalam	നാളെ തന്നെ അവന്റെ യാത്ര ആരംഭിക്കാന് അവന് പദ്ധതിയിട്ടു *[He planned to start his journey tomorrow itself]* അവന്റെ യാത്ര നാളെ തന്നെ ആരംഭിക്കാനായിരുന്നു അവന്റെ പദ്ധതി *[His plan was to start his journey tomorrow itself]*	P
	ഒ. രാജഗെ·ാപാ**ല്**എം.എ**ല്**.എയായിസത്യപ്രതിജ്ഞചയെ്തു *[O. Rajagopal was sworn in as legislator]* കരേളാനിയമസഭയിലങ്ങെദ്ഭയബി.ജെ.പിഎം.എ**ല്**.എഒ. രാജഗെ·ാപാ**ല്**സത്യപ്രതിജ്ഞചയെ്തു *[The first BJP MLA of Kerala Legislative Assembly O. Rajagopal was sworn in]*	SP
	ഇന്ത്യയുടെദെശേീയഗാനംരചിച്ചത്രബീന്ദ്രനാഥ്ടാഗെ·ാ**ര്**ആണ് *[India's national Anthem is written by Rabindranath Tagore]* രബീന്ദ്രനാഥ്ടാഗെ·ാരിന്റകെ്യതിയായഗീതാഞ്ഛലിക്ക്നെ·ാബെ**ല്**സമ്മാനംലഭിച്ചിട്ടുണ്ട് *[Rabindranath Tagore won the Nobel Prize for his work Gitanjali]*	NP
Punjabi	ਕਾਬੁਲ ਦੇ ਹੋਟਲ ਤੇ ਅੱਤਵਾਦੀ ਹਮਲਾ। *A Kabul hotel was attacked by the terrorists.* ਅੱਤਵਾਦੀਆਂ ਦੁਆਰਾ ਕਾਬੁਲ ਦੇ ਹੋਟਲ ਤੇ ਕੀਤਾ ਗਿਆ ਹਮਲਾ। *The terrorists attacked a hotel in Kabul*	P
	ਪੁਲੀਸ ਅਧਿਕਾਰੀ ਮੁਹੰਮਦ ਮੁਤਾਬਕ ਦੋਵੇਂ ਭਰਾਵਾਂ ਵਿਚਕਾਰ ਕਾਰੋਬਾਰ ਨੂੰ ਲੈ ਕੇ ਝਗੜਾ ਸੀ। *According to the police officer, there was a dispute over trade among two brothers.* ਦੋਵੇਂ ਭਰਾਵਾਂ ਵਿਚਕਾਰ ਕਾਰੋਬਾਰ ਨੂੰ ਲੈ ਕੇ ਝਗੜਾ ਸੀ। *There was a dispute over trade between two brothers*	SP
	ਅਮਰਨਾਥਤੇ ਵੈਸ਼ਨੋ ਦੇਵੀ ਯਾਤਰਾ ਨੂ ਭਾਰੀ ਬਾਰਿਸ਼ ਚਲਦਿਆ ਰੋਕ ਦਿਤਾ ਗਯਾ ਹੈ। *Travels to Amarnath and Vaishnodevi were stopped because of heavy rain* ਅਮਰਨਾਥ ਗੁਫਾ ਭਗਵਾਨ ਸ਼ਿਵ ਦੇ ਪ੍ਰਮੁੱਖ ਧਾਰਮਿਕ ਥਾਂਵਾਂ ਵਿੱਚੋਂ ਇੱਕ ਹੈ। *Amarnath cave is one of the major religious site of Lord Shiva*	NP

4.2 Evaluation Metrics

The evaluation metrics used for subtask 1 and subtask 2 were slightly different because of the uniqueness of the tasks. To evaluate runs for subtask 1, we used accuracy and F-score values. The *Accuracy* (1) and *F1 − score* (2) for subtask 1 were calculated as follows:

$$Accuracy = \frac{Number\ of\ correct\ instances}{Total\ number\ of\ instances} \tag{1}$$

$$Precision_P = \frac{Number\ of\ correct\ paraphrases}{Number\ of\ detected\ paraphrases}$$

$$Recall_P = \frac{Number\ of\ correct\ paraphrases}{Number\ of\ reference\ paraphrases}$$

Subsequently, $F1 - score$ can be calculated as:

$$F1 - score_P = \frac{2 \times Precision_p \times Recall_p}{Precision_p + Recall_p} \qquad (2)$$

The subscript p refers to paraphrase (P) class for the subtask 1. Similarly, *Accuracy* and $F1 - score$ for the non-paraphrase class could be calculated.

To evaluate runs for subtask 2, we used *Accuracy* and $macro - F\ score$. Since it is a multiclass classification task, *Accuracy* is equal to $micro\ precision$, $micro - recall$ and $micro - F\ measure$. The $macro - F\ score$ (3) could be computed as:

$$Macro - P = \frac{Precision_P + Precision_{NP} + Precision_{SP}}{Number\ of\ classes}$$

$$Macro - Re = \frac{Recall_P + Recall_{NP} + Recall_{SP}}{Number\ of\ classes}$$

$$Macro - F1\ score = \frac{2 \times Macro - P \times Macro - R}{Macro - P + Macro - R} \qquad (3)$$

Where $Macro - P$ and $Macro - R$ are macro precision and macro recall, which is used to calculate $Macro - F1\ score$.

5 Development of Paraphrase Corpus for Indian Languages

The shared task on Detecting Paraphrases in Indian Languages (DPIL)[3] required participants to identify sentential paraphrases in four Indian languages, namely Hindi, Tamil, Malayalam, and Punjabi. The corpora creation task for these Indian languages started with collecting news articles from various web-based news sources. The collected dataset was further cleaned from any noise or informal information. Apart from cleaning, some sentences required spelling corrections and text transformations. After removing all the irregularities, the dataset was annotated according to the paraphrases phenomena (Paraphrase, Non-Paraphrase, Semi-Paraphrase) present in each sentence pair. Annotation tags used were P, SP, and NP corresponding to Paraphrase, Semi-Paraphrase, and Non-Paraphrase. Post-graduate students, language experts, and linguist for each language were handled the annotation process. An initial annotation process was done by the post-graduate students. Additionally, the annotated labels were further proofread by a language expert and then again by a linguistic expert (Two-step Proofreading). The annotated dataset proofread by the linguistic expert was converted to Extensible Markup Language (XML) format. Figure 1 shows the sample data format.

---

[3] http://nlp.amrita.edu/dpil_cen/

Tables 1 and 2 includes examples of Paraphrase, Semi-Paraphrase, and Non-Paraphrase for Hindi, Tamil, Malayalam and Punjabi Language. Where "P", "SP" and "NP" are the tags used for Paraphrase, Semi-Paraphrase, and Non-Paraphrase. The English translation for each sentence pairs is given for the non-native speakers to understand the meaning. It can be seen that paraphrased sentence pairs contain the same information, Semi paraphrased sentence pairs overlaps only the partial information between them and Non-Paraphrases conveys totally different information.

```xml
<?xml version="1.0" encoding="UTF-8"?>
<Data version="1.0" name="AmritaCEN_DPIL.TAM.TASK2">
  - <Corpus domain="NEWS">
      <Language>Tamil</Language>
    - <Paraphrase pID="TAM0001">
        <Sentence1>சங்கராபுரம் தொகுதியில் போட்டியிடும் ஸ்டாலின் நடைபயணமாக சென்று பிரசாரம் செய்தார்.</Sentence1>
        <Sentence2>தி.மு.க., வேட்பாளர் ஸ்டாலின் போட்டியிடும் சங்கராபுரம் தொகுதியில் சின்ன சேலம் பகுதியில் நடைபயணமாக சென்று ஓட்டு
           சேகரித்தார்.</Sentence2>
        <Class>P</Class>
      </Paraphrase>
    - <Paraphrase pID="TAM0002">
        <Sentence1>கேரள மாநிலம் திருச்சூரில் கூடல்மாணிக்கம் கோயில் திருவிழா துவங்கியது.</Sentence1>
        <Sentence2>கூடல்மாணிக்கம் கோயில் திருவிழா கோலாகலமாக துவங்கியது.</Sentence2>
        <Class>P</Class>
      </Paraphrase>
```

Fig. 1. Sample data format

5.1   Corpora Statistics

The paraphrase corpus was further analyzed for certain parameters such as the number of sentence pairs for each class (P, NP, and SP), an average number of words per sentence per task, and overall vocabulary size. The statistics for the number of sentence pairs in testing and training phase for each subtask is given in the Table 3.

Table 3. Statistics for sentence pairs in subtask 1 and 2

Language	Subtask-1 (in pairs)		Subtask-2 (in pairs)	
	Train	Test	Train	Test
Tamil	2500	900	3500	1400
Malayalam	2500	900	3500	1400
Hindi	2500	900	3500	1400
Punjabi	1700	500	2200	750

The average number of words per sentence along with an average pair length for subtask 1 and subtask 2 is given in Table 4.

The overall vocabulary size (Subtask 1 & Subtask 2) for training as well as testing for all the languages is shown in the form of line chart in Fig. 2. Notably, the vocabulary size for Hindi & Punjabi languages is less compared with Tamil and Malayalam. This is because of the agglutinative nature of Tamil and Malayalam. Due to this phenomenon, Tamil and Malayalam languages end up with having unique words and hence larger vocabulary.

Table 4. The average number of words per sentence for Subtask 1 and 2

Language	Subtask-1			Subtask-2		
	Sentence 1	Sentence 2	Pair	Sentence 1	Sentence 2	Pair
Hindi	16.058	16.376	16.217	17.78	16.48	17.130
Tamil	11.092	12.044	11.568	11.097	11.777	11.437
Malayalam	9.253	9.035	9.144	9.414	8.449	8.932
Punjabi	19.485	19.582	19.534	20.994	19.699	20.347

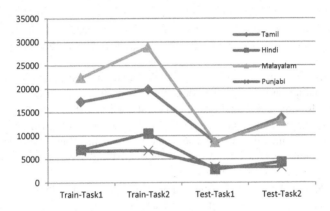

Fig. 2. Overall vocabulary size

6   System Descriptions and Results

A total of 35 teams registered for the DPIL shared task and out of those, 11 teams successfully submitted their runs. A brief description of the methodologies used by each team is given in the following subsection. Figure 3 shows the submitted and registered participants in each language.

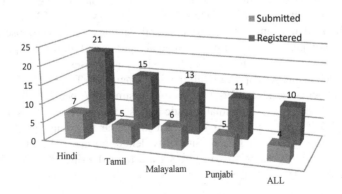

Fig. 3. Overall vocabulary size

6.1 Participants System Descriptions

The brief description of the techniques used by all the teams to submit the runs for the shared task are as follows:

- **ANUJ:** This team participated only in the Hindi language. They pre-processed the sentence using stemmer, *Soundex*, synonym handler. After that, they extracted features using overlapping words and normalized IDF scores. Finally, the Random forest classifier is used for classification.
- **ASE:** This team competed only for Hindi Language. They extracted the features using POS tags and stemming information. The semantic similarity metric is employed which extracts the word synonyms from WordNet to check whether the compared words are synonyms. Finally, decision tree classifier is used to detect paraphrases.
- **BITS_PILANI:** This team participated in the Hindi language paraphrase task. They attempted paraphrase detection with different classifiers and finally used Logistic Regression for Subtask-1 and Random Forest for Subtask-2.
- **CUSAT-TEAM:** This team competed only for Malayalam Language. They stemmed words and calculated the sentence vector using Bag-of-Words model and find out the similarity score between sentences. Finally, they set a threshold for determining the appropriate class.
- **CUSAT_NLP:** This team also participated only for Malayalam Language. They used identical tokens, matching lemmas and synonyms for finding the similarity between sentences. They also utilized in-house Malayalam Wordnet to replace the synonyms. Finally, the similarity score is compared with a threshold value to identify the exact class.
- **HIT2016:** This team participated in all the four languages. Cosine Distance, Jaccard Coefficient, Dice Distance and METEOR features are used and classification is done based on Gradient Boosting Tree. They experiment various aspects of the classification method for detecting paraphrases.
- **JU_NLP:** This team competed in all the four languages. They used similarity based features, word overlapping features and scores from machine translation evaluation metrics to find out the similarity scores between the pair of sentences. They tried with three different classifiers, namely Naïve Bayes, SVM, and SMO.
- **KEC@NLP:** This team participated in Tamil language only. They used existing Tamil Shallow parser to extract morphological features and utilizing Support Vector Machine and Maximum Entropy for classifying paraphrases.
- **KS_JU:** This team participated in all the four languages. They have used different lexical and semantic level (Word embeddings) similarity measures for computing features and used the multinomial logistic regression model as a classifier.
- **NLP-NITMZ:** This team also participated in all the four languages. They used external features based on Jaccard Similarity, length normalized Edit Distance and Cosine Similarity. Finally, this feature-set are trained using Probabilistic Neural Network (PNN) to detect the paraphrases.

6.2   Overall Results

As announced during the shared task, we have given **Sarwan award** for top performers in each language. The top-performing team on each language is given in Table 5. The overall results of all the participating teams can be seen in Table 6. For representation purpose, we have truncated evaluation measures (Precision, Recall, and Accuracy) to two digits[4].

Table 5. Top performers in each language

Punjabi	Hindi	Malayalam	Tamil	Rank
0.932 (HIT)	**0.907 (Anuj)**	**0.785 (HIT)**	**0.776 (HIT)**	**First**
0.922 (JU_KS)	0.896 (HIT)	0.729 (JU_KS)	0.741 (KEC)	Second
0.913 (JU)	0.876 (JU_KS)	0.713 (NITMZ)	0.727 (NIT-MZ)	Third

Table 6. The overall result for Subtask 1 and Subtask 2

Team name	Language	Subtask 1				Subtask 2			
		P	R	F1	Acc	P	R	MacF1	Acc
Anuj	**Hindi**	**0.95**	**0.90**	**0.91**	**0.9200**	**0.90**	**0.90**	**0.90**	**0.9014**
ASE	Hindi	0.41	0.35	0.34	0.3588	0.35	0.37	0.35	0.3542
ASE*	Hindi	0.82	0.97	0.89	0.8922	0.67	0.67	0.67	0.6660
BITS-P	Hindi	0.91	0.90	0.89	0.8977	0.72	0.71	0.71	0.7171
CU-NLP	Mal	0.83	0.72	0.75	0.7622	0.52	0.51	0.51	0.5207
CU-TEAM	Mal	0.79	0.88	0.76	0.8044	0.48	0.52	0.46	0.5085
DAVPBI[#]	Punjabi	0.95	0.92	0.94	0.9380	0.82	0.77	0.73	0.7466
HIT2016	Hindi	0.97	0.84	0.89	0.8966	0.90	0.90	0.89	0.9000
HIT2016	**Mal**	**0.84**	**0.87**	**0.81**	**0.8377**	**0.75**	**0.75**	**0.74**	**0.7485**
HIT2016	**Punjabi**	**0.95**	**0.94**	**0.94**	**0.9440**	**0.96**	**0.95**	**0.92**	**0.9226**
HIT2016	**Tamil**	**0.82**	**0.87**	**0.79**	**0.8211**	**0.76**	**0.74**	**0.73**	**0.7550**
JU-NLP	Hindi	0.75	0.99	0.74	0.8222	0.70	0.69	0.68	0.6857
JU-NLP	Mal	0.58	0.99	0.16	0.5900	0.62	0.41	0.30	0.4221
JU-NLP	Punjabi	0.95	0.94	0.94	0.9420	0.93	0.92	0.88	0.8866
JU-NLP	Tamil	0.57	1.00	0.09	0.5755	0.59	0.51	0.43	0.5507
KS_JU	Hindi	0.94	0.89	0.90	0.9066	0.85	0.85	0.84	0.8521
KS_JU	Mal	0.83	0.82	0.79	0.8100	0.66	0.66	0.65	0.6614
KS_JU	Punjabi	0.95	0.94	0.95	0.9460	0.93	0.92	0.89	0.8960
KS_JU	Tamil	0.79	0.85	0.75	0.7888	0.68	0.67	0.66	0.6735
NLP@KEC	Tamil	0.82	0.87	0.79	0.8233	0.69	0.67	0.66	0.6857
NLP-NITMZ	Hindi	0.92	0.92	0.91	0.9155	0.80	0.77	0.76	0.7857
NLP-NITMZ	Mal	0.8	0.94	0.79	0.8344	0.65	0.62	0.60	0.6243
NLP-NITMZ	Punjabi	0.95	0.94	0.94	0.9420	0.85	0.83	0.80	0.8120
NLP-NITMZ	Tamil	0.8	0.92	0.79	0.8333	0.66	0.66	0.63	0.6571

* *Due to some formatting issues, this team re-submitted the output after the deadline.*
# *This team didn't submit the working notes.*

---

[4] It does not affect the result of the participating teams

Table 7. Various features used by the participants

Features	Anuj	ASE	BITS-P	CU-NLP	CU-TEAM	HIT2016	JU-NLP	KS_JU	KEC	NITMZ
POS		✓		✓					✓	
Stem/Lemma	✓	✓	✓	✓	✓			✓		
Stop words	✓	✓			✓					
Word Overlap	✓						✓	✓		
Synonym	✓	✓		✓						
Cosine				✓	✓	✓	✓	✓		✓
Jaccord						✓	✓			✓
Levinstin		✓								✓
METEOR/BLEU						✓	✓			
Others	IDF		Soundex	WordNet	BoW	N-gram	Dice	word2vec	Morph	

7 Discussions

Out of the 11 teams which submitted their runs, 10 teams successfully submitted their working notes. There were four teams which participated in all the four languages and rest of the teams (3-Hindi, 2-Malayalam, and 1-Tamil) participated in only one language. Two out of ten teams used the threshold based method to detect the paraphrases, the remaining teams used machine learning based approaches. The different types of feature set used by participant teams are illustrated in Table 7. Most of the teams used the common similarity based features like cosine, Jaccard, and only two teams used the Machine Translation evaluation metrics, BLEU and METEOR as features. Very few teams used the synonym replacement and Wordnet features. For Tamil language, team KEC@NLP used the morphological information as features to the machine learning-based classifier. The KS_JU team created the word2vec embeddings with the help of additional in-house unlabeled data and found out the semantic similarity features which were used as features in the classifier. The top-performing team (HIT-2016) for the three languages used the character n-gram based features and they experimented the results for different n-gram size.

We calculated F1-measure and accuracy for evaluating the submissions of the teams. The accuracy of the Task-2 is comparably low with the accuracy of Task-1 due to the complexity of the task. In general, the accuracy obtained by runs submitted for Tamil and Malayalam language is low as compared to the accuracy obtained by Hindi and Punjabi language. This is due to the agglutinative nature of the Dravidian languages.

8 Conclusions and Future Scope

In this overview paper, we explained the dataset of paraphrase corpus and evaluation results of subtask-1 and subtask-2 of Detecting Paraphrases in Indian Languages (DPIL) shared task held at the 8th Forum for Information Retrieval (FIRE) Conference-2016. A total number of 35 teams registered in which 11 teams submitted their runs successfully. The corpora developed for the shared task is the first publicly available paraphrase detection corpora for Indian languages. Detecting paraphrases and semantic similarity in Indian languages is a challenging task because the morphological variations and semantic relations in Indian languages are more crucial to understand. Discrepancies can be found in manually annotated paraphrase corpus, to revise the annotation feedbacks are welcome and appreciated. Our detailed experiment analysis provides fundamental insights into the performance of paraphrase identification in Indian languages. Overall, HIT-2016 (Heilongjiang Institute of Technology) got the first place in Tamil, Malayalam, and Punjabi languages and Anuj (Sapient Global Markets) got the first place in Hindi. In general, Tamil and Malayalam language accuracy is low as compared to the accuracy obtained for Hindi and Punjabi language. As a future work, we plan to extend the task to analyze the performance of cross-genre and cross-lingual paraphrases for more Indian languages. Detecting paraphrases in social media content of Indian languages, plagiarism detection and the use of paraphrases in Machine Translation evaluation are also interesting areas for further study.

Acknowledgement. First, we would like to thank FIRE 2016 organizers for giving us an opportunity to organize the shared task on Detecting Paraphrases for Indian Languages (DPIL). We would like to extend our gratitude to the advisory committee members Prof. Ramanan, RelAgent Pvt. Ltd and Prof. Rajendran S, Computational Engineering and Networking (CEN) for actively supporting us throughout the track. We would like to thank our PG students at CEN for helping us in creating the paraphrase corpora.

References

1. Dolan, W.B., Brockett, C.: Automatically constructing a corpus of sentential paraphrases. In: Proceedings of IWP, October 2005
2. Xu, W., Callison-Burch, C., Dolan, W.B.: SemEval-2015 task 1: paraphrase and semantic similarity in Twitter (PIT). In: Proceedings of SemEval (2015)
3. Xu, W., Ritter, A., Callison-Burch, C., Dolan, W.B., Ji, Y.: Extracting lexically divergent paraphrases from Twitter. Trans. Assoc. Comput. Linguist. **2**, 435–448 (2014)
4. Pronoza, E., Yagunova, E., Pronoza, A.: Construction of a Russian paraphrase corpus: unsupervised paraphrase extraction. In: Braslavski, P., Markov, I., Pardalos, P., Volkovich, Y., Ignatov, Dmitry I., Koltsov, S., Koltsova, O. (eds.) RuSSIR 2015. CCIS, vol. 573, pp. 146–157. Springer, Cham (2016). https://doi.org/10.1007/978-3-319-41718-9_8
5. Potthast, M., Stein, B., Barrón-Cedeño, A., Rosso, P.: An evaluation framework for plagiarism detection. In: Proceedings of the 23rd International Conference on Computational Linguistics: Posters, pp. 997–1005. Association for Computational Linguistics, August 2010
6. Rus, V., Banjade, R., Lintean, M.C.: On paraphrase identification corpora. In: LREC, pp. 2422–2429 (2014)
7. Kothwal, R., Varma, V.: Cross lingual text reuse detection based on keyphrase extraction and similarity measures. In: Majumder, P., Mitra, M., Bhattacharyya, P., Subramaniam, L. V., Contractor, D., Rosso, P. (eds.) FIRE 2010-2011. LNCS, vol. 7536, pp. 71–78. Springer, Heidelberg (2013). https://doi.org/10.1007/978-3-642-40087-2_7
8. Mahalakshmi, S., Anand Kumar, M., Soman, K.P.: Paraphrase detection for Tamil language using deep learning algorithm. Int. J. Appl. Eng. Res. **10**(17), 13929–13934 (2015)
9. Idicula, S.M.: Fingerprinting based detection system for identifying plagiarism in Malayalam text documents. In: 2015 International Conference on Computing and Network Communications (CoCoNet), pp. 553–558. IEEE, December 2015

10. Mathew, D., Idicula, S.M.: Paraphrase identification of Malayalam sentences-an experience. In: 2013 Fifth International Conference on Advanced Computing (ICoAC), pp. 376–382. IEEE, December 2013
11. Kahane, S.: The meaning-text theory. Dependency Valency Int. Handb. Contemp. Res. **1**, 546–570 (2003)

Anuj@DPIL-FIRE2016: A Novel Paraphrase Detection Method in Hindi Language Using Machine Learning

Anuj Saini[1(✉)] [iD] and Aayushi Verma[2] [iD]

[1] Sapient Global Markets, Gurugram, India
asaini13@sapient.com
[2] Hays Business Solutions, Noida, India
aayushi291091@gmail.com

Abstract. Every language possesses plausible several interpretations. With the evolution of web, smart devices and social media it has become a challenging task to identify these syntactic or semantic ambiguities. In Natural Language Processing, two statements written using different words having same meaning is termed as paraphrasing. At FIRE 2016, we have worked upon the problem of detecting paraphrases for the given Shared Task DPIL (Detecting Paraphrases in Indian Languages) in Hindi Language specifically. This paper proposes a novel approach to identify if two statements are paraphrased or not using various machine learning algorithms like Random Forest, Support Vector Machine, Gradient Boosting and Gaussian Naïve Bayes on the given training data set of two subtasks. In cross validation experiments, Random Forest outperforms the other methods with F1-score of 0.94. We have extended our work by adding few more features and using the former best classifier resulting in improvement of F1-score by 1%. The experimental results depict that our algorithm got the highest F1-score and accuracy and hence, secured the first rank in Hindi language in this shared task among all participants. Our novel approach can be used in various applications such as question-answering system, document clustering, machine translation, text summarization, plagiarism detection and many more.

Keywords: Paraphrase detection · Machine learning
Natural language processing · Soundex · Semantic similarity · Random forest

1 Introduction and Related Work

With the plethora of information generated by the web these days, it is challenging to understand the semantics of different languages when each language has its own scripts and linguistic rules. Hindi language is still in its early stage when concerning natural language processing and applications [1]. Currently significant amount of research work has already been done for English language but there is a huge scope for Hindi language. Paraphrases are sentences or phrases which convey the same meaning using different words [2]. Paraphrase detection is an important building block in Natural Language Processing (NLP) pipeline [9]. Previously, many researchers have investigated ways of

© Springer International Publishing AG 2018
P. Majumder et al. (Eds.): FIRE 2016 Workshop, LNCS 10478, pp. 141–152, 2018.
https://doi.org/10.1007/978-3-319-73606-8_11

automatically detecting paraphrases on formal texts [3]. Various state-of-the-art para-phrase identification techniques have been summarized in an excellent manner by ACL [4]. The objective of our work is motivated by the shared task of DPIL organized by the Forum for Information Retrieval Evaluation (FIRE 2016). There were two subtasks given for the classification problem. Subtask 1 is to classify two Hindi sentences into two classes: P (Paraphrased) or NP (Non-Paraphrased). Subtask 2 is to classify them into three classes which are P (Paraphrased), SP (Semi-Paraphrased) or NP (Non-Paraphrased). For detecting paraphrases, it is very important to understand the language at an initial stage. Starting from tokenization, stemming, lemmatization, stop words, phonetics and POS tags etc. need to be identified before comparing two texts. And as machine learning algorithms works on numeric data, so it's important to convert the textual data into corresponding numbers known as text vectors. A vector denotes the numerical representation of text comparison of two sentences. We have generated a set of vectors for each data point using first two steps of our proposed approach and trained the model in the third step to get the results.

The rest of the paper is organized as follows. Section 2 gives the description of the training dataset provided by the organizing committee. Section 3 presents the proposed approach for paraphrase detection. Experimental results and evaluation has been carried out in Sect. 4. Section 5 concludes our research work along with the future scope.

2 Data Set Description

The evaluation corpora developed for the shared task has been divided into two different subtasks. There was a total of 2500 data points in the training set with 2 classes P and NP to be used for classification in Subtask 1, whereas Subtask 2 had 3 classes (P, NP and SP) and a total of 3500 data points. A detail distribution of classes and its count for both the tasks is mentioned in Table 1.

Table 1. Classes and its count for SubTask 1 and SubTask 2

Class	SubTask 1	SubTask 2
P	1500	1500
NP	1000	1000
SP	–	1000

Each data point contains a pID, a unique id for each data point and two Hindi sentences and their final tagged Class. The initial analysis of the data surfaced some noise, majorly in NP class. A few examples of false negatives and false positives have been identified and listed down in Table 2. Here the examples for class NP and class P denotes false negatives and false positives respectively.

We have accepted this noise present in the given training data without any filtering of such misclassified records and trained model on all the data points.

Table 2. False positives and false negatives in the dataset

pID	Sentence1	Sentence2	Class
HIN2802	रविशंकर ने कहा मुझे लगता है कि आईएसआईएस कोई पीस टॉक नहीं चाहता	मुझे लगता है कि आईएसआईएस कोई पीस टॉक नहीं चाहता: रविशंकर	NP
HIN2852	पाक के फॉरेन सेक्रेटरी एजाज अहमद चोधरी मंगलवार को हार्ट ऑफ एशिया के ऑफिशियल्स की बैठक में भाग लेने के लिए भारत पहुंच रहे हैं	पाकिस्तान के विदेश सचिव एजाज अहमद चोधरी हैदराबाद हाउस में हार्ट ऑफ एशिया सम्मेलन में भाग लेंगे	NP
HIN2958	इस किताब में कांग्रेस उपाध्यक्ष राहुल गांधी को करिश्माई नेता भी बताया गया है	इस किताब में कांग्रेस उपाध्यक्ष राहुल गांधी को करिश्माई नेता भी बताया गया और इसको लेकर लोकसभा में बुधवार को सत्तापक्ष और विपक्ष के बीच काफी नोकझोंक हुई	NP
HIN3032	बॉलीवुड अभिनेत्री बिपाशा बसु ने शनिवार को एक निजी समारोह में करण सिंह ग्रोवर के साथ शादी रचाई	बॉलीवुड एक्ट्रैस बिपाशा बसु और करण सिंह ग्रोवर ने शनिवार को मुंबई में की शादी	NP
HIN0230	मुद्राकोष में बढ़ेगा भारत का रुतबा	ऐएमएफ के दस बड़े सदस्य देशों में भारत भी शामिल	P

3 The Proposed Method

The proposed approach includes three sub-processes which are text preprocessing, feature generation and classification model. Text preprocessing is done in various steps such as encoding, tokenization, stemming, soundex, stop word removal, handling synonyms and n-grams. Feature generation involves the creation of eight new features which will be used as an input to the classifier for classification of paraphrases. Classification model includes the model training using the four machine learning algorithms. All the three steps are summarized in the proposed flow diagram in Fig. 1 and described in the below sub-section.

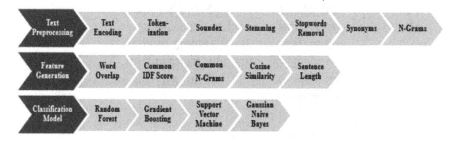

Fig. 1. Proposed flow diagram

3.1   Text Preprocessing

Generally, text preprocessing is considered as the first step to handle text-data that involves cleaning and extracting valuable information from texts. In this paper, we have incorporated following preprocessing techniques which would further help in building the features.

- **Text Encoding**
  Here, the sentences are encoded using standard UTF-8 encoding that handles scripting of Hindi language.
- **Tokenization**
  In this step, the sentences are tokenized into words i.e. dividing the text into a sequence of words termed as tokens. NLTK library of Python is used to perform tokenization.
- **Soundex**
  We have applied custom set of rules for phonetics. The normalization of phonetics has been done using soundex algorithm [10]. It looks for specific characters and replaces them with their corresponding metaphor characters. For example,

न् न or ज़ ज

- **Stemming**
  We have applied some set of customized rules for stemming into its basic form. A set of Hindi suffixes characters were removed to get normalized Hindi word. For example,

Table 3. Steps of text preprocessing

PreProcessing	Input	Preprocessed
Tokenization	कपिल शर्मा फोर्स	[कपिल, शर्मा, फोर्स]
Soundex	हजअर लोट	हज़अर लौट
Stemming	अनियमितताओं, दिल्ली	अनियमित, दिल्ल
Stop Words Removal	काफी निराश था और ड्रेसिंग रूम में लोटते हुए रोने लगा	काफी निराश ड्रेसिंग रूम लोटते हुए रोने लगा
Synonyms	इंडिया आखिरी	भारत फाइनल
N-Grams	कपिल शर्मा फोर्स	[कपिल शर्मा, शर्मा फोर्स]

[ो","ें","ू","ु","ीं",िं","ा"][कर","ाओ",िए","ाई","ाए","ने","नी","ना","ते","ेों","ती","ता",
ोों","ाों","ाों","ेों"]
[ाकर","ाइए","ाईं","ाया","ेगी","ेगा","ोगी","ोगे","ाने","ाना","ाते","ाती","ाता","तीं","ा
ओं","ाएं","ुओं","ुएं","ुआं"]

- **Stop Words Removal**
  We have removed irrelevant words from the sentences using a standard list of 164 Hindi Stop words. For example,

$$[सारा, से, सो, ही, हुआ, हुई, हुए]$$

- **Synonyms**
  We have used Hindi WordNet, an extensive lexical dictionary of Hindi language having 40 K ~ synsets, to fetch synonyms for Hindi words. It was developed by researchers at the Center for Indian Language Technology, Computer Science and Engineering Department, IIT Bombay and we have downloaded it from the mentioned link in [5].
- **N-Grams**
  N- consecutive words in a sentence is considered as a feature to extract n-grams. We have considered the value of N = 2 i.e. Bigrams as the average length of sentences is small.
  All the text preprocessing steps have been summarized with examples in the below Table 3.

3.2 Feature Generation

Generating features from the text is one of the challenging task of natural language processing and text analytics. It is difficult to extract several types of features from a sentence. In our proposed approach, we tried to extract various key features from the sentences to make our machine understand the syntactic and lexical behavior of the text. The following sub-section includes the features which are generated after text pre-processing in the form of vectors to be passed as an input to the classifier.

- **Word Overlap**
  It is the number of common tokens amongst two sentences. These tokens have been generated by comparing the preprocessed tokens after removing the stop words and then taking intersection of them symbolized as follows.

$$\text{Tokens (sentence 1)} \cap \text{Tokens (sentence 2)}$$

- **Normalized Word Overlap**
  We have normalized the common tokens generated in the first feature to compute the proportion of commonality of tokens between two sentences. The value will be in the range of 0 and 1. It is 0 when there are no common tokens between two sentences and 1 if all tokens between the two sentences are the same. Mathematically, it has been calculated by dividing the common tokens by number of unique tokens in both the sentences as shown below.

$$\text{Common tokens}/ \\ \text{Unique Tokens (sentence 1, sentence 2)}$$

- **Common IDF Score**
  Sum of IDF scores of common tokens from two sentences is used as numeric similarity vector.

$$\Sigma \text{IDF score (common tokens)}$$

IDF (Inverse Document Frequency) is defined as inverse of document frequency which is used to identify the importance of a token in the given corpus. Represented as:

$$idf_t = log\frac{N}{df_t} \tag{1}$$

Here a document is an individual sentence. At first IDF has been calculated for all tokens and kept for reference. Then during feature generation process, IDF values of common tokens have been considered and are used as a feature to capture the importance of rarely occurring terms.

- **Normalized Common IDF Score**
  Here the proportion of IDF score of common tokens between two sentences is computed for normalization and used as a vector. It gives us normalized common IDF score ranges between 0 and 1. It can be calculated as follows.

$$\text{IDF of Common tokens}/ \\ \text{Total IDF of Unique tokens (sentence 1, sentence 2)}$$

- **Common N-Grams**
  It is the number of common bigrams (N = 2) between two sentences generated during the text preprocessing step calculated just like word overlap. It is used to capture the importance of n-consecutive words together and is symbolized as follows:

  $$\text{Bigrams (sentence 1)} \cap \text{Bigrams (sentence 2)}$$

- **Normalized Common N-Grams**
  Here we have normalized the common bigram tokens generated in the previous feature and it also ranges between 0 and 1. It has been computed as follows:

  $$\text{Common Bigrams} / \\ \text{Unique Tokens (sentence 1, sentence 2)}$$

- **Cosine Similarity**
  The cosine similarity is calculated between two vectors which are generated from binary vectors of the sentences denoting the presence or absence of the word. It has been computed by the dot product of the vectors divided by the modulus of both the sentence vectors and it is mathematically denoted as follows:

  $$similarity = \cos \theta = \frac{A.B}{|A||B|} = \frac{\sum_{i=1}^{n} A_i B_i}{\sqrt{\sum_{i=1}^{n} A_i^2} \sqrt{\sum_{i=1}^{n} B_i^2}} \tag{2}$$

  Higher the value more will be the similarity score for two sentences [8].

- **Sentences Length**
  It denotes the count of number of tokens in sentence 1 and sentence 2 as separate columns. This feature is used to capture the complexity of sentence in terms of number of words used in a sentence, as shorter length denotes less complexity and vice versa.

3.3 Classification Model

Features generated in Sect. 3.2 have been used as training data to train the classifiers using Python Scikit library [14]. Here, we have used four popular machine learning algorithms which are random forest, support vector machine, naive bayes and gradient boosting and compared their respective performances. Since, random forest being an ensemble learning method outperforms the other individual methods [15], is implemented by growing many classification trees and having them "vote" for a final decision according to a majority role [6]. We have also focused on tuning its hyper parameters to enhance the predictive ability of the model. Key parameters are as follows:

- n_estimators
  These are the number of trees that we want to build before having the vote for the final decision. More the number of trees better the performance however it also increases the time complexity.

- max_depth
  It is the maximum depth of the tree which needs to be tuned.
- min_samples_leaf
  These are the minimum number of samples or observations required in a terminal node of the tree.
- min_samples_split
  These are the minimum number of samples or observations needed in a node to be considered for splitting [7].

We have selected the best set of hyper parameters for Random Forest using Grid Search of Scikit library [14] which resulted in the following values n_estimators – 500, max_depth – 10, min_samples_leaf – 4 and min_samples_split – 4 and trained our training data. Overall training time for model is less than 1 s on quad-core Machine with 8 GB of RAM. For other classification models, default values of the hyper parameters are taken given in the scikit library. The training time of other models is comparatively more than Random Forest model.

4 Experimental Results

We have used 10-fold cross-validation method to compute overall accuracy for the system. In this work three evaluation metrics have been considered which are precision, recall and f1-score [12]. We have calculated the values of the evaluation parameters for all the four respective algorithms Random Forest, Gradient Boosting, SVM and Gaussian Naïve Bayes. For the subtask 1 we have got the overall accuracy of 0.92 with F1 score of 0.94 maximum for Random Forest algorithm (Previous) with the proposed approach performed in the shared task, described in the paper [13]. Those experimental results were the highest among all the participants of the shared task. Hence, we have incorporated more features to the top ranked Random Forest classifier for the extended work mentioned in this paper. The experimental results depict significant improvement in the system performance with the F1 score of 0.95 for Random Forest (Extended). Detailed performance matrix of the model for subtask 1 is given as below in Table 4 for the prediction of 2 classes.

The same approach is used for Subtask 2 which had same problem for the prediction of 3 classes. With 3 classes and larger training set of 3500 data points we have got overall accuracy of 0.85 with 10-folds cross validation method and F1 score of 0.91 which is again highest for Random forest algorithm (Previous). Significant improvement in results have been found after extending the work by the training of additional features on Random Forest algorithm. Detailed summary of performance matrix of subtask 2 is given in Table 5.

The comparison of results of all the 7 participants who have implemented their paraphrase detection approach for Hindi language is shown in the following Figs. 2, 3, 4 and 5 for overall accuracy and F1 scores respectively. It is clearly visible that our approach outperforms the work done by other participants resulting in scoring top rank in the Hindi language. Detailed summarization of results can be found in [12].

Table 4. SubTask 1 scores summary

Class	Precision	Recall	F1-score	Algorithm
P	0.95	0.93	0.95	Random forest (extended)
NP	0.91	0.92	0.91	
Avg/Total	0.93	0.92	0.93	
P	0.94	0.93	0.94	Random forest (previous)
NP	0.90	0.91	0.90	
Avg/Total	0.92	0.92	0.92	
NP	0.93	0.91	0.92	Gradient boosting
P	0.87	0.89	0.88	
Avg/Total	0.9	0.9	0.9	
NP	0.92	0.84	0.88	SVM
P	0.79	0.89	0.84	
Avg/Total	0.87	0.86	0.86	
NP	0.92	0.94	0.93	Gaussian Naïve Bayes
P	0.91	0.88	0.9	
Avg/Total	0.92	0.92	0.92	

Table 5. SubTask 2 scores summary

Class	Precision	Recall	F1-score	Algorithm
NP	0.91	0.91	0.91	Random forest (extended)
P	0.83	0.82	0.82	
SP	0.83	0.83	0.83	
Avg/Total	0.86	0.85	0.86	
NP	0.90	0.91	0.91	Random forest (previous)
P	0.81	0.80	0.80	
SP	0.83	0.82	0.82	
Avg/Total	0.85	0.85	0.85	
NP	0.89	0.90	0.89	Gradient boosting
P	0.79	0.80	0.79	
SP	0.84	0.81	0.83	
Avg/Total	0.85	0.85	0.85	
NP	0.89	0.82	0.86	SVM
P	0.74	0.67	0.70	
SP	0.68	0.82	0.74	
Avg/Total	0.79	0.78	0.78	
NP	0.87	0.93	0.9	Gaussian Naïve Bayes
P	0.68	0.73	0.71	
SP	0.76	0.62	0.68	
Avg/Total	0.78	0.79	0.78	

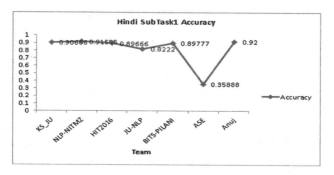

Fig. 2. SubTask 1 accuracy results comparison

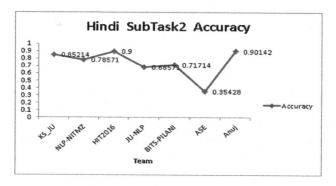

Fig. 3. SubTask 2 accuracy results comparison

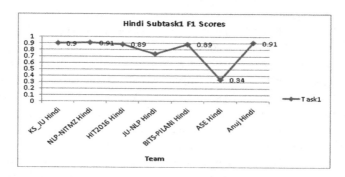

Fig. 4. SubTask 1 F1 score results comparison

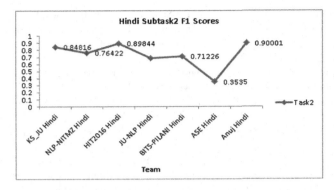

Fig. 5. SubTask 2 F1 score results comparison

5   Conclusion

In this paper, we have proposed a novel approach for the detection of Hindi paraphrases which is a very important building block of semantic text analysis. Building a
question answering system, document clustering, knowledge extraction, plagiarism
detection, building ontologies etc. are the potential applications for paraphrase identification in NLP [11]. After comparing all the four machine learning algorithms used in
our model, Random Forest has given best results with F1 score of 0.94 for subtask 1
and 0.91 for subtask 2. Our novel approach got the highest F1 score and accuracy for
Hindi language enabling us to achieve first rank among all the participants of the shared
task. By adding few more noteworthy features and training the model using the previous best classifier, F1 score got further improved by 1%. We can extend our work by
incorporating Part of Speech tagging in feature generation which plays a key role in
paraphrase detection, as nouns and verbs are key elements for paraphrasing. Named
Entity Recognition and Word2Vec model can also be considered in our future work as
it could improve the overall system performance.

Acknowledgments. We would like to thank the organizers of FIRE 2016 for conducting this
shared task on Detecting Paraphrases for Indian Languages (DPIL) and building the paraphrase
corpora. We would also like to thank Sapient Corporation and Hays Business Solutions for
giving us an opportunity to work and explore the world of text analytics.

References

1. Sethi, N., Agrawal, P., Madaan, V., Singh, S.K.: A novel approach to paraphrase Hindi
   sentences using natural language processing. Indian J. Sci. Technol. 9(28), July 2016. https://
   doi.org/10.17485/ijst/2016/v9i28/98374
2. Kumar, N.: A graph based automatic plagiarism detection technique to handle artificial word
   reordering and paraphrasing. In: Gelbukh, A. (ed.) CICLing 2014. LNCS, vol. 8404,
   pp. 481–494. Springer, Heidelberg (2014). https://doi.org/10.1007/978-3-642-54903-8_40

3. Xu, W., Callison-Burch, C., Dolan, W.B.: SemEval-2015 task 1: paraphrase and semantic similarity in Twitter (PIT). In: Proceedings of the 9th International Workshop on Semantic Evaluation (SemEval 2015), Denver, Colorado, June 4–5, pp. 1–11. Association for Computational Linguistics (2015)
4. https://www.aclweb.org/aclwiki/index.php?title=Paraphrase_Identification_(State_of_the_art)
5. http://www.cfilt.iitb.ac.in/wordnet/webhwn/downloaderInfo.php
6. Zhang, W., Zeng, F., Wu, X., Zhang, X., Jiang, R: A comparative study of ensemble learning approaches in the classification of breast cancer metastasis. In: International Joint Conference on Bioinformatics, Systems Biology and Intelligent Computing (2009)
7. Banfield, E.R., Lawrence, O.H., Kevin, W.B., Kegelmeyer, W.P.: A comparison of decision tree ensemble creation techniques. IEEE Trans. Pattern Anal. Mach. Learn. **29**(1) (2007)
8. Verma, A., Arora, A.: Reflexive hybrid approach to provide precise answer of user desired frequently asked question. In: 2017 7th International Conference on Cloud Computing, Data Science and Engineering-Confluence, pp. 159–163. IEEE, January 2017
9. Sundaram, M.S., Anand Kumar, M., Soman, K.P.: AMRITA CEN@ SemEval-2015: paraphrase detection for Twitter using unsupervised feature learning with recursive autoencoders. In: SemEval-2015, p. 45 (2015)
10. Mahalakshmi, S., Anand Kumar, M., Soman, K.P.: Paraphrase detection for Tamil language using deep learning algorithm. Int. J. Appl. Eng. Res. **10**(17), 13929–13934 (2015)
11. Socher, R., Huang, E.H., Pennin, J., Manning, C.D., Ng, A.Y.: Dynamic pooling and unfolding recursive autoencoders for paraphrase detection. In: Advances in Neural Information Processing Systems, pp. 801–809 (2011)
12. Anand Kumar, M., Singh, S., Kavirajan, B., Soman, K.P.: DPIL@FIRE2016: overview of shared task on detecting paraphrases in Indian languages. In: Working notes of FIRE 2016 - Forum for Information Retrieval Evaluation, Kolkata, India, December 7–10, CEUR Workshop Proceedings (2016). http://ceur-ws.org/
13. http://ceur-ws.org/Vol-1737/T6-8.pdf
14. http://scikit-learn.org/stable/
15. Verma, A., Mehta, S.: A comparative study of ensemble learning methods for classification in bioinformatics. In: 2017 7th International Conference on Cloud Computing, Data Science and Engineering-Confluence, pp. 155–158. IEEE, January 2017

Learning to Detect Paraphrases in Indian Languages

Kamal Sarkar[⊠] [iD]

Department of Computer Science and Engineering,
Jadavpur University, Kolkata, India
jukamal2001@yahoo.com

Abstract. In this paper, we present a system that detects paraphrases in Indian Languages- Hindi, Punjabi, Malayalam and Tamil. Our paraphrase detection method uses machine learning algorithms such as multinomial logistic regression and support vector machines trained with a variety of features which are basically various lexical and semantic level similarities between two sentences in a pair. With our developed paraphrase detection system, we participate in the shared Task on detecting paraphrases in Indian Languages (DPIL) organized by Forum for Information Retrieval Evaluation (FIRE) in 2016. This shared task consisted of two tasks-Task1 and Task2. We participated in task1 and task2 both for all four Indian Languages. We participate in the shared task with the system that uses multinomial logistic regression model and it was officially evaluated by the organizers of the contest against the test set released for the FIRE 2016 shared task on DPIL. After the conference, we enhance our system using another machine learning algorithm-Support Vector Machines and compare its performance with our previous systems. We present in this paper the description of our system, its performance in the shared task and its enhancement using Support Vector Machines. Our evaluation of the system based on the overall average system performance including task1 and task2 over all four languages reveals that the performance of our system is comparable to the best system participated in the shared task.

Keywords: Paraphrasing · Multinomial logistic regression model
Sentence similarity · Hindi language · Punjabi language · Malayalam language
Tamil language · SVM

1 Introduction

Two text segments are said to be paraphrase of each other if they are semantically equivalent. The concept of paraphrasing has been defined in [1] as follows:

"The concept of paraphrasing is most generally defined on the basis of the principle of semantic equivalence: A paraphrase is an alternative surface form in the same language expressing the same semantic content as the original form."

© Springer International Publishing AG 2018
P. Majumder et al. (Eds.): FIRE 2016 Workshop, LNCS 10478, pp. 153–165, 2018.
https://doi.org/10.1007/978-3-319-73606-8_12

Paraphrases may occur at various levels of granularity:

- lexical paraphrases (synonyms, hyponyms etc.),
- phrasal paraphrase (phrasal fragments sharing the same semantic content),
- sentential paraphrases (for example, *I finished my work, I completed my assignment*).

The task of paraphrasing can be broadly categorized as paraphrase generation and paraphrase recognition.

The most common applications of paraphrasing are the automatic generation of query variants, query expansion by paraphrasing techniques to enhance performance of information retrieval systems [2–8]. Ravichandran and Hovy [9] applied semi-supervised learning techniques to generate several paraphrase patterns for each question type and use them in an open-domain question answering system (QA system). Riezler et al. [10] use a query expansion technique that expands a query by generating n-best paraphrases for the query and incorporating any novel words in the paraphrases to expand the original query.

Paraphrase generation techniques have also been used for evaluating various NLP (Natural Language Processing) tasks such as machine translation and multi-document summarization where system performance is evaluated by comparing the system generated output with the gold standard. Since manual creation of references is a laborious task, many researchers have used paraphrase generation techniques for generating variants of paraphrases which have been utilized for evaluating summarization and machine translation output [11, 12].

Callison-Burch et al. [13] uses phrase level paraphrasing to improve a statistical phrase-based machine translation system. When a phrase of a sentence does not have any translation in the look up table, they use the translation of one of paraphrases of any source phrase.

Like paraphrase generation, paraphrase recognition is also an important task which has been recently popular due to the fact that it can be applied in several NLP applications such as Plagiarism detection, text-to-text generation and information extraction. Plagiarism detection is another important application which uses the paraphrase recognition technique to detect the sentences which are paraphrases of others. Paraphrase generation is a process that can assign a quantitative measurement to the semantic similarity of two phrases [14] or even two given pieces of text [15, 16]. In other words, the paraphrase recognition task is to detect or recognize which sentences in the two texts are paraphrases of each other [17–23]. The latter formulation of the task has become popular in recent years [24] and paraphrase generation techniques that can be benefited immensely from this task.

Redundancy is a very important issue for a multi-document summarization task where a cluster of related documents are summarized and many sentences coming from different documents in the cluster may convey the same semantic content. So, it is necessary to remove redundancy to maximize diverse information in summary. Barzilay and McKeown [25] use sentence fusion technique to eliminate the redundancy present in a given set of sentences and to generate a single coherent sentence. Sekine [26] shows how to use paraphrase recognition to cluster together extraction patterns to improve the cohesion of the extracted information.

Paraphrase recognition is also relevant for another recently proposed natural language processing task, textual entailment recognition [27–30]. Textual entailment can be defined as follows:

A piece of text T is said to entail a hypothesis H if humans reading T will infer that H is most likely true.

Paraphrasing techniques mentioned above are mostly applied on English language. Almost no such attempt has been made for detecting paraphrases in Indian languages. Most probably, the major difficulty in the task of detecting paraphrases in Indian Languages is the unavailability of annotated corpora. The publicly available and the most commonly used corpus for paraphrase detection is the MSRP corpus[1] which contains 5,801 English sentence pairs from news articles manually labelled with 67% paraphrases and 33% non-paraphrases. The shared task on Semantic Textual Similarity conducted as a part of SemEval-2012[2] was targeted to create benchmark datasets for the similar kind of task, but its main focus was to develop systems that can examine the degree of semantic equivalence between two sentences unlike paraphrase detection which determines yes/no decision for given pair of sentences. But all these tasks were designed mainly for English language. The shared task on detecting Paraphrases in Indian Languages (DPIL) @FIRE 2016 is a good effort towards creating benchmark data for paraphrases in Indian Languages. This shared task consists of two tasks: task1 is to classify a given pair of sentences in Indian language as paraphrases (P) or non-paraphrases (NP) and task2 is to identify whether a given pair of sentences are completely equivalent (E) or roughly equivalent (RE) or not equivalent (NE). Four Indian Languages- Hindi, Punjabi, Malayalam and Tamil were considered in this shared task.

We describe in the Sect. 2 our proposed method used to implement our system participated in the shared task. The description of the data, evaluation of the system and the results are presented in Sect. 3. In Sect. 4, we conclude and describe future plan for system enhancement.

2 Our Proposed Method

We view the paraphrase detection problem as classification problem. Given a pair of sentences, the task1 of paraphrase detection is to classify the pair of sentences into any two categories: paraphrase (P) or non-paraphrase (NP). According to this, task1 is a two class problem and task2 is a three class problem which is to classify a given pair of sentences into one of three categories: completely equivalent (E) or roughly equivalent (RE) or not equivalent (NE).

Since the problems are basically a classification problem, any traditional classifier can be used for implementing our system. We have used multinomial logistic regression classifier with ridge estimator for both task1 and task2 for developing the system with which we participate in the shared task. After the conference is over, we also used Support Vector Machines as a classifier to enhance the system performance. For

---

[1] https://www.microsoft.com/en-us/download/confirmation.aspx?id=52398.

[2] https://www.cs.york.ac.uk/semeval-2012/task6/index.html.

training the classifiers, we have used training data consisting of a collection of sentence pairs in Indian language where each labeled pair of sentences is considered as a training instance. Features are extracted from the training pairs. We consider a variety of features for representing sentence pairs. The features which we have used for implementing our system are described in the subsequent subsections:

2.1   Features

Since task is to recognize whether a given pair of sentences is paraphrase, semi-paraphrase or not-paraphrase, we think that similarity between the pair can be the important features for paraphrase recognition. We have used various similarity measures as the features. Features are extracted from the training pairs.

Cosine Similarity. To compute cosine similarity between two sentences in a pair, we represent each sentence using a bag-of-words model. Then cosine similarity is computed between two vectors corresponding to the sentences in the pair. To obtain the vector representations of the sentences in a pair, we initially extract the set of distinct words in the pair and each word in joined word set corresponds to a component of the vector representing a sentence. The size of the vector is n where n is $|S_1 \cup S_2|$, S_1 is the set of words in the sentence 1 and S_2 is the set of words in sentence 2. Each sentence in a pair is mapped to vector of length n. If the vector V for sentence 1 is $<v_1, v_2 .....v_n>$ and the vector U for sentence 2 is $<u_1, u_2 ...u_n>$, where v_i and u_i are the values of i-th word feature in sentence 1 and sentence 2 respectively, the cosine similarity between two sentences is computed as follows:

$$Sim_1(S_1, S_2) = cosine(V, U) = \frac{v_1 u_1 + v_2 u_2 + ...v_n u_n}{\sqrt{v_1^2 + v_2^2 + ...v_n^2}\sqrt{u_1^2 + u_2^2 + ...u_n^2}} \quad (1)$$

Here the vector component v_i in vector V is basically the TF * IDF weight of the corresponding word.

Word Overlap based Similarity. We have also used the word overlap based similarity measure as a feature for paraphrase detection. If two sentences in the pair are S1 and S2, the similarity based on word overlap (Jaccard similarity) is computed as follows:

$$Sim_2(S_1, S_2) = \frac{2 * |S_1 \cap S_2|}{|S_1| + |S_2|} \quad (2)$$

Where $|S_1 \cap S_2|$ is the number of exact word matches (without stemming) between two sentences. $|S|$ is the length of sentence S in terms of words.

Stemmed Word Overlap based Similarity. Since the most Indian languages are highly inflectional, stemming can be useful while computing similarity between two sentences. Since accurate stemmers are also not available for Indian languages, we applied a lightweight approach to stemming. Our stemming process is applied while comparing two words to find a match. It works as follows:

- *Input*: two words
- *Output*: match or not a match
- Steps:
  - Find the matched portions and unmatched portions of two words. Say, the matched portion and unmatched of the first word is X and Y1 respectively and so are X and Y2 respectively for the second word. Here the matched portion of the both words is X because the matched portions are the same for both words.
  - If we find that X is greater than or equal to a threshold *T1* and the minimum of Y1 and Y2 (unmatched portions of word1 and word2) is less than or equal to a threshold *T2*, we assume that there exists a match between word1 and word2.

Stemmed word overlap similarity between two sentences is computed using Eq. (2) with the only difference in word matching criteria, that is, computation of stemmed word overlap measure checks matching between any pair of words based on the above stated algorithm.

For our system implementation, we set *T1* to 3 and *T2* to 2. We indicate such similarity between two sentences S_1 and S_2 as $Sim_3(S_1, S_2)$.

N-gram based Similarity. The similarity measures mentioned in the earlier subsections compare sentences based on bag-of-words model and individual word matching which do not take into account the context of occurrences of words. We consider word n-gram based sentence similarity as one of the features for paraphrase detection. The n-gram based similarity between two sentences S_1 and S_2 is computed as follows:

$$Sim_4(S_1, S_2) = \frac{2 * c}{a + b} \qquad (3)$$

Where
$c = \#$ of n $-$ grams matches between S_1 and S_2
$a = \#$ of n $-$ grams in S_1
$b = \#$ of n grams in S_2

Since unigram based sentence similarity measure is exactly similar with Word Overlap Based Similarity measure discussed earlier in this section, here we have only considered bigrams (n = 2) based similarity as another feature for paraphrase detection.

Semantic Similarity. When comparing two sentences based on simple word match, similarity between them may not be detected due to word mismatch problem. So, we measure semantic similarity between two sentences and use it as a feature for paraphrase detection. To compute semantic similarity between sentences, we depend on the semantic match between the words in the sentences. To determine whether two words are semantically matched or not, we use cosine similarity between word vectors for the corresponding word pair. The word vectors have been obtained using word2vec models [31]. Word2vec is a group of related models used to produce word embedding [32, 33]. Word2vec takes as its input a large corpus of text and produces a high-dimensional space where each unique word in the corpus is assigned a corresponding vector in the space. Such representation of words into vectors positions the word in the vector space such that words that share common contexts are positioned in close proximity to one another in the space.

We have used word2vec model available in Python for computing word vectors for the words. We have used *gensim word2vec* model under Python platform with dimension set to 50, *min_count* to 5 (when *min_count* is set to 5, all words with total frequency lower than this are ignored). The training algorithm used for developing word2vec model is *CBOW* (Continuous Bag of words). The other parameters of word2vec model are set to default values.

If the cosine similarity between the word vectors for the two given words is greater than a threshold value, we consider these two words are semantically similar. We set the threshold value to 0.8.

To train Word2Vec model, we add a small amount of additional news data to the training data released for DPIL shared task and thus we create the corpus used for training Word2Vec model. Size of the corpora used to compute word vectors for the different languages is as follows:

For Hindi, 1.93 MB (8752 sentences), for Punjabi, 1.5 MB (5848 sentences), for Tamil, 2.20 MB (7847 sentences) and for Malayalam, 2.12 MB (7448 sentences).

We compute semantic similarity between two sentences as follows:

$$Sim_5(S_1, S_2) = \frac{2 * e}{f + g} \tag{4}$$

Where:

$e = \#$ of words semantically matches between S_1 and S_2

$f = \#$ words in S_1

$g = \#$ of words in S_2

2.2   Machine Learning Algorithms Used for Paraphrase Detection

We have used multinomial logistic regression and the Support Vector Machines as the classifier for paraphrase detection task. At the time of the contest, we used only multinomial logistic regression model [34, 35]. But after the conference is over, we have applied SVM as the classifier to enhance the system performance.

We have chosen multinomial logistic regression classifier and SVM present in WEKA. WEKA is machine learning workbench consists of many machine learning algorithms for data mining tasks [36]. The multinomial logistic regression classifier is present in WEKA with the name "logistic". For SVM, we have used SMO, a support vector classifier present in WEKA. SMO is an implementation of a support vector classifier which is trained using Sequential Minimal optimization algorithm presented in [37].

We set the "ridge" parameter to 0.4 for all our experiments. The other parameters of the classifiers are set to default values.

The SMO version of SVM present in WEKA is configured as follows:

- Task1: Cost parameter, C = 10 and kernel type: polynomial kernel with exponent set to 2
- Task 2: Cost parameter, C = 15 and kernel type: polynomial kernel with exponent set to 2.

3   Evaluation and Results

3.1   Description of Datasets and Data Representation

We have trained and tested our systems using the datasets obtained from the organizers of the shared task on detecting paraphrases in Indian Languages (DPIL) held in conjunction with FIRE 2016 @ ISI – Kolkata. The datasets for four Indian languages - (1) Hindi, (2) Punjabi, (3) Tamil and (4) Malayalam, are released. For each language, two paraphrase detection tasks task1 and task2 were defined. Data sets were separately designed for Task1 and task 2. The description of the datasets is shown in Tables 1 and 2.

Table 1. Description of data sets for Task1

Language	Training data size	Test data size
Hindi	2500	900
Punjabi	1700	500
Malayalam	2500	900
Tamil	2500	900

The training data sets consist of sentence pairs and their labels and the test data sets consist of the sentence pairs to be labeled. To make the data machine understandable, we map each training pair of sentences to a pattern vector based on the features discussed in Sect. 2.1 and then the pattern vector is labeled with "P" (paraphrase) or "NP" (not-paraphrase) or "SP" (semi-paraphrase or roughly paraphrase) according to the label of the corresponding sentence pair. Thus all labeled pattern vectors for the corresponding sentence pairs in the training set for an Indian language are used to train each classifier. Each test pair of sentences is also represented as the pattern vector in the similar way and then the obtained test pattern vector is submitted to the trained classifier for finding its label.

Table 2. Description of data sets for Task2

Language	Training data size	Test data size
Hindi	3500	1400
Punjabi	2200	750
Malayalam	3500	1400
Tamil	3500	1400

3.2   Evaluation

For evaluating the system performance, two evaluation metrics - Accuracy and F-measure have been used by the organizers of the contest. Accuracy is defined as follows:

$$\text{Accuracy} = \frac{\text{\# of correctly classified Pairs}}{\text{Total \# of Pairs}} \tag{5}$$

The accuracy calculation formula used to calculate accuracy for Task1 was the same as that for Task2.

The metric used by the organizers of the contest to calculate F-measure for Task1 was not the same as that used for Task2. The F-measure used for evaluating task1 is defined as follows:

F1-Score = F1 measure of Detecting Paraphrases = F1- score over P class only.

F-measure for the task2 is defined as:

F1-Score = Macro F1 Score which is an average of F1 scores of all three classes - P, NP and SP.

3.3   Results

For system development and evaluation, the training data and test data [38] released for the DPIL shared task@FIRE 2016[3] have been used.

The official results of the various systems participated in Task1 and Task 2 of the contest are shown in Tables 3 and 4 respectively. Along with the official results, we have also shown in the tables the post conference results obtained by our developed SVM based system (the team name is indicated in the tables by KS_JU(SVM)).

As we can see from the tables, no system performs equally well in both the tasks-task1 and task2 across all languages. Some systems have performed well in some languages on task1 and some other systems have performed well in some other languages on the same task. This is also true for task2.

It is also evident from the tables that only 4 teams out of 11 participated teams submitted their systems for all four languages- Hindi, Punjabi, Malayalam and Tamil and the remaining 7 teams participated in only one of the four languages.

We have shown in the tables in bold font the performance scores highest in a particular task for a particular language. It is also evident from the tables that the most systems perform well on Punjabi and Hindi languages. But they show relatively poor performance in Tamil and Malayalam languages. We think that the main reason for achieving the better performances in Punjabi and Hindi language domain is the nature of training and testing data sets supplied for those languages. Most likely, that is why the most participating systems perform almost equally well for Punjabi and Hindi languages.

Another reason for having poor performance for Tamil and Malayalam may be the complex morphology of these languages. We have computed the relative rank order of the participating teams based on overall average performance on task1 and task2 in all four languages (simple average of F1-scores obtained by a team on task1 and task2 over all four languages). Since only four teams have participated in all four languages, we have only shown rank order of these four teams in Table 5. As we can see from

---

[3] http://nlp.amrita.edu/dpil_cen/.

Table 5, our system (Team code: KS_JU) obtains the second best accuracy among the four systems which participated in shared task@DPIL.

The post conference enhancement of our system by replacing multinomial logistic regression by SMO gives slight improvement in the overall score. We have indicated in Table 5 our enhanced system by KS_JU(SVM) to distinguish it from our original team code (KS_JU) assigned at time of participation in the shared task. The details of the system with team code: HIT 2016 whose performance is comparable with our proposed SVM based system (in terms of overall average performance), can be found in [39].

Like our proposed approach, HIT 2016 [39] also formalizes paraphrase detection task as a classification problem. It uses Gradient Boosting Tree to detect paraphrases.

Table 3. Results obtained for Task 1 by the various participating teams @DPIL 2016 and our system that uses SVM. In the table, "Malay" indicates Malayalam and "Pun" indicates Punjabi language

Team name	Language	Task	Accuracy	F1 score/macro
KS_JU	Hindi	Task1	0.90666	0.9
KS_JU	Malay	Task1	0.81	0.79
KS_JU	**Pun**	**Task1**	**0.946**	**0.95**
KS_JU	Tamil	Task1	0.78888	0.75
KS_JU(SVM)	Hindi	Task1	0.91	0.90
KS_JU(SVM)	Malay	Task1	0.82	0.79
KS_JU(SVM)	**Pun**	**Task1**	**0.982**	**0.982**
KS_JU(SVM)	Tamil	Task1	0.7911	0.747
NLP-NITMZ	Hindi	Task1	0.91555	0.91
NLP-NITMZ	Malay	Task1	0.83444	0.79
NLP-NITMZ	Pun	Task1	0.942	0.94
NLP-NITMZ	Tamil	Task1	0.83333	0.79
HIT2016	Hindi	Task1	0.89666	0.89
HIT2016	**Malay**	**Task1**	**0.83777**	**0.81**
HIT2016	Punjabi	Task1	0.944	0.94
HIT2016	**Tamil**	**Task1**	**0.82111**	**0.79**
JU-NLP	Hindi	Task1	0.8222	0.74
JU-NLP	Malay	Task1	0.59	0.16
JU-NLP	Punjabi	Task1	0.942	0.94
JU-NLP	Tamil	Task1	0.57555	0.09
BITS-PILANI	Hindi	Task1	0.89777	0.89
DAVPBI	Punjabi	Task1	0.938	0.94
CUSAT_TEAM	Malay	Task1	0.80444	0.76
ASE	Hindi	Task1	0.35888	0.34
NLP@KEC	**Tamil**	**Task1**	**0.82333**	**0.79**
Anuj	**Hindi**	**Task1**	**0.92**	**0.91**
CUSAT_NLP	Malay	Task1	0.76222	0.75

Table 4. Results obtained for Task 2 by the various participating teams @DPIL 2016 and the system that uses SVM. In the table, "Malay" indicates Malayalam and "Pun" indicates Punjabi language

Team name	Language	Task	Accuracy	F1 score/macro F1 score
KS_JU	Hindi	Task2	0.85214	0.84816
KS_JU	Malay	Task2	0.66142	0.65774
KS_JU	Pun	Task2	0.896	0.896
KS_JU	Tamil	Task2	0.67357	0.66447
KS_JU(SVM)	Hindi	Task2	0.905	0.905
KS_JU(SVM)	Malay	Task2	0.6557	0.65
KS_JU(SVM)	Pun	Task2	0.8987	0.8970
KS_JU(SVM)	Tamil	Task2	0.6843	0.6727
NLP-NITMZ	Hindi	Task2	0.78571	0.76422
NLP-NITMZ	Malay	Task2	0.62428	0.60677
NLP-NITMZ	Pun	Task2	0.812	0.8086
NLP-NITMZ	Tamil	Task2	0.65714	0.63067
HIT2016	Hindi	Task2	0.9	0.89844
HIT2016	**Malay**	**Task2**	**0.74857**	**0.74597**
HIT2016	**Pun**	**Task2**	**0.92266**	**0.923**
HIT2016	**Tamil**	**Task2**	**0.755**	**0.73979**
JU-NLP	Hindi	Task2	0.68571	0.6841
JU-NLP	Malay	Task2	0.42214	0.3078
JU-NLP	Pun	Task2	0.88666	0.88664
JU-NLP	Tamil	Task2	0.55071	0.4319
BITS-PILANI	Hindi	Task2	0.71714	0.71226
DAVPBI	Pun	Task2	0.74666	0.7274
CUSAT_TEAM	Malay	Task2	0.50857	0.46576
ASE	Hindi	Task2	0.35428	0.3535
NLP@KEC	Tamil	Task2	0.68571	0.66739
Anuj	**Hindi**	**Task2**	**0.90142**	**0.90001**
CUSAT_NLP	Malay	Task2	0.52071	0.51296

Gradient boosting is a machine learning technique which produces a prediction model in the form of an ensemble of weak prediction models. It builds the model in a stage-wise fashion and it generalizes them by allowing optimization of an arbitrary differentiable loss function. Gradient boosting tree is an ensemble of weak prediction models which are basically decision trees. The system HIT 2016 has used Gradient Boosting Tree with a feature set that includes a set of the Meteor evaluation metrics commonly used in machine translation domain.

Table 5. Overall average performance of systems including task1 and task2 both over all four languages- Hindi, Punjabi, Malayalam and Tamil

Team name	Overall average F1-score
HIT2016	**0.84**
KS_JU(SVM)	0.82
KS_JU	0.81
NLP-NITMZ	0.78
JU-NLP	0.53

4 Conclusion

In this work, we implement a paraphrase detection system that can detect paraphrases in four Indian Languages- Hindi, Punjabi, Tamil and Malayalam. We use various lexical and semantic level similarity measures as the features for paraphrase detection task. We view paraphrase detection problem as a pattern classification problem and we use multinomial logistic regression model and SVM for the classification task. Our model performs relatively better on task1 than on task2.

Our system has the scope for further improvement in the following ways:

- Word2Vec models requires large corpus for proper representation of word meaning, but while computing we have used a small amount of corpus for each language. Use of large corpus for computing word vectors may improve semantic similarity measure leading to improving system performance.
- Most Indian languages are highly inflectional. So, use of morphological analyzer/ more accurate stemmer or lemmatizer may improve the system performance.

Acknowledgments. This research work has received support from the project entitled "Design and Development of a System for Querying, Clustering and Summarization for Bengali" funded by the Department of Science and Technology, Government of India under the SERB scheme.

References

1. Madnani, N., Dorr, B.J.: Generating phrasal and sentential paraphrases: a survey of data-driven methods. Comput. Linguist. **36**(3), 341–387 (2010)
2. Culicover, P.W.: Paraphrase generation and information retrieval from stored text. Mech. Transl. Comput. Linguist. **11**(1–2), 78–88 (1968)
3. Sparck-Jones, K., Tait, J.I.: Automatic search term variant generation. J. Doc. **40**(1), 50–66 (1984)
4. Beeferman, D., Berger, A.: Agglomerative clustering of a search engine query log. In: Proceedings of the ACM SIGKDD International Conference on Knowledge Discovery and Data mining, Boston, MA, pp. 407–416 (2000)
5. Jones, R., Rey, B., Madani, O., Greiner, W.: Generating query substitutions. In: Proceedings of the World Wide Web Conference, Edinburgh, pp. 387–396 (2006)

6. Sahami, M., Heilman, T.D: A web-based kernel function for measuring the similarity of short text snippets. In: Proceedings of the World Wide Web Conference, Edinburgh, pp. 377–386 (2006)

7. Metzler, D., Dumais, S., Meek, C.: Similarity measures for short segments of text. In: Amati, G., Carpineto, C., Romano, G. (eds.) ECIR 2007. LNCS, vol. 4425, pp. 16–27. Springer, Heidelberg (2007). https://doi.org/10.1007/978-3-540-71496-5_5

8. Shi, X., Yang, C.C.: Mining related queries from web search engine query logs using an improved association rule mining model. JASIST 58(12), 1871–1883 (2007)

9. Ravichandran, D., Hovy, E.: Learning surface text patterns for a question answering system. In: Proceedings of ACL, Philadelphia, PA, pp. 41–47 (2002)

10. Riezler, S., Vasserman, A., Tsochantaridis, I., Mittal, V.O., Liu, Y.: Statistical machine translation for query expansion in answer retrieval. In: Proceedings of ACL, Prague, pp. 464–471 (2007)

11. Owczarzak, K., Groves, D., Genabith, J.V., Way, A.: Contextual bitext-derived paraphrases in automatic MT evaluation. In: Proceedings on the Workshop on Statistical Machine Translation, New York, NY, pp. 86–93 (2006)

12. Zhou, L., Lin, C.-Y., Hovy. E.: Re-evaluating machine translation results with paraphrase support. In: Proceedings of EMNLP, Sydney, pp. 77–84 (2006)

13. Callison-Burch, C., Koehn, P., Osborne M.: Improved statistical machine translation using paraphrases. In: Proceedings of NAACL, New York, NY, pp. 17–24 (2006)

14. Fujita, A., Sato, S.: A probabilistic model for measuring grammaticality and similarity of automatically generated paraphrases of predicate phrases. In: Proceedings of COLING, Manchester, pp. 225–232 (2008)

15. Corley, C., Mihalcea, R.: Measuring the semantic similarity of texts. In: Proceedings of the ACL Workshop on Empirical Modeling of Semantic Equivalence and Entailment, Ann Arbor, MI, pp. 13–18 (2005)

16. Uzuner, O., Katz, B.: Capturing expression using linguistic information. In: Proceedings of AAAI, Pittsburgh, PA, pp. 1124–1129 (2005)

17. Brockett, C., Dolan, W.B.: Support vector machines for paraphrase identification and corpus construction. In: Proceedings of the Third International Workshop on Paraphrasing, Jeju Island, pp. 1–8 (2005)

18. Marsi, E., Krahmer, E.: Explorations in sentence fusion. In: Proceedings of the European Workshop on Natural Language Generation, Aberdeen, pp. 109–117 (2005)

19. Wu, D.: Recognizing paraphrases and textual entailment using inversion transduction grammars. In: Proceedings of the ACL Workshop on Empirical Modeling of Semantic Equivalence and Entailment, Ann Arbor, MI, pp. 25–30 (2005)

20. Cordeiro, J., Dias, G., Brazdil, P.: A metric for paraphrase detection. In: Proceedings of the Second International Multi-Conference on Computing in the Global Information Technology, Guadeloupe, p. 7 (2007a)

21. Cordeiro, J., Dias, G., Brazdil, P.: New functions for unsupervised asymmetrical paraphrase detection. J. Softw. 2(4), 12–23 (2007b)

22. Das, D., Smith, N.A.: Paraphrase identification as probabilistic quasi-synchronous recognition. In: Proceedings of ACL/IJCNLP, Singapore, pp. 468–476 (2009)

23. Malakasiotis, P.: Paraphrase recognition using machine learning to combine similarity measures. In: Proceedings of the ACL-IJCNLP 2009 Student Research Workshop, Singapore, pp. 27–35 (2009)

24. Dolan, B., Dagan, I. (eds.): Proceedings of the ACL Workshop on Empirical Modeling of Semantic Equivalence and Entailment, Ann Arbor, MI. ACL (2005)

25. Barzilay, R., McKeown, K.R.: Sentence fusion for multi-document news summarization. Comput. Linguist. 31(3), 297–328 (2005)

26. Sekine, S.: On-demand information extraction. In: Proceedings of COLING-ACL, Sydney, pp. 731–738 (2006)
27. Dagan, I., Glickman, O., Magnini, B.: The PASCAL recognising textual entailment challenge. In: Quiñonero-Candela, J., Dagan, I., Magnini, B., d'Alché-Buc, F. (eds.) MLCW 2005. LNCS (LNAI), vol. 3944, pp. 177–190. Springer, Heidelberg (2006). https://doi.org/10.1007/11736790_9
28. Bar-Haim, R., Dagan, I., Dolan, B., Ferro, L., Giampiccolo, D., Magnini, B., Szpektor, I. (eds.): Proceedings of the Second PASCAL Challenges Workshop on Recognizing Textual Entailment, Venice (2007)
29. Sekine, S., Inui, K., Dagan, I., Dolan, B., Giampiccolo, D., Magnini, B. (eds.): Proceedings of the ACL-PASCAL Workshop on Textual Entailment and Paraphrasing. Association for Computational Linguistics, Prague (2007)
30. Giampiccolo, D., Dang, H., Dagan, I., Dolan, B., Magnini, B. (eds.): Proceedings of the Text Analysis Conference (TAC): Recognizing Textual Entailment Track, Gaithersburg, MD (2008)
31. Gensim-Deep learning with word2vec. https://radimrehurek.com/gensim/models/word2vec.html, Retrieved in 2016
32. Mikolov, T., Chen, K., Corrado, G.S., Dean, J.: Efficient estimation of word representations in vector space. In: ICLR Workshop Papers (2013)
33. Mikolov, T., Sutskever, I., Chen, K., Corrado, G.S., Dean, J.: Distributed representations of words and phrases and their compositionality. In: NIPS, pp. 3111–3119 (2013)
34. Sarkar, K.: KS_JU@DPIL-FIRE2016: detecting paraphrases in indian languages using multinomial logistic regression model. eprint arXiv:1612.08171 (2016)
35. Sarkar, K.: KS_JU@DPIL-FIRE2016: detecting paraphrases in indian languages using multinomial logistic regression model. In: Working notes of FIRE 2016 - Forum for Information Retrieval Evaluation, Kolkata, India, 7–10 December, pp. 250–255 (2016)
36. Hall, M., Frank, E., Holmes, G., Pfahringer, B., Reutemann, P., Witten, I.H.: The WEKA data mining software: an update. SIGKDD Explor. 11(1), 10–18 (2009)
37. Platt, J.C.: Sequential minimal optimization: a fast algorithm for training support vector machines. In: SchOlkopf, B., Burges, C.J.C., Smola, A.J. (eds.) Advances in Kernel Methods- Support Vector Learning, pp. 185–208. M.I.T. Press (1999)
38. Anand Kumar, M., Singh, S., Kavirajan, B., Soman, K. P.: DPIL@FIRE2016: overview of shared task on detecting Paraphrases in indian languages. In: Working notes of FIRE 2016 - Forum for Information Retrieval Evaluation, Kolkata, India, 7–10 December, CEUR Workshop Proceedings (2016). CEUR-WS.org
39. Kong, L., Chen, K., Tian, L., Hao, Z., Han, Z., Qi, H.: HIT2016@DPIL-FIRE2016: detecting paraphrases in Indian Languages based on gradient tree boosting. In: Working Notes of FIRE 2016 - Forum for Information Retrieval Evaluation, Kolkata, India, 7–10 December, pp. 260–265 (2016)

Sentence Paraphrase Detection Using Classification Models

Liuyang Tian[1] , Hui Ning[1] , Leilei Kong[2(✉)] ,
Kaisheng Chen[2] , Haoliang Qi[2] , and Zhongyuan Han[2]

[1] School of Computer Science and Technology,
Harbin Engineering University, Harbin 150001, China
[2] School of Computer Science and Technology,
Heilongjiang Institute of Technology, Harbin 150050, China
`kongleilei1979@gmail.com`

Abstract. In this paper, we address on the task of sentence paraphrase detection which is focused on deciding whether the two sentences have the relationship of paraphrase. A supervised learning strategy for paraphrase detection is described whereby the two sentences are classified to decide the paraphrase relationship and using only the lexical features operated at n-gram as the classification features. Gradient Boosting, K-Nearest Neighbor, Decision Tree and Support vector machine are chosen as the classifiers. The performance of the classification method is compared and the features are analyzed to determine which of them are most important for paraphrase detection. Evaluation is performed on the corpus of 2016 Detecting Paraphrase in Indian Languages task proposed by Forum of Information Retrieval Evaluation (DPIL-FIRE2016). The experimental results show that the Gradient Boosting can achieve the highest Overall Score. By using the learned classifier, we got the highest F1 measure for both Task1 and Task2 on Malayalam and Tamil, and the highest F1 measure for Task2 on Punjabi in DPIL-FIRE2016.

Keywords: Sentence paraphrase detection · Classification
Gradient Tree Boosting · Lexical features · Indian Languages

1 Introduction

Sentence paraphrase means the same meaning of a sentence is expressed in another sentence using different words. Detecting sentence paraphrase is an important and challenging task. It is difficult to achieve a better performance [1]. Detecting paraphrase has attracted the attention of researchers in recent years. It is widely used in paraphrase generation and extraction, machine translation, Q&A and plagiarism detection.

Paraphrase is defined as the restatement of a text or passages in an alternative way by Huang [1]. In the task of Detecting Paraphrase in Indian Languages of the Forum Information Retrieval Evaluation 2016(DPIL-FIRE2016)[1], the paraphrase is described as "the same meaning of a sentence is expressed in another sentence using different words".

---

[1] http://nlp.amrita.edu/dpil_cen/

© Springer International Publishing AG 2018
P. Majumder et al. (Eds.): FIRE 2016 Workshop, LNCS 10478, pp. 166–181, 2018.
https://doi.org/10.1007/978-3-319-73606-8_13

Paraphrase detection is focused on sentence level paraphrase identification, to classify them as paraphrase (P) and not paraphrase (NP), or completely equivalent (E), roughly equivalent (RE) and not equivalent (NE) [2].

The paraphrased sentences always retain the same meaning and usually obfuscated by manipulating the text and changing most of its appearance. The words in the original sentence is replaced with synonyms/antonyms, and short phrases are inserted to change the appearance, but not the idea of the text [3]. Otherwise, the sentence reduction, combination, restructuring, paraphrasing, concept generalization, and concept specification also are used to paraphrase the sentence.

Intuitively, paraphrase task can be seen as a classification problem and the classification problem can be concerned about the following:

(1) Which classification method can be effectively applied to the paraphrase identification tasks?
(2) Which features can be used for classification?

For the first problem, we compare some classical approaches, such as Gradient Boosting, K-Nearest Neighbor, Decision Trees and Support Vector Machines, to decide experimentally which one is more suitable for this task.

For the second problem, we choose only the lexical features operated at the word level, Word-based N-Gram (WNG), as the fingerprints to represent a sentence. The various similarity computation based on WNG are chosen as the classification features. Simple WNGs may be constructed by using word-unigram, word-bigram, word-trigram or larger.

Using the training and testing corpora of Detecting Paraphrase in Indian Languages proposed by FIRE, we rigorously evaluate various aspects of our classification methods for detecting paraphrase.

The rest of this paper is organized as follows. In Sect. 2, we discuss the related work of paraphrase detection. In Sect. 3, we analyze the problem of sentence paraphrase detection taking the Indian Languages as examples, introduce the classification method we selected in this paper, and our feature set. In Sect. 4, we report the experimental results and compare the performance of different classification methods. The last section we conclude our study.

2 Related Work

Paraphrase detection is a rather challenging task because it is difficult to assess the semantic similarity of potential content and to understand the morphological changes of the language. Many research focused on this task. We mainly divided into two parts to introduce the work of predecessors, including the sentence feature description and classification model selection.

In order to facilitate the observation, we will be predecessors of features and classification methods gathered in table. As shown in Table 1.

Table 1. Various Features used by the researchers

Features	McClendon	Dolan	Lintean	Socher	Hu and Lu	Fernando	Rus
Morphological		√	√	√			
Word overlap	√						
Word order	√		√				
Syntactic		√	√	√			√
WordNet		√	√			√	
String similarity	√	√				√	
other	N-gram				Word2Vec		Word2Vec
Classifier	SVM	SVM	d2dSim	RAEs	CNN	Threshold	Threshold

McClendon (2014) use ten different NLP modules to decide whether two sentences are paraphrases. These modules can be broken into three different categories, each examining different aspects of the sentence: word overlap, word order and n-grams. Then they use SVM for classification [5].

Dolan (2005) use string similarity features, morphological variants, WorldNet lexical, Encarta thesaurus, composite features as feature set to generate corpus. The corpus was created using heuristic extraction techniques in conjunction with an SVM-based classifier to select likely sentence-level paraphrases from a large corpus of topic clustered news data [6].

Lintean (2009) propose an approach that quantifies both the similarity and dissimilarity between two sentences. The similarity and dissimilarity is assessed based on Lexico semantic information, i.e., word semantics, and syntactic information in the form of dependencies, which are explicit syntactic relations between words in a sentence. Then, they compute a dependency similarity score (d2dSim) using the word-to-word similarity metrics for classification [7].

Socher (2011) introduce a method based on recursive auto encoders (RAE). The RAEs are based on an unfolding objective and learn feature vectors for phrases in syntactic trees. These features are used to measure the word and phrase similarity between two sentences [8]. Hu and Lu (2014) propose Convolutional neural network models for matching two sentences; the proposed models not only nicely represent the hierarchical structures of sentences with their layer by-layer composition and pooling, but also capture the rich matching patterns at different levels. They use the embedding of words (often trained beforehand with unsupervised methods) as features [9].

Fernando (2008) described a semantic similarity approach for paraphrase identification which makes extensive use of word similarity information derived from WordNet. The approach is evaluated using the Microsoft Research Paraphrase Corpus [10]. Rus and McCarthy (2008) described an approach to paraphrase identification with Lexico-Syntactic Graph. The approach to recognizing textual entailment is based on the idea of subsumption. For example, an object A subsumes an object B, if A is more general than B, or B is more specific than A. The effectiveness of the proposed method is verified by the original MS paraphrase corpus [11].

In the FIRE2016 @ DPIL task, many teams have also proposed a variety of methods. For example, the ANUJ team obtains the features by overlapping words and normalized IDF scores, and then uses the random forest classification model to classify them [12]; KS_JU team uses different word and semantic level of similarity measure (Word embedding) to calculate the features, and then use the logical regression model for classification [13]. KEC @ NLP team uses the existing Tamil shallow analyzer to extract the sentence morphological features, and then use SVM and the maximum entropy model to identify [14]. The NLP-NITMZ team uses Jaccard similarity, normalized editing distance and Cosine similarity as features, and then uses probabilistic neural networks (PNN) to identify [15].

For the methods based on the supervised learning, it is lack of the research to compare the performance on the public available corpus for paraphrase detection task. This paper addresses the performance comparison of different classification method and different features to discover which ones are more suitable for paraphrase detection.

3   Sentence Paraphrase Detection Based on Classification

In this section, we take the FIRE2016 @ DPIL task as an example to analyze the main problems, the formal definition of the paraphrase task, and then briefly introduce the classification of our selected model to obtain the best performance method; the last detailed some of the features used in this paper.

3.1   Problem Analysis

As we have discussed in above section, paraphrase identification is difficult to detect. The traditional similarity computing methods, such as Cosine Distance, Jaccard Coefficient, Dice Distance, may be ineffective for paraphrase. Figure 1 exemplifies the paraphrase cases.

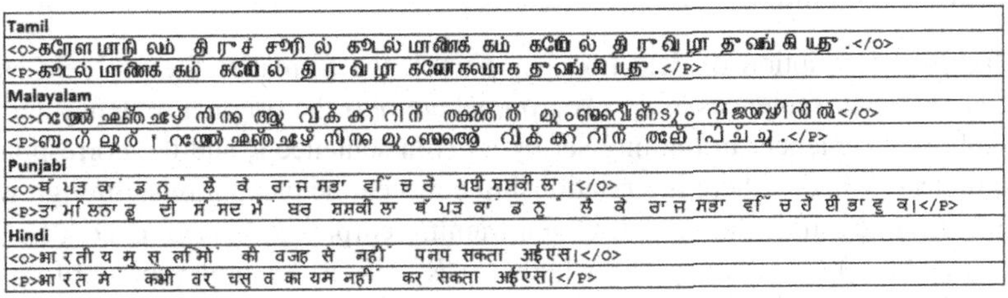

Fig. 1. A paraphrase cases

From Fig. 1, we can see that the two sentences having the paraphrasing relationship are different in their appearance. Furthermore, we conduct the analysis on 1000 randomly selected cases with paraphrase relationship on Malayalam sub corpora and all four languages corpora. Figure 2 displays the distribution with Jaccard Coefficient and METEOR-F1.

It is easy to detect from Fig. 2 that the scores of Jaccard coefficient are all very low, the average score is only 0.1332. Considering the rewriting properties of the paraphrase sentences, it is not enough to consider only the similarity of sentences. By analyzing it, we believe that more features are needed.

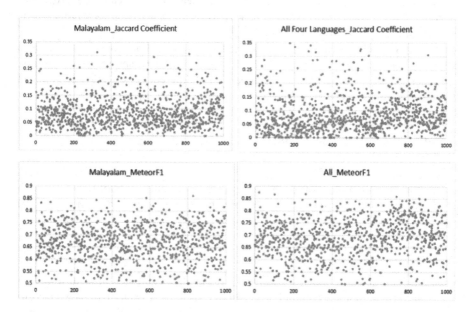

Fig. 2. Score distribution of Jaccard coefficient on Malayalam (up) sub corpora and all four languages corpora (down)

3.2   Problem Definition

According the description of detection paraphrase, we formalize the problem as follows. Denote a pair sentences as $s_i = (o_i, p_i)$, where o_i is the original sentence and p_i is the paraphrased sentence. In training set by a given sentence s_i and the corresponding label to indicate whether there is a relationship between the paraphrases, through which we can learn a classification model. Given training corpus is defined as $D = \{(x_1, y_1), (x_2, y_2), \ldots, (x_i, y_i), \ldots, (x_n, y_n)\}$, where $x_i \in R^N$ is a feature vector of s_i and $x_i = (x_i^{(1)}, x_i^{(2)}, \ldots, x_i^{(n)})^T, i = 1, 2, \ldots, N$. We use a function to get each xi defined as follows.

$$x_{(i)} = \Phi(o_i, p_i) \tag{1}$$

Where, $x_{(i)} = \Phi(o_i, p_i)$ is a mapping onto feature that describes the paraphrase between the i-th original sentence o_i and the paraphrased sentence p_i.

And y_i is the label of x_i to denote the category of each x_i. For the task 1, we define $y_i \in \{P, NP\}$, and for task 2, we define $y_i \in \{E, RE, NE\}$.

Then the framework of learning problem can be depicted in Fig. 3.

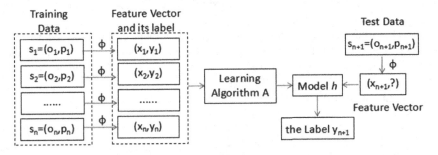

Fig. 3. The framework of detection paraphrase

Then, given D as training data, the learning system will learn a conditional probability P(Y|X) based on the training data. Then given a new input x_{n+1}, the classification system gives the corresponding output label y_{n+1} according to the learning classifier.

3.3   Classification Based Methods

Decision Trees
Decision Trees (DTs) are a non-parametric supervised learning method used for classification and regression [16]. The goal is to create a model that predicts the value of a target variable by learning simple decision rules inferred from the data features.

Moreover, the decision tree model needs to consider the order of selection of feature node, the common measure method including: Information Gain and Gini Impurity. Information entropy is one of the most common metrics to measure the purity of samples. Given a sample set D, the proportion of sample k is $p_k(k = 1,2,...,|y|)$. The information entropy of D is defined as:

$$Ent(D) = -\sum_{k=1}^{|y|} p_k \log_2^{p_k} \qquad (2)$$

The same information gain is defined as follows:

$$Gain(D, a) = Ent(D) - \sum_{v=1}^{V} \frac{|D^v|}{|D|} Ent(D^v) \qquad (3)$$

Where, a is a discrete attribute, and v is the possible value of the attribute.

K-Nearest Neighbors
K-Nearest Neighbor (KNN) algorithm is used to measure different characteristics of distance value between classification algorithm [17]. For example, there is a training dataset, we know that the samples of each data and the corresponding relationship

between the classification of the input data. After comparing characteristics of each feature and sample data corresponding to the new data, then the algorithm to extract the classification label the samples feature most similar data. We only select the sample set before the k most similar data.

The algorithm used to compute the nearest neighbors can be divided as three categories: BallTree, KDTree and Brute-force Search. In this experiment, we selected the most appropriate algorithm based on the values passed to fit method. And the distance metric is the Minkowski distance.

The Minkowski distance is defined as:

$$L(x_i, x_j) = \left(\sum_{l=1}^{n} |x_i^{(l)} - x_j^{(l)}|^2 \right)^{\frac{1}{2}} \tag{4}$$

Where, X as feature space, $x_i, x_i \in X$, $x_i = (x_i^{(1)}, x_i^{(2)}, \ldots, x_i^{(n)})^T$, $x_j = (x_j^{(1)}, x_j^{(2)}, \ldots, x_j^{(n)})^T$.

SVM

Support vector machine (SVM) are a set of supervised learning methods used for classification, regression and outliers detection. The support vector machines are effective in high dimensional spaces and still effective in cases where number of dimensions is greater than the number of samples [18]; And, we use the kernel trick in the model. The basic idea is a nonlinear transformation of the input space (Euclidean space Rn) corresponds to a feature space (Hilbert space H). Therefore, this classification problem can be completed by solving the linear support vector machine in the feature space. In this experiment, we use the Gauss kernel function:

$$K(x, z) = \exp\left(-\frac{||x - z||^2}{2\delta^2} \right) \tag{5}$$

And the corresponding support vector machine is a radial basis function classifier. In this case, the classification decision function is defined as:

$$f(x) = sign\left(\sum_{i=1}^{N_s} a_i^* y_i \exp\left(-\frac{||x - z||^2}{2\delta^2} \right) + b^* \right) \tag{6}$$

Where, $a^* = (a_1^*, a_2^*, \ldots, a_n^*)^T$ is the solution of dual problem, and b^* is the solution of the original problem. $T = [(x_1, y_1), (x_2, y_2), \ldots, (x_N, y_N)]$ is the training set on the feature space.

Gradient Tree Boosting

The gradient boosting algorithm was originally proposed by Freidman in 2001 [19, 20]. Its core is that each tree is learned from the residuals of all previous trees. The residual estimate is defined as follows:

$$r_{mi} = -\left[\frac{\partial L(y_i, f(x_i))}{\partial f(x_i)}\right]_{f(x)=f_{m-1}(x)} \tag{7}$$

Where, $L(y, f(x))$ is the loss function. $f(x)$ is a classification of decision tree.

The negative gradient of the loss function in the current model is used as an approximation of the residuals in the boosting tree algorithm, and then a classification tree is fitted.

Finally, they can be combined, they can be weighted (the greater the error rate of the base classifier weight value is smaller, the smaller the error rate of the base classifier weight value), or let them vote to get a final model.

Gradient Boost and traditional Boost are very different; it is calculated every time to reduce the last residual. In order to reduce these residuals, a new model can be established in the gradient direction of the residual reduction. Therefore, in the Gradient Boost, each new model is established in order to make the previous model residuals to the gradient direction reduction, and the traditional boost algorithm on the correct, the wrong sample weight is very different.

3.4   Features

Set $d = \{(w_1, d), (w_2, d),\ldots, (w_n, d)\}$, where (w_i, d) refers to the i-th word in d, and n is the words number in d. We exploit the Word-based n-gram (WNG) to represents d as a collection of words. For the feature vector $x_{(i)}$, we define the WNG similarity-based features to capture the matching degree of o_i and p_i.

Jaccard Coefficient: This method was first used to measure the intersection of two thesauruses in information retrieval, although this method has defects, without considering the word frequency, but wins in simple and practical. Here we will do N-gram processing on the two sentences. Each sentence as a thesaurus will be used to measure the similarity of sentence. The formula is defined as follows:

$$JC(o, p) = \frac{|o \cap p|}{|o \cup p|} \tag{8}$$

Cosine Similarity: This method is the cosine of the angle by using two n-dimensional vector values to calculate their similarity. This method is often used to compare documents in text mining. Here we firstly do N-gram processing on two sentences, the term-frequency sentence as the dimension of vector, and then calculate the text similarity of two sentences. This feature is considered the frequency of the words in the sentence. The formula is defined as follows:

$$CS(\vec{x}_i, \vec{y}_i) = \frac{\vec{o}_i \cdot \vec{p}_i}{||\vec{o}_i|| \cdot ||\vec{p}_i||} \tag{9}$$

Dice Coefficient: Similar to the Jaccard coefficient, this method is also used for information retrieval. After N-gram treatment, with the common words of two sentences and the length of two sentences to calculate the similarity of two sentences. The formula is defined as follows:

$$DC(s,r) = \frac{2 \cdot common(o,p)}{len(o) + len(p)} \tag{10}$$

Reference the METEOR measure used in machine translation [4], we design the following six features to combine the lexical similarity. The specific formula is defined as follows:

METEOR Precision:

$$P = \frac{common(o,p)}{len(p)} \tag{11}$$

METEOR Recall:

$$R = \frac{common(o,p)}{len(o)} \tag{12}$$

METEOR F1: The harmonic value of precision and recall.

$$F1 = \frac{2PR}{R+P} \tag{13}$$

METEOR F-mean: The harmonic mean value of precision and recall.

$$F - mean = \frac{10PR}{R+9P} \tag{14}$$

METEOR Penalty: The len (chunks) is the number of the matching number of each chunk.

$$Penalty = 0.5 * \left(\frac{len(chunks)}{common(o,p)} \right)^3 \tag{15}$$

METEOR score: The overall METEOR score.

$$Score = Fmean * (1 - Penalty) \tag{16}$$

The METEOR score is harmonic mean value of the chunks matching decomposition and the characterization matching decomposition quality. Finally, we get the score.

4 Experiments

4.1 Task Description

The FIRE2016@DPIL task divides the paraphrase task into two subtasks, as described below:

The task1 is: given a pair of sentences from newspaper domain, the task is to classify them as paraphrase (P) or not paraphrase (NP).

The task2 is: given two sentences from newspaper domain, the task is to identify whether they are completely equivalent (E) or roughly equivalent (RE) or not equivalent (NE).

4.2 Dataset

The dataset used in our experiment comes from the evaluation data published in the FIRE2016@DPIL task. The data set is mainly extracted from the news newspaper. A detailed description of the data set can refer to http://nlp.amrita.edu/dpil_cen/.

The data set is divided into two different subsets: Task1 and Task2. Each subset contains four different categories of Indian language: Tamil, Malayalam, Hindi and Punjabi. The Task1-set contains 12400 samples, including 9200 training samples and 3200 test samples, and the Task2-set contains 17650 samples, including 12700 training samples and 4950 test samples. The statistics of training and testing data is shown in Tables 2 and 3.

Table 2. Corpus statistics of DPIL 2016 on Task1

Language		Train					Test				
		Hin	Mal	Pun	Tam	All	Hin	Mal	Pun	Tam	All
Sample number		2500	2500	1700	2500	9200	900	900	500	900	3200
Avg terms	Blank	32	18	39	24	27	32	19	43	23	28
	4 g	126	166	150	175	155	120	181	164	176	160

Table 3. Corpus statistics of DPIL 2016 on Task2

Language		Train					Test				
		Hin	Mal	Pun	Tam	All	Hin	Mal	Pun	Tam	All
Sample number		3500	3500	2200	3500	12700	1400	1400	750	1400	4950
Avg terms	Blank	34	18	41	24	28	42	19	41	28	31
	4 g	131	164	156	178	158	154	177	157	207	176

4.3 Evaluation Metrics

In this experiment, the evaluation criteria used were Accuracy and F1 values. For easy understanding, we first introduce several measurement indicators [21].

TP: The sample is true, and the results obtained are positive.
FP: The sample is false, and the results obtained are positive.
FN: The sample is false, and the results obtained are negative.
TN: The sample is true, and the results obtained are negative.
According to the above measure metrics, Precision and Recall are defined as follows:

$$\text{Precision} = \frac{TP}{TP + FP} \tag{17}$$

$$\text{Recall} = \frac{TP}{TP + FN} \tag{18}$$

The main evaluation metrics adopted by DPIL is Accuracy and F1 measure defined as follows:

$$\text{Accuracy} = \frac{TP + TN}{TP + \text{FN} + FP + TN} \tag{19}$$

$$F1 = \frac{2 \times \text{Pr}\,ecision \times \text{Re}call}{\text{Pr}\,ecision + \text{Re}call} \tag{20}$$

4.4 Experimental Settings

Pre-processing
For the training set and the test set, we first remove the illegal characters. The new choose two kinds of word processing methods, one is the space word segmentation, and the other is n-gram segmentation. According to a priori knowledge, we know that through the Chinese or English string for n-gram segmentation, the Chinese or English information can be based on keyword fuzzy query [22, 23]. So we apply the n-gram segmentation method to this task. This method avoids the problem of exact match based on keywords. The segmentation of the sentence can be calculated by editing distance, cosine similarity and Jaccard coefficients to calculate the degree of similarity of the sentence; the data is cleaned to achieve fuzzy matching. For example, Fig. 4 shows an example of 4-gram. In the experiments, the n is set empirically.

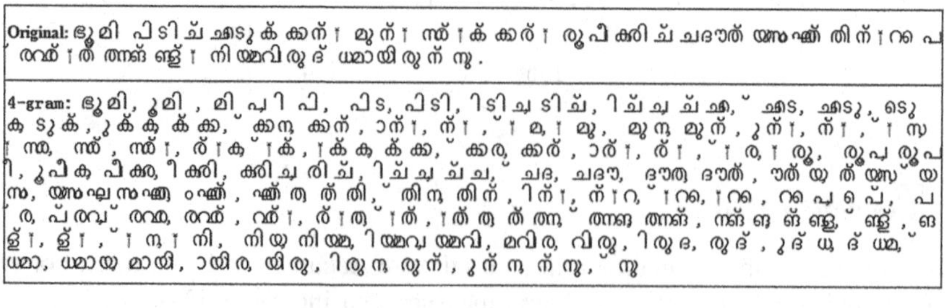

Fig. 4. The example of 4-gram

Parameter Tuning

In this experiment, we compared a number of different supervised classification methods. The supervised method include: Gradient Tree Boosting, Support Vector Machines, KNN, and Decision Trees. This section briefly describes the parameter settings for several classification methods, as shown in Table 4.

Table 4. Parameter information of classification model

Shorter form	Full name	Parameter
GTB	Gradient tree boosting	loss = 'deviance', learning_rate = 0.1 min_samples_split = 2, n_estimators in task1: 55 (Malayalam), 20 (Tamil), 45 (Hindi), 10 (Punjabi); n_estimators In task2: 40 (Malayalam), 20 (Tamil), 45 (Hindi), 25 (Punjabi)
KNN	K-Nearest neighbor	n_neighbors = 5, weights = 'uniform', leaf_size = 30, p = 2, metric = 'minkowski', n_jobs = 1
DT	Decision trees	criterion = 'gini', splitter = 'best', max_depth = None, min_samples_split = 2, min_samples_leaf = 1, min_impurity_split = 1e-07
SVM	Support vector machines	C = 1.0, kernel = 'rbf', degree = 3, shrinking = True, tol = 0.001, cache_size = 200

In the parameter adjustment experiments, the training data set were randomly divided into two parts, as training data, as another part of the test data. When the classification method is a Gradient Tree Boosting, we adjust the value of the parameter n_estimators in four languages according to the training data set. The parameter n_estimators is the number of iterations in the model boosting phase. For the other parameters of the classification model involved in Table 3, see default values in sklearn.

4.5 Experimental Results

The experimental results are divided into two parts:

In the first part, we show and analyze several classification methods in four languages respectively on the accuracy and F1. In the second part, we show the results of our work in the FIRE2016 @ DPIL task and compare the results of some best teams.

As can be seen from Table 5, in task1, the difference of highest F1 Measure of all kinds of language between the four Classification models is not obvious, except for DT. GTB and SVM achieved the best performance accuracy (0.91) and F1 Measure (0.93) in general, but the performance difference between the two is not obvious. The accuracy and F1 Measure have the same distribution.

As can be seen from Table 6, the score of GTB in task 2 is generally higher than other classification models, accuracy (0.80), F1 (0.80).The accuracy and F1 Measure also have the same distribution. So GTB is better in generalization performance.

The experimental results of the evaluation corpus.

Table 5. Comparisons of different classification model on task1

Task1	Accuracy					F1 measure				
	Mal	Tam	Hin	Pun	All	Mal	Tam	Hin	Pun	All
GTB	0.8906	0.9502	0.9003	0.9908	0.9133	0.9105	0.9581	0.9173	0.9922	0.9286
KNN	0.8979	0.9494	0.9010	0.9899	0.9052	0.9165	0.9580	0.9178	0.9913	0.9216
DT	0.8531	0.9278	0.8653	0.9852	0.8668	0.8771	0.9395	0.8866	0.9875	0.8875
SVM	0.8958	0.9550	0.9080	0.9925	0.9134	0.9174	0.9625	0.9256	0.9937	0.9290

Table 6. Comparisons of different classification model on task2

Task2	Accuracy					F1 measure				
	Mal	Tam	Hin	Pun	All	Mal	Tam	Hin	Pun	All
GTB	0.7222	0.7863	0.8440	0.9835	0.8034	0.7275	0.7888	0.8437	0.9834	0.8059
KNN	0.7133	0.7771	0.8399	0.9849	0.7814	0.7178	0.7821	0.8401	0.9849	0.7833
DT	0.6439	0.7184	0.7849	0.9746	0.7221	0.6430	0.7191	0.7849	0.9746	0.7218
SVM	0.7373	0.7889	0.8269	0.9624	0.7933	0.7456	0.7948	0.8301	0.9627	0.7985

In the FIRE2016 @ DPIL task, we chose the Gradient Tree Boosting model. Table 6 shows the experimental results published excerpts from FIRE2016 party evaluation of participating teams in relatively good few participating teams. Our team is HIT2016. From Table 7, we can easily observe the performance differences of each team.

As can be seen from Table 7, our method in this evaluation task has made three languages first. The experimental results show that the GTB method has achieved the best Accuracy in Malayalam in Task 1 and Malayalam, Tamil, Punjabi in Task 2. The method achieves the best F1 index in Malayalam, Tamil in Task 1 and Task 2 and Punjabi in Task 2.

Table 7. Experimental results on DPIL@FIRE2016

Team	Accuracy				F1 measure			
	Mal	Tam	Hin	Pun	Mal	Tam	Hin	Pun
(a) Task1 sub corpus								
HIT2016	0.8377	0.8211	0.8966	0.9440	0.8100	0.7900	0.8900	0.9400
KS_JU	0.8100	0.7888	0.9066	0.9460	0.7900	0.7500	0.9000	0.9500
NIT-MZ	0.8344	0.8333	0.9155	0.9420	0.7900	0.7900	0.9100	0.9400
JU-NLP	0.5900	0.5755	0.8222	0.9420	0.1600	0.0900	0.7400	0.9400
Anuj	-	-	0.9200	-	-	-	0.9100	-
NLP@KEC	-	0.8233	-	-	-	0.7900	-	-
(b) Task2 sub corpus								
HIT2016	0.7486	0.7550	0.9000	0.9226	0.7460	0.7398	0.8984	0.9230
KS_JU	0.6614	0.6735	0.8521	0.8960	0.6578	0.6645	0.8482	0.8960
NLP-NITMZ	0.6243	0.6571	0.7857	0.8120	0.6068	0.6307	0.7642	0.8086
JU-NLP	0.4221	0.5507	0.6857	0.8866	0.3078	0.4319	0.6841	0.8866
Anuj	-	-	0.9014	-	-	-	0.9000	-
NLP@KEC	-	0.6857	-	-	-	0.6674	-	-

Effect of word segmentation

For the word segmentation, we utilize two processing methods. One is based on the space to do the word segmentation, and the other is based on n-gram.

On the n-gram word segmentation, we selected N from 1 to 10, the results shown in Fig. 5. The experimental results show that when N is 4, the experiment will get a better performance.

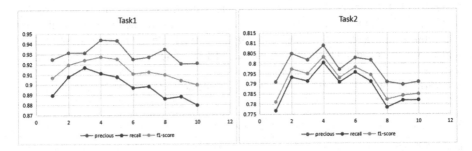

Fig. 5. Comparison of different N-gram in task2

In order to facilitate the observation, we only show the results of the two different pretreatment on the GTB model. We compare the two kinds of word segmentation methods in Table 8.

From Table 8, we can observe the result of two kinds of pretreatment methods is not much difference. But from the Malayalam language can be seen clearly, the n-gram method is better than method of space. In task1, the Best F1 performance of Malayalam is 0.91, and in task2, F1 performance of Malayalam is 0.73. Overall, the n-gram method is slightly better than the space, so we use n-gram method in the experiments to deal with the India corpus.

Table 8. Comparison of two different preprocessing

	4-gram				Space segmentation			
	Mal	Tam	Hindi	Pun	Mal	Tam	Hindi	Pun
Task1								
Precision	0.8993	0.9587	0.9235	0.9884	0.8771	0.9543	0.9340	0.9911
Recall	0.9301	0.9606	0.9187	0.9921	0.9279	0.9574	0.9289	0.9921
Accuracy	0.8957	0.9517	0.9054	0.9885	0.8785	0.9469	0.9178	0.9901
F1	0.9143	0.9596	0.9210	0.9902	0.9017	0.9558	0.9314	0.9916
Task2								
Precision	0.7298	0.7873	0.8499	0.9810	0.7135	0.7917	0.8553	0.9814
Recall	0.7370	0.7918	0.8484	0.9808	0.7227	0.7949	0.8545	0.9813
Accuracy	0.7370	0.7918	0.8484	0.9808	0.7227	0.7949	0.8545	0.9813
F1	0.7309	0.7878	0.8483	0.9808	0.7134	0.7923	0.8541	0.9813

5   Conclusions

In the field of natural language processing, paraphrase detection is a very challenging task. In this study, we selected feature sets based on the lexical features operated at n-gram, and use four classification models to verify whether the feature set is valid, such as: Gradient Tree Boosting, SVM, KNN, and DT. From the results, the feature is very competitive. In general, the performance of the GTB method is superior to other methods, and the core of the method is that each iteration is based on the last residual drop. So we chose the GTB method as our model, and we used the model to get the first of the three languages in FIRE2016 @ DPIL. Overall, the approach was very competitive and achieved the highest Accuracy and F1 measure among all task participants.

Acknowledgments. This work is supported by Social Science Fund of Heilongjiang Province (NO. 16XWB02).

References

1. Huang, E.: Paraphrase detection using recursive autoencoder (2011). http://nlp.stanford.edu/courses/cs224n/2011/reports/ehhuang.pdf
2. Anand Kumar, M., Singh, S., Kavirajan, B., et al.: DPIL@FIRE2016: overview of shared task on detecting paraphrases in Indian Languages. In: Working notes of FIRE 2016–Forum for Information Retrieval Evaluation, Kolkata, India, 7–10 December 2016
3. Alzahrani, S.M., Salim, N., Abraham, A.: Understanding plagiarism linguistic patterns, textual features, and detection methods. IEEE Trans. Syst. Man Cybern. Part C (Appl. Rev.) **42**(2), 133–149 (2012)
4. Banerjee, S., Lavie, A.: METEOR: an automatic metric for MT evaluation with improved correlation with human judgments. In: Proceedings of the ACL Workshop on Intrinsic and Extrinsic Evaluation Measures for Machine Translation and/or Summarization, vol. 29, pp. 65–72 (2005)
5. McClendon, J.L., Mack, N.A., Hodges, L.F.: The use of paraphrase identification in the retrieval of appropriate responses for script based conversational agents. In: FLAIRS Conference (2014)
6. Dolan, W.B., Brockett, C.: Automatically constructing a corpus of sentential paraphrases. In: Proceedings of IWP (2005)
7. Lintean, M., Rus, V.: Paraphrase identification using weighted dependencies and word semantics. In: Twenty-Second International FLAIRS Conference (2009)
8. Socher, R., Huang, E.H., Pennin, J., et al.: Dynamic pooling and unfolding recursive autoencoders for paraphrase detection. In: Advances in Neural Information Processing Systems, pp. 801–809 (2011)
9. Hu, B., Lu, Z., Li, H., et al.: Convolutional neural network architectures for matching natural language sentences. In: Advances in Neural Information Processing Systems, pp. 2042–2050 (2014)
10. Fernando, S., Stevenson, M.: A semantic similarity approach to paraphrase detection. In: Proceedings of the 11th Annual Research Colloquium of the UK Special Interest Group for Computational Linguistics, pp. 45–52 (2008)

11. Rus, V., McCarthy, P.M., Lintean, M.C., McNamara, D.S., Graesser, A.C.: Paraphrase identification with lexico-syntactic graph subsumption. In: FLAIRS Conference, pp. 201–206 (2008)
12. Saini, A., Gurgaon, H.: Anuj@DPIL-FIRE2016: a novel paraphrase detection method in Hindi Language using machine learning. In: FIRE (Working Notes), pp. 270–274 (2016)
13. Sarkar, K.: KS_JU@DPIL-FIRE2016: detecting paraphrases in Indian Languages using multinomial logistic regression model. arXiv preprint arXiv:1612.08171 (2016)
14. Thangarajan, R., Kogilavani, S.V., Karthic, A., et al.: KEC@ DPIL-FIRE2016: detection of paraphrases on Indian Languages (2016)
15. Sarkar, S., Saha, S., Bentham, J., et al.: NLP-NITMZ@DPIL-FIRE2016: Language independent paraphrases detection. In: FIRE (Working Notes), pp. 256–259 (2016)
16. Friedl, M.A., Brodley, C.E.: Decision tree classification of land cover from remotely sensed data. Remote Sens. Environ. **61**(3), 399–409 (1997)
17. Peterson, L.E.: K-nearest neighbor. Scholarpedia **4**(2), 1883 (2009)
18. Wu, T.F., Lin, C.J., Weng, R.C.: Probability estimates for multi-class classification by pairwise coupling. J. Mach. Learn. Res. **5**(Aug), 975–1005 (2004)
19. Friedman, J.H.: Greedy function approximation: a gradient boosting machine. Ann. Stat. 1189–1232 (2001)
20. Friedman, J.H.: Stochastic gradient boosting. Comput. Stat. Data Anal. **38**(4), 367–378 (2002)
21. Li, H.: Statistical learning methods. Tsinghua University Press, Beijing (2012). (in Chinese)
22. Li, C., Lu, J., Lu, Y.: Efficient merging and filtering algorithms for approximate string searches. In: ICDE, pp. 257–266 (2008)
23. Wang, J., Li, G., Feng, J.: Fast-join: an efficient method for fuzzy token matching based string similarity join. In: ICDE, pp. 458–469 (2011)

Feature Engineering and Characterization of Classifiers for Consumer Health Information Search

D. Thenmozhi$^{(\boxtimes)}$, P. Mirunalini, and Chandrabose Aravindan

Department of Computer Science and Engineering, SSN College of Engineering,
Kalavakkam, Chennai, India
{theni_d,miruna,aravindanc}@ssn.edu.in

Abstract. Health information search (HIS) is the process of seeking health awareness information on the Internet by health professionals and consumers. Identifying whether the retrieved text is relevant to consumer query and identifying whether it supports, opposes or is neutral to the claim made by the query are challenging tasks in HIS. In this paper, we present our methodology to address these two tasks using supervised learning approaches by performing feature engineering and characterization of classifiers. We have used seven variations including an ensembling approach and hierarchical boosting by incorporating statistical feature selection to different set of features and have determined the best solutions to the two tasks. We have evaluated our methods using CHIS@FIRE2016 data set. We have obtained accuracies of 82.4% for the first challenge using hierarchical boosting and 61.48% for the second using ensembling method. These results are promising when compared with those of other systems.

Keywords: Consumer Health Information Search · Machine learning
Classification · Feature selection · Hierarchical boosting

1 Introduction

Information retrieval (IR) is the process of obtaining information relevant to a given query from a collection of resources. The Internet is a major source for retrieving information for all domains. Health care is one of the domains where health professionals and consumers seek for information from the Internet. Consumer Health Information Search (CHIS) is the process of retrieving health related information from the Internet by common people to get some health awareness information. The existing search engines retrieve information based on keywords resulting in a large number of irrelevant information which may not satisfy CHIS users. For example, if a user wants to know whether a carrot is helpful for eye sight, he/she may pose a query "carrot improves eye sight" to search engines. However, all the information retrieved by a search engine may not satisfy his/her need. Hence, it is necessary for an information retrieval system

© Springer International Publishing AG 2018
P. Majumder et al. (Eds.): FIRE 2016 Workshop, LNCS 10478, pp. 182–196, 2018.
https://doi.org/10.1007/978-3-319-73606-8_14

to extract only relevant information for the user. Further, identifying whether such relevant information support or oppose the user query is also an important task.

Surveys on CHIS related work have been reported by Cline et al. [3], Zhang et al. [30] and Fiksdal et al. [4]. They have analyzed diverse purposes and diverse users on CHIS. Goeuriot et al. [5] analyzed the CHIS users based on varying information needs, varying medical knowledge and varying language skills. However, different kinds of users seek for health related information from the Web by posing different types of queries. The retrieval performance may be improved by assisting the consumers to reformulate the query with more precise and domain specific terms [17,26,28], and by categorizing the retrieved information into relevant or irrelevant [12].

In this work, we have focused on the shared task of CHIS@FIRE2016 [16] which aims to identify a text as relevant or irrelevant for a query. CHIS@FIRE2016 is a shared task on Consumer Health Information Search (CHIS) and it is part of Forum for Information Retrieval Evaluation (FIRE). The goal of CHIS task is to research and develop techniques to support users in complex multi-perspective health information queries[1]. This shared task has two sub tasks. Given a CHIS query, and a set of text associated with that query, the first sub-task is to classify whether the sentences in the set of text are relevant to the CHIS query or not. The relevant sentences are those from that text, which are useful in providing an answer to the query. The second sub-task is to further classify the relevant sentences as supporting, opposing or neutral to the claim made by the query. Our focus is on providing best solutions to both the sub-tasks of CHIS@FIRE2016 through feature engineering and classifier characterization.

2   Related Work

Much research has been carried out in consumer health information search (CHIS) in recent years. Researchers analyzed the behaviour of the CHIS users [3,4,30] and the challenges in searching for information [5]. The query construction, query reformulation, and ranking of search result may improve the performance of CHIS. This section reviews the related work for CHIS.

2.1   Query Reformulation

Several researchers presented algorithms for reformulating queries to improve health information search. Zeng [28] recommended additional query terms by computing the semantic distance among concepts related to the user's initial query based on concept co-occurrences in the medical domain. The semantic distance is calculated based on the degree of relevance which is computed from the frequency score of concepts and their co-occurences. Soldaini et al. [17] proposed a methodology to bridge the gap between layperson and expert vocabularies by

---

[1] https://sites.google.com/site/multiperspectivehealthqa/home.

providing appropriate medical expressions for unfamiliar terms. Their approach adds the expert expression to the queries submitted by the users which they call as query clarifications. They have used a supervised approach to select the most appropriate synonym mapping for each query to improve the performance. Keselman et al. [10] supported the users with query formulation support tools and suggested additional or alternative query terms to make the query more specific. They also educate the consumers to learn medical terms by providing interactive tools. Yunzhi et al. [26] proposed a methodology for query expansion using hepatitis ontology. They compute semantic similarity using an ontology for finding the similarity of retrieval terms to improve the retrieval performance. Several researchers analyzed how consumers try to reformulate queries to improve the search performance. Toms and Latter [23] reported that consumers follow trial-and-error process to formulate queries. Sillence et al. [15] stated that the queries are reformulated using Boolean operators by the consumers to alter search terms. Many researchers [6,18,27] analyzed the behaviour of CHIS user which help to reformulate a query for improving the performance of the retrieval.

2.2 Machine Learning Approaches for Health Information Search

Several researchers used machine learning approaches in health information search. Zhang et al. [29] used a machine learning approach for rating the quality of depression treatment web pages using evidence-based health care guidelines. They used a Naive Bayes classifier to rate the web pages. Nerkar and Gharde [12] proposed a supervised approach using support vector machine to classify the semantic relations between disease and treatment. The best treatment for a disease is identified by applying a voting algorithm. Automatic mapping of concepts from text in clinical report to a reference terminology is an important task in health information search systems. Casteno et al. [2] presented a machine learning approach to normalise bio-medical terms normalization for which they used a hospital thesaurus database.

Much work has been reported on query construction and query reformulation to improve the performance of consumer health information search. However, very few works have been reported on categorizing the retrieved information into relevant or irrelevant.

2.3 Approaches Used in CHIS@FIRE2016

A total of nine teams participated in the CHIS task held at FIRE 2016. Indurthi and Oota [7] used a deep neural network over binary bag-of-phrase features for the CHIS tasks. However, they used manually selected features and hence the method may not work for other datasets. Sarkar et al. [14] implemented a support vector machine with polynomial kernel to classify the data. They used features such as part-of-speech matching and neighborhood matching for classification. However, this approach does not work well for Task 2. Jalan et al. [8] proposed a machine learning approach using several classifiers on doc2vec and tf-idf based ensemble representation of the data. Veena et al. [24] used a support-vector-machine and the features extraced by word-embedding and keyword generation techniques for classification. Sankhavara [13] and Hua Yang [25] used query expansion and ranking method for the CHIS tasks. However, these methods may not be generalizable for other queries. Barati et al. [1] used a random forest classifier by extracting distributional semantic features using the non-negative matrix factorization technique for the CHIS tasks. However, their distributional semantic representation method does not give good results due to the large dimensions of data. Thenmozhi et al. [22] proposed a decision tree approach using χ^2 feature selection for the CHIS tasks. However, they have not focused on Task 2. Suresh Kumar and Naveen [19] used average of measures namely, cosine similarity, Jaccard co-efficient and TF-IDF score to find the relevance nature for Task 1. They used n-gram features and support vector machine for Task 2 classification. However, their approach using similarity measures does not give good results.

In this paper, we aim to improve the performance of both the CHIS tasks through feature engineering and characterization of classifiers.

3   Proposed Approach

We have implemented a supervised machine learning approach for both the CHIS tasks. An overview of our approaches is given below.

- Preprocess the given text
- Extract features for training data
- Select features using χ^2 feature selection
- Build models using different classifiers
- Apply hierarchical boosting and ensembling of classifiers
- Predict class label for the test instance as "relevant" or "irrelevant" using the model. Also, predict as "support", "oppose" or "neutral" for the instance.

The steps are explained in detail in the sequel.

3.1   Feature Extraction

The given text is preprocessed before extracting the features by removing punctuations like ",", –, ',', _ and by replacing the term such as "n't" with "not", "&" with "and", "'m" with "am", and "'ll" with "will". The terms of the each sentence in the given training text are annotated with parts of speech information such as noun, verb, determiner, adjectives and adverbs. In general, keyterms/features are extracted from the noun information. However, in medical domain, adjectives may also contribute to the keyterms. For example, the sentence "Skin cancer is more common in people with light colored skin who have spent a lot of time in the sunlight." is relevant to the query "skin cancer". In this sentence, the adjective "light colored" is also important along with the nouns namely cancer, skin and sunlight to identify the sentence as relevant. Hence, all the nouns and adjectives from the training data are extracted as features. These constitute the conceptual features. We have considered all forms of nouns (NN^*) namely noun-singular (NN), noun-plural (NNS) and proper noun (NNP), and all forms of adjectives (JJ^*) namely adjective (JJ), adjective-comparative (JJR) and adjective-superlative (JJS) to extract the conceptual features. Sometimes, the relational features that are extracted from the verb parts of the text also may contribute in identifying whether a sentence is relevant to the query or not. All forms of verbs (VB^*) namely verb-base (VB), verb-third person singular-present (VBZ), verb-past (VBD) and verb-past particile (VBN) are used to extract such relational features. The extracted terms are lemmatized to bring them to their root forms. The feature set is constructed by eliminating all duplicate terms from the extracted terms.

3.2   Features Selection

The number of features extracted by our methodology may be high. All of them may not be helpful for classifications. We have used a technique which computes chi-square values for selecting the relevant features from the extracted features. This χ^2 method selects the features that have strong dependency on the categories by using the average or maximum χ^2 statistic value.

Since Task 1 has only two categories, we form a 2×2 feature-category contingency table which is called as CHI table for every feature f_i. This table is used to count the co-occurrence observed frequency (O) of f_i for every category C and $\neg C$. Each cell at position (i, j) contains the observed frequency O(i, j), where $i \in \{f_i, \neg f_i\}$ and $j \in \{C, \neg C\}$.

Similarly, for Task 2 we form a 2×3 CHI table for every feature f_i.

The expected frequencies (E) for every feature f_i, when they are assumed to be independent, can be calculated from the observed frequencies (O). The observed frequencies are compared with the expected frequencies to measure the dependency between the feature and the category. The expected frequency E(i, j) is calculated from the observed frequencies (O) using the Eq. 1 for Task 1 and Eq. 2 for Task 2.

$$E(i,\ j) = \frac{\Sigma_{a \in \{f_i, \neg f_i\}} O(a, j) \Sigma_{b \in \{C, \neg C\}} O(b, j)}{n} \tag{1}$$

where i represents whether the feature f_i is present or not, j represents whether the instance belongs to C or not, and n is the total number of instances.

The expected frequencies namely $E(f_i, C), E(f_i, \neg C), E(\neg f_i, C)$ and $E(\neg f_i, \neg C)$ are calculated using Eq. 1 for Task 1.

$$E(i,\ j) = \frac{\Sigma_{a \in \{f_i, \neg f_i\}} O(a, j) \Sigma_{b \in \{C_1, C_2, C_3\}} O(b, j)}{n} \tag{2}$$

The expected frequencies namely $E(f_i, C_1), E(f_i, C_2), E(f_i, C_3), E(\neg f_i, C_1), E(\neg f_i, C_2)$ and $E(\neg f_i, C_3)$ are calculated using Eq. 2 for Task 2.

Then the χ^2 statistical value for each feature f_i is calculated using the Eqs. 3 and 4.

$$\chi^2_{stat} f_i = \Sigma_{i \in \{f_i, \neg f_i\}} \Sigma_{j \in \{C, \neg C\}} \frac{(O(i,j) - E(i,j))^2}{E(i,j)} \tag{3}$$

$$\chi^2_{stat} f_i = \Sigma_{i \in \{f_i, \neg f_i\}} \Sigma_{j \in \{C_1, C_2, C_3\}} \frac{(O(i,j) - E(i,j))^2}{E(i,j)} \tag{4}$$

The set of features for which the χ^2_{stat} value is greater than $\chi^2_{crit(\alpha=0.05, df=1)}$: 3.841 are considered to be significant features for Task 1 and those features are selected for building a model using a classifier. The set of features for which the χ^2_{stat} value is greater than $\chi^2_{crit(\alpha=0.05, df=2)}$: 5.991 are considered to be significant features for Task 2 and those features are selected for building a model.

The process to select χ^2 features from the extracted features for Task 1 is given in Algorithm 1. The process to select χ^2 features for Task 2 is given in Algorithm 2.

Algorithm 1. χ^2 Feature Selection for Task 1

Input: Training data T, Set of features F
Output: Set of χ^2 features F_{chi_1}
1: Let Chi feature set $F_{chi_1} = \emptyset$
2: **for** (each $f_i \in F$) **do**
3:     **for** (each category $C \in [relevant, irrelevant])$ **do**
4:         Construct 2×2 feature-category contingency table (CHI table) with the observed co-occurrence frequencies (O) of f_i and C using T and F
5:         Calculate the expected frequencies (E) using CHI table
    $E(i, j) = \frac{\Sigma_{a \in \{f_i, \neg f_i\}} O(a,j) \Sigma_{b \in \{C, \neg C\}} O(b,j)}{n}$
6:         Calculate χ^2 value of f_i for C
    $\chi^2_{stat} f_i = \Sigma_{i \in \{f_i, \neg f_i\}} \Sigma_{j \in \{C, \neg C\}} \frac{(O(i,j) - E(i,j))^2}{E(i,j)}$
7:     **end for**
8:     **if** $\chi^2_{stat} f_i >= \chi^2_{crit(\alpha=0.05, df=1)}$: 3.841 **then**
9:         Add f_i to F_{chi_1}
10:     **end if**
11: **end for**
12: Return feature set F_{chi_1}

3.3   Building Models

The set of selected features along with the class labels, namely relevant and irrelevant, from training data are used to build a model using a classifier for Task 1. The features along with the class labels namely support, oppose and neutral are used to build a model for Task 2. Any well known classifier such as J48, Random Forest, Sequential minimal optimization (SMO), Naive Bayes, or Support Vector Machines (SVM) may be used to build the models.

Algorithm 2. χ^2 Feature Selection for Task 2

Input: Training data T, Set of linguistic features F
Output: Set of χ^2 features F_{chi_2}
1: Let Chi feature set $F_{chi_2} = \emptyset$
2: **for** (each $f_i \in F$) **do**
3:      **for** (each category $C \in [support, oppose, neutral]$) **do**
4:          Construct 2×3 CHI table with the observed co-occurrence frequencies (O) of f_i and C using T and F
5:          Calculate the expected frequencies (E) using CHI table
   $$E(i, \ j) = \frac{\Sigma_{a \in \{f_i, \neg f_i\}} O(a,j) \Sigma_{b \in \{C_1, C_2, C_3\}} O(b,j)}{n}$$
6:          Calculate χ^2 value of f_i for C
   $$\chi^2_{stat} f_i = \Sigma_{i \in \{f_i, \neg f_i\}} \Sigma_{j \in \{C_1, C_2, C_3\}} \frac{(O(i,j) - E(i,j))^2}{E(i,j)}$$
7:      **end for**
8:      **if** $\chi^2_{stat} f_i >= \chi^2_{crit(\alpha=0.05, df=2)} : 5.991$ **then**
9:          Add f_i to F_{chi_2}
10:     **end if** .
11: **end for**
12: Return feature set F_{chi_2}

A hierarchical boosting technique may be used to enhance the performance of the classification. In this boosting approach, a two-level classifier can be employed. In the first level, a model is built and the examples with a high confidence score (based on cross validation accuracies) are accepted. A second level model is built using only the rejected examples. A model may also be built by ensembling different classifiers in an appropriate manner after analyzing their performances using different set of features. The implementation details are provided in the next section.

4   Implementation

We have implemented several variations of our methodology in Java for the Shared Task on Consumer Health Information Search (CHIS) Tasks. The data set used to evaluate the task consists of five queries and a set of training data and test data for each query. The queries, number of training instances, and number of test instances are given in Table 1. The actual ground truth has been provided along with the data. Though not all queries are statements and also some statements may not have yes or no answers, we have considered the ground truth as such for evaluation.

We have implemented seven variations of our methodology. They are

1. Method 1: All conceptual features without feature selection
2. Method 2: Selected conceptual features with χ^2 feature selection
3. Method 3: All conceptual and relational features without feature selection
4. Method 4: Selected conceptual and relational features with χ^2 feature selection

Table 1. Data set for CHIS task

Query no.	Query	No. of sentences	
		Training	Test
Q1	Does sun exposure cause skin cancer	341	88
Q2	E-Cigarettes	413	64
Q3	Vitamin-C common cold	278	74
Q4	Women should take HRT	246	72
Q5	MMR-Vaccine lead to autism	259	58

5. Method 5: Restricted feature selection
6. Method 6: Hierarchical boosting
7. Method 7: Ensemble of Classifiers

We have annotated the given sentences using the Stanford POS tagger[2] which uses the Penn Treebank tag set. For the first variation, all forms of nouns and adjectives are considered as conceptual features. Then the features are lemmatized. We have used the Stanford lemmatizer to bring the features to their root form. Likewise, the features are extracted from all the training instances. Duplicates are eliminated to obtain a set of features for building the models.

We have used five classifiers namely J48, Random Forest, SMO, Naive Bayes, and SVM to build the models with the extracted features. To implement the classifiers, we have used the Weka API[3].

We have performed 10-fold cross validation on the training data. The cross validation accuracies for the queries are summarized in Table 3.

In the second variation, we have selected a set of features which significantly contribute to identify the classes from the conceptual features. To select the features, we have used the χ^2 method described in the previous section. We have constructed the CHI table for each feature f_i. For example, the CHI table which shows the observed frequencies for the feature "estrogen", with respect to the query "HRT" (Task 1) is given in Table 2.

Table 2. CHIS table for the feature "Estrogen" with respect to the query "HRT"

	Relevant	Irrelevant
Estrogen	39	14
¬Estrogen	167	26

The total number of training instances are 246 for the query "HRT". The expected frequencies are calculated from the CHI table values using Eq. 1.

---

[2] http://nlp.stanford.edu/software/tagger.shtml.
[3] http://www.java2s.com/Code/Jar/w/Downloadwekajar.htm.

Table 3. 10-fold cross validation accuracies (%)

Method	Query	Task 1					Task 2				
		J48	RF	SMO	NB	SVM	J48	RF	SMO	NB	SVM
Method 1	Q1	80.65	80.35	78	76.83	56.89	62.46	61.58	60.70	62.46	46.63
	Q2	69.98	74.33	69.49	70.94	70.94	53.03	61.74	60.29	61.74	39.95
	Q3	78.78	76.98	77.34	79.14	74.82	48.92	55.76	50	53.24	39.93
	Q4	85.37	86.18	86.59	82.11	83.74	54.07	63.82	56.91	58.13	55.28
	Q5	81.47	81.08	86.10	83.4	80.31	54.83	62.93	64.86	63.71	36.68
	Average	79.25	79.78	79.5	78.5	73.34	54.66	61.17	58.55	59.86	43.69
Method 2	Q1	78.59	81.23	77.13	75.37	77.71	66.28	68.03	63.05	64.52	65.17
	Q2	67.8	71.67	72.64	73.61	70.94	52.3	55.21	53.51	58.6	55.69
	Q3	82	78.42	80.22	79.5	82.37	56.12	53.25	55.04	55.04	54.68
	Q4	84.96	85.77	84.96	83.74	83.74	63	54.07	60.16	59.35	54.47
	Q5	79.15	77.99	79.54	74.52	80.31	51.74	55.6	58.69	58.30	52.9
	Average	78.5	79.08	78.9	77.35	79.01	57.89	57.23	58.09	59.16	55.98
Method 3	Q1	76.25	81.53	76.83	76.54	56.89	61.58	65.1	64.22	64.81	46.63
	Q2	69	74.09	73.12	73.37	70.94	49.64	59.56	61.26	58.35	39.95
	Q3	77.7	78.42	80.22	79.86	74.82	48.56	60.43	52.16	55.04	39.93
	Q4	88.62	86.99	89.84	81.3	83.74	51.22	60.98	60.57	60.57	55.28
	Q5	79.13	80.31	84.94	84.17	80.31	52.9	64.86	63.71	63.32	36.68
	Average	78.14	80.27	80.99	79.05	73.34	52.78	62.19	60.38	60.42	43.69
Method 4	Q1	76.25	80.65	76.54	76.54	76.54	66.86	66.86	63.34	61.29	62.46
	Q2	71.67	74.82	74.09	77.48	70.94	50.12	54.72	57.39	58.35	56.17
	Q3	82.01	78.42	79.5	79.5	79.5	55.76	53.24	56.12	56.47	55.04
	Q4	90.28	85.37	86.59	82.1	83.74	57.72	55.28	57.72	59.76	54.88
	Q5	76.83	76.83	79.54	73.36	80.31	53.28	55.98	58.69	59.46	56.37
	Average	79.41	79.22	79.25	77.8	78.21	56.75	57.22	58.65	59.07	56.98
Method 5	Q1	77.42	80.35	78.59	76.54	56.89	59.53	63.93	66.28	64.22	46.63
	Q2	70.46	75.54	73.61	74.09	70.94	52.3	61.99	63.68	62.23	39.95
	Q3	79.86	80.22	79.14	79.5	74.82	47.84	60.79	51.8	56.12	39.93
	Q4	85.37	86.99	87.4	81.3	83.74	53.25	61.38	56.5	63.82	55.28
	Q5	79.92	80.7	84.94	85.71	80.31	55.6	67.18	66.8	66.8	36.68
	Average	78.61	80.76	80.74	79.43	73.34	53.70	63.05	61.01	62.64	43.69

The expected frequencies obtained for the feature "Estrogen" are 44.0, 8.0, 161.0 and 31.0. The $\chi^2_{stat}(Estrogen)$ is computed using Eq. 2 as 6.098236 which is greater than $\chi^2_{crit(\alpha=0.05, df=1)}$: 3.841. Thus, this "Estrogen" feature is selected as a candidate feature for building a model.

The cross validation accuracy obtained by this variation for the queries are summarized in Table 3.

In our third variation, we have used all the conceptual and relational features that are extracted to build models. The cross validation accuracies for the tasks by this method using various classifiers are summarized in Table 3.

We have selected features from all the conceptual and relational features using χ^2 feature selection in the fourth variation and built models using the five classifiers. The cross validation accuracy for the tasks by this method using various classifiers are summarized in Table 3.

To eliminate some commonly used relational features which may reduce the performance of the classifiers, feature selection is done only for the relational features in the fifth variation. The cross validation accuracy for the tasks by this variation using various classifiers are summarized in Table 3.

In the hierarchical boosting approach, a model is constructed from the selected features, from which a rejection frame work is obtained by identifying the rejection rate. The rejection rate is determined from the cross validation accuracy of the training data by varying different thresholds from 0.8 to 1 at the interval 0.1. The rejection rate from cross validation accuracy with $\delta = 0.8$ is 39%, with $\delta = 0.9$ is 49% and with $\delta = 1.0$ is 81%. Hence, we have chosen $\delta = 0.8$ as the rejection rate to obtain the rejection frame work for Task 1. A second level model using J48 classifier is built using the examples rejected in the first phase. The cross validation accuracy obtained from this model for Task 1 is 85.2% which is higher than the other 5 models. However, the cross validation accuracy obtained for Task 2 is 51.7% which is lower than the other 5 models.

The class label for a test instance is predicted using the first model. If the prediction probability is more than 0.8, then the prediction is accepted, otherwise the class label is predicted using the second model.

In the seventh variation, ensemble of classifiers is done. We have implemented this variation as given below.

- Characterize the classifiers based on the first five variations.
- For each classifier,
    - measure the performance using cross validation accuracy of the training data.
    - determine the model among the five variations which gives higher cross validation accuracy.
    - predict the class labels for the test instances using that model.
- Assign final label for the test instance based on majority voting method.
    - For Task 1, the label is assigned as "relevant" if more than 2 classifiers classified the instance as "relevant", otherwise, the label is assigned as "irrelevant".
    - For Task 2, the category "support", "oppose" or "neutral" is assigned as the label for the instance if more than 2 classifiers classified into a category. When more than one category gets the majority, then the label predicted with higher confidence value will be assigned as the label for the instance.

The classifiers and the model for which they outperform are reported in Table 4.

It is observed from Table 4 that χ^2 feature selection is significantly contributing to improve the performance of all the classifiers. However, the performance of

Table 4. The models selected for ensembling

Classifiers	Model selected	
	Task 1	Task 2
J48	Method 4	Method 2
RF	Method 5	Method 5
SMO	Method 5	Method 5
NB	Method 5	Method 5
SVM	Method 2	Method 4

classifiers namely RF, SMO and NB are improved when χ^2 feature selection is applied only to the relational features, whereas J48 and NB classifiers performed better with both relational and conceptual features.

In the ensemble approach, we have used all the five models specified in Table 4 to predict the class labels of instances for both the tasks. Then the final label is assigned for the instances based on majority voting. In case of task 2, tie if any is broken based on the confidence scores of the classifiers.

5   Results and Discussion

The results obtained using all the variations of our approach for the tasks are given in this section. We have evaluated the performance of our methodologies using the metrics accuracy and class-specific F1-measures. The performance of our method with all the seven variations on evaluating with the test data for tasks 1 and 2 are shown in Tables 5 and 6 resectively.

Table 5. Results of approaches for task 1

Classifier	F1(irrelevant)	F1(relevant)	Accuracy
J48	**48.65**	85.46	81.3
RF	23.94	83.02	75.62
SMO	29.07	80.30	72.11
NB	32.94	79.65	72.35
SVM	28.38	85.63	81.48
Ensembling method	29.60	84.67	78.804
Boosting method	39.41	**86.65**	**82.372**

It is observed from Table 5 that the boosting method performs better than ensembling method in terms of Accuracy and F1 for both the classes. The boosting method also gives higher values for Accuracy and F1(relevant) than all the

Table 6. Results of approaches for task 2

Classifier	F1(oppose)	F1(support)	F1(neutral)	Accuracy
J48	37.41	37.51	26.79	52.74
RF	50.34	49.83	40.70	57.95
SMO	**55.62**	59.39	38.62	53.88
NB	45.71	54.69	34.2	53.55
SVM	30.45	41.84	38.53	49
Ensembling method	52.03	**59.87**	**41.24**	**61.48**
Boosting method	27.80	36.42	34.16	43.15

other individual classifiers. However, J48 gives higher F1 score for "irrelevant" class.

It is observed from Table 6 that the ensembling method performs better than boosting method in terms of Accuracy and F1 for all the classes namely "oppose", "support" and "neutral". The ensembling method also gives higher values for Accuracy, F1(support) and F1(neutral) than all the other individual classifiers. However, SMO gives higher F1 score for "oppose" class.

We have performed a statistical test, namely k-fold paired t-test, to show whether the improvement in performance is significant or not. The boosting method performs better than ensembling method for Task 1. However, the p-values obtained for F1(irrelevant), F1(relevant) and accuracy are 0.293051738, 0.187281861 and 0.082844 respectively which show that the improvement is not significant and hence both these methods may be used for Task 1. In the case of Task 2, the ensembling method performs better than boosting method. The p-values obtained for F1(oppose), F1(support), F1(neutral) and accuracy are 0.00882888, 0.050222055, 0.249660299 and 0.018305 respectively. This shows that

Table 7. Accuracy comparison for the tasks

Method	Accuracy	
	Task 1	Task 2
Amrita_fire_CEN [1]	68.12	38.53
JNTUH [19]	54.84	55.43
Fermi [7]	77.04	54.87
JU_KS_Group [14]	73.39	33.64
Techie challangers [8]	73.03	52.47
Amrita_cen [24]	52.47	34.64
Yang [25]	69.33	53.99
Sankhavara [13]	70.28	37.96
Our Approach	**82.4**	**61.48**

the ensembling method significantly improves the performance and hence this method may be more suitable for Task 2.

Finally, we have compared our results, in terms of accuracy, with those of other teams who have participated in CHIS@FIRE2016 task. The results are shown in Table 7, and it can be observed that our current approach outperforms the other approaches reported in the workshop.

6   Conclusions

We have presented a methodology and its variations for identifying whether the given text are relevant or irrelevant to a query in health care domain. Feature engineering has been done and performance of different classifiers with different variations of feature sets have been studied. A χ^2 feature selection method is used to select the most significant features. We have implemented five variations of our methodology based on the features used by the classifiers. The five variations are conceptual features, which include nouns and adjectives, with & without feature selection, conceptual & relational features, which include verbs also, with & without feature selection, and all the conceptual features with selected relational features. In all the variations, we have constructed feature vectors from training data and models are built using five classifiers namely J48, Random Forest, SMO, Naive Bayes, and SVM. The models are used to predict whether the test instances are "relevant" or "irrelevant" to the query or to predict whether test instances "support", "oppose" or "neutral" to the claim made by the query. In addition, we have proposed a hierarchical boosting approach and an ensembled approach which combines the best models to improve the classification performance.

We have used the data set given by CHIS@FIRE2016 shared task to evaluate our methodology. We have obtained the accuracy of 82.4% for Task 1 of CHIS@FIRE2016 shared task using hierarchical boosting approach and 61.48% for Task 2 using the ensembled approach. The boosting method in Task 1 performs better than the ensembling method in terms of accuracy and F1-score for both "irrelevant" and "relevant" classes. In Task 2, the ensembling method performs better than the boosting method in terms of accuracy and F1-score for "oppose", "support" and "neutral" classes. Statistical test, namely k-fold paired t-test, shows that the improvement in Task 1 is not significant and hence both boosting and ensembling methods may be explored further in the future for Task 1. However, the t-test shows that the ensembling method significantly improves the Task 2 performance. Also, our approach gives better performance than the other approaches reported at CHIS@FIRE2016 for both the tasks.

At present we have used POS information with χ^2 feature selection to extract and select the features respectively. Further, the features may be extracted based on the predicate information of the text [20, 21] in future. The CHIR value [9, 11] may be calculated from χ^2 value to select more relevant features. Deep learning algorithms using the word embedding techniques like Word2Vec or Glove may be explored in the future for these CHIS tasks. User profile based retrieval may also be explored.

Acknowledgments. We thank the management of SSN Institutions for funding the High Performance Computing (HPC) lab where this work is being carried out. We also thank the CHIS organizers for the data sets and the anonymous reviewers for their constructive comments and suggestions.

References

1. Barathi Ganesh, H.B., Anand Kumar, M., Soman, K.P.: Distributional semantic representation in health care text classification. In: International Conference on Forum of Information Retrieval and Evaluation, pp. 201–204. CEUR-Working Notes of FIRE (2016)
2. Castano, J., Berinsky, H., Park, H., Pérez, D., Avila, P., Gambarte, L., Benitez, S., Luna, D., Campos, F., Zanetti, S.: A machine learning approach to clinical terms normalization. In: ACL 2016, p. 1 (2016)
3. Cline, R.J., Haynes, K.M.: Consumer health information seeking on the internet: the state of the art. Health Educ. Res. **16**(6), 671–692 (2001)
4. Fiksdal, A.S., Kumbamu, A., Jadhav, A.S., Cocos, C., Nelsen, L.A., Pathak, J., McCormick, J.B.: Evaluating the process of online health information searching: a qualitative approach to exploring consumer perspectives. J. Med. Internet Res. **16**(10), e224 (2014)
5. Goeuriot, L., Jones, G.J., Kelly, L., Müller, H., Zobel, J.: Medical information retrieval: introduction to the special issue. Inf. Retr. **19**(1–2), 1–5 (2016)
6. Hong, Y., de la Cruz, N., Barnas, G., Early, E. Gillis, R.: A query analysis of consumer health information retrieval. In: Proceedings of the AMIA Symposium, p. 1046. American Medical Informatics Association (2002)
7. Indurthi, V., Oota, S.R.: Relevance detection and argumentation mining in medical domain. In: International Conference on Forum of Information Retrieval and Evaluation, pp. 214–216. CEUR-Working Notes of FIRE (2016)
8. Jalan, R.S., Priyatam, P.N., Varma, V.: Consumer health information system. In: International Conference on Forum of Information Retrieval and Evaluation, pp. 217–220. CEUR-Working Notes of FIRE (2016)
9. Janaki Meena, M., Chandran, K.: Naive Bayes text classification with positive features selected by statistical method. In: International Conference on Autonomic Computing and Communications, pp. 28–33. IEEE (2009)
10. Keselman, A., Browne, A.C., Kaufmann, D.R.: Consumer health information seeking as hypothesis testing. J. Am. Med. Inform. Assoc. **15**(4), 484–495 (2008)
11. Li, Y., Luo, C., Chung, S.M.: Text clustering with feature selection by using statistical data. IEEE Trans. Knowl. Data Eng. **20**(5), 641–652 (2008)
12. Nerkar, B.E., Gharde, S.S.: Best treatment identification for disease using machine learning approach in relation to short text. IOSR J. Comput. Eng. (IOSR-JCE) **16**(3), 5–12 (2014)
13. Sankhavara, J.: Team DA_IICT at consumer health information search@ FIRE2016. In: International Conference on Forum of Information Retrieval and Evaluation, pp. 226–227. CEUR-Working Notes of FIRE (2016)
14. Sarkar, K., Das, D., Banerjee, I., Kumari, M., Biswas, P.: JU_KS_Group@ FIRE 2016: consumer health information search. In: International Conference on Forum of Information Retrieval and Evaluation, pp. 208–213. CEUR-Working Notes of FIRE (2016)

15. Sillence, E., Briggs, P., Fishwick, L., Harris, P.: Trust and mistrust of online health sites. In: Proceedings of the SIGCHI Conference on Human Factors in Computing Systems, pp. 663–670. ACM (2004)
16. Sinha, M., Mannarswamy, S., Roy, S.: CHIS@FIRE: overview of the CHIS track on consumer health information search. In: Working Notes of FIRE 2016 - Forum for Information Retrieval Evaluation, Kolkata, India, 7–10 December 2016, pp. 193–196. CEUR Workshop Proceedings. CEUR-WS.org (2016)
17. Soldaini, L., Yates, A., Yom-Tov, E., Frieder, O., Goharian, N.: Enhancing web search in the medical domain via query clarification. Inf. Retr. J. 19(1–2), 149–173 (2016)
18. Spink, A., Yang, Y., Jansen, J., Nykanen, P., Lorence, D.P., Ozmutlu, S., Ozmutlu, H.C.: A study of medical and health queries to web search engines. Health Inf. Libr. J. 21(1), 44–51 (2004)
19. Suresh Kumar, S., Naveen, L.: Relevance and support calculation for health information. In: International Conference on Forum of Information Retrieval and Evaluation, pp. 205–207. CEUR-Working Notes of FIRE (2016)
20. Thenmozhi, D., Aravindan, C.: An automatic and clause based approach to learn relations for ontologies. Comput. J. 59(6), 889–907 (2016)
21. Thenmozhi, D., Aravindan, C.: Paraphrase identification by using clause based similarity features and machine translation metrics. Comput. J. 59(9), 1289–1302 (2016)
22. Thenmozhi, D., Mirunalini, P., Aravindan, C.: Decision tree approach for consumer health information search. In: International Conference on Forum of Information Retrieval and Evaluation, pp. 221–225. CEUR-Working Notes of FIRE (2016)
23. Toms, E.G., Latter, C.: How consumers search for health information. Health Inform. J. 13(3), 223–235 (2007)
24. Veena, P.V., Remmiya Devi, G., Anand Kumar, M., Soman, K.P.: AMRITA_CEN@ FIRE 2016: consumer health information search using keyword and word embedding features. In: International Conference on Forum of Information Retrieval and Evaluation, pp. 197–200. CEUR-Working Notes of FIRE (2016)
25. Yang, H., Gonlves, T.: UEVORA@ 2016 FIRE CHIS. In: International Conference on Forum of Information Retrieval and Evaluation, pp. 228–232. CEUR-Working Notes of FIRE (2016)
26. Yunzhi, C., Huijuan, L., Shapiro, L., Travillian, R.S., Lanjuan, L.: An approach to semantic query expansion system based on hepatitis ontology. J. Biol. Res.-Thessaloniki 23(1), 11 (2016)
27. Zeng, Q., Kogan, S., Ash, N., Greenes, R., Boxwala, A.: Characteristics of consumer terminology for health information retrieval. Methods Inf. Med. 41(4), 289–298 (2002)
28. Zeng, Q.T.: Assisting consumer health information retrieval with query recommendations. J. Am. Med. Inform. Assoc. 13(1), 80–90 (2006)
29. Zhang, Y., Cui, H., Burkell, J., Mercer, R.E.: A machine learning approach for rating the quality of depression treatment web pages. In: iConference 2014 Proceedings (2014)
30. Zhang, Y., Wang, P., Heaton, A., Winkler, H.: Health information searching behavior in MedlinePlus and the impact of tasks. In: Proceedings of the 2nd ACM SIGHIT International Health Informatics Symposium, pp. 641–650. ACM (2012)

Identification of Relevance and Support
for Consumer Health Information

Suresh Kumar Sanampudi[1(✉)] and Naveen Kumar Laskari[2]

[1] Jawaharlal Nehru Technological University Hyderabad, Hyderabad, India
sureshsanampudi@jntuh.ac.in
[2] BVRIT College of Engineering for Women, Hyderabad, India

Abstract. With a rapid growth of queries posted for the search on internet that were related to medical information raised the need of acquiring the right and relevant information related to those queries. The information systems available at present are providing the documents that matches the user query, but to check whether they really matches the queries is becoming a difficult task for the layman. This is because the consumer does not have any knowledge related to Medical records and its nomenclature. Consumer Health Information Search (CHIS) is a track organized to cater the need of medical information search. As a part of this track two tasks were designed. (1) Given a query and a document containing a set of sentences, the task is to identify whether the sentence selected is relevant/irrelevant to the query posted. (2) To identify whether the sentence selected from the document is supporting the query or opposing the query or is in neutral state. The solution of Task_1 is achieved by selecting the similarity scores as a feature. The mean of this similarity scores were computed to identify the relevant nature of the sentence to the query. Task 2 is viewed as a multiple classification problem and is solved by making use of C-Support Vector Machine Classifier. The model was tested on data set provided by the CHIS track organizers. The results obtained by our model that was designed for task_1 were not to the satisfactory level when compared to the results of other track participants. For Task 2 C-support vector machine model is applied. In that Tf-idf score is used as a feature for the model. Results obtained for task_2 obtained the highest accuracy scores when compared with the other models submitted by different participants of the track.

Keywords: C-support vector machines · Cosine similarity
Jaccard co-efficient · Semantic similarity · Tf-Idf

1 Introduction

As a part of satisfying the information need of medical related queries posted by a consumer, a track was designed by the name consumer health information search (CHIS) in the forum for information retrieval extraction (FIRE) 2016. CHIS track include two subtasks to perform. The first task involves the identification of relevant nature of the sentence with that of the given query.

P. Majumder et al. (Eds.): FIRE 2016 Workshop, LNCS 10478, pp. 197–205, 2018.
https://doi.org/10.1007/978-3-319-73606-8_15

For example:

Q1:   *Can e-cigarettes cause lung cancer.*

S1:   *Using electronic cigarettes has the same short-term effects on the lungs as smoking conventional tobacco cigarettes, a study finds.*

S2:   *Toxicologists view drops in the gas as a marker of inflammation that signals airway damage.*

Given a query Q1 and the set of sentences, the task is to identify whether the sentences S1 and S2 are relevant to the given query or not. In the given sentences S1 is relevant to the Query Q1 while the S2 is not relevant. To identify this it requires to hypothesize whether the obtained search results are relevant or not which intern is a frustrating action to do it manually.

The solution to this task is identified by using various similarity measures to see how relevant a sentence is for a given query. Different similarity measures [4–6] have been used to solve the problem defined in task_1. The several similarity Scores were computed between the query and sentences given in the document collection. The average of these scores were identified. A threshold is fixed at a value which was decided after analyzing the scores obtained for different sentences and based on that it is decided whether the sentence is relevant to query or not.

Once the relevant nature of the sentence is obtained by task 1, while the second task identifies the support nature of the sentence with that of the given query. It identifies whether the retrieved sentence is supporting the query or opposing the query or neutral to it.

For example:

S3:   *Physicians were more likely to recommend e-cigarettes when their patients asked about them, or when the physician believed e-cigarettes were safer than smoking standard cigarettes.*

S4:   *Last week, researchers reported that smoking e-cigarettes provides more toxins than real cigarettes.*

S5:   *Safety and risks associated with the e-cigarettes were always a topic of discussion since it was first launched in the Chinese markets in 2004.*

Obtained the relevant sentences S3, S4 and S5, the task lies in classifying which of these sentences are supporting the Query Q1 positively and Opposing the Query or acting Neutral to Q1. The solution to this problem is viewed as a multiple classification problem which needs to categorize the sentence into three classes, i.e., positive/negative/neutral. This problem is solved by making use of C-support vector classification technique. Tf-Idf score is used as a feature component to derive feature vector. Radial bias Function (RBF) kernel is used that make use of two parameters C and γ. The best values for parameters C and γ are obtained using cross validation by performing grid search. The model designed was used on training data to fix the values which are further used on test data to predict the classes.

The remaining part of the paper is ordered as follows. Section 2 discuss about methods used to find the relevance computation between the query and the sentence given int the document collection. Section 3 elucidate implementation of achieving the support nature of a relevant sentence with respect to that of a given query. Section 4 elaborates the dataset provided. Section 5 concludes the paper.

2 Relevance Identification

Given a CHIS query and a set of sentences associated with the query, the task is to identify whether these sentences are relevant/irrelevant to the query. The solution to this task was obtained by computing various similarity measures between the given query and the sentence collection. Similarity between query and sentence collection was computed both in syntactic and semantic aspect. The similarity measure reflects the degree of closeness or separation of the target objects. Choosing an appropriate similarity measure was important for information retrieval task. In general, similarity measures plot the distance or similarity between the symbolic descriptions of two objects into a single numeric value [5]. Solution to CHIS task-1 is designed using cosine similarity, Jaccard coefficient, TF-IDF similarity which gave relevance with respect to syntactic nature of sentence and word overlapping in order to find semantical relevance. These similarity measures were explained in the following subsections.

2.1 Cosine Similarity

Cosine similarity is a measure computed by representing sentences and query are represented as term vectors. The bag-of-words were used as feature selection for finding the similarity. The cosine similarity is quantified as cosine angle between the query and a sentences vector. Cosine similarity is the most widespread similarity measures applied to check similarity between a pair of textual information.

Given a Sentence collection (S) and query (Q), the similarity coefficient between them is computed using following formula:

$$SC1\left(\vec{S}, \vec{Q}\right) = \frac{\vec{S} \cdot \vec{Q}}{|\vec{S}| \times |\vec{Q}|} \tag{1}$$

Where $\vec{S}$ *and* $\vec{Q}$ are vector representation of sentence and query.

2.2 Jaccard Coefficient

Jaccard coefficient is a measure that identifies the similarity measures between finite sample sets. It is defined as the cardinality of the intersection of sets divided by the cardinality of the union of the sample sets [3]. For text similarity Jaccard coefficient compares the sum of weight of shared terms to the sum of weights terms that are present in either of the document but are not shared terms. The formal definition is:

$$SC2\left(\vec{S}, \vec{Q}\right) = \frac{\vec{S} \cdot \vec{Q}}{|\vec{S}|^2 + |\vec{Q}|^2 - \vec{S} \cdot \vec{Q}} \tag{2}$$

Where $\vec{S}$ *and* $\vec{Q}$ are vector representation of sentence and query.

2.3   Tf-Idf Score

Term Frequency-Inverse Document frequency (Tf-Idf) measures are a broad class of functions that uses frequency of word occurrences as a feature vector which are used to compute the similarity of the sentences with that of given query. The basic idea is that, if a word appears most frequently in text then the word is most indicative towards the topicality of the text. The less frequently a word appears in a document collection, the greater is its power to categorize between relevant or irrelevant.

The similarity function:

$$SC3(S, Q) = \sum_{w \in Q \cap R} \log\left(tf_{w,Q} + 1\right) \log(tf_{w,S} + 1) \log\left(\frac{N+1}{df_w + 0.5}\right) \tag{3}$$

Where $tf_{w,Q}$ is the number of times word w appears in query sentence Q; $tf_{w,S}$ is the number of times word w appears in sentence S; N is the total number of sentences in the collection; and df_w is the number of sentences that w appears in.

2.4   Word Overlapping

Word overlapping is a measure used to find the semantical relevance of a sentence with that of given query. To compute the similarity score for each sentence, a raw semantic vector is derived with the help of lexical database; and also a word order vector is formed for each of the sentences using the same information from lexical database. Each word in a sentence contributes differently to the complete meaning of the whole sentence, the importance of a word is weighted by using information content obtained by combining the raw semantic information from the dataset, a semantic vector is found for each of the two sentences [3]. Semantic similarity is computed based on the two semantic vectors. A word order similarity is computed using two word order vectors. Finally, the overall similarity is derived by combining word order similarity and semantic similarity and thus obtained score was given an id as SC4.

The mean of these scores were computed as follows:

$$SC(Q, S) = \frac{SC1 + SC2 + SC3 + SC4}{4} \tag{4}$$

The mean of all these score were calculated, after analyzing the scores obtained for each of the sentences. A threshold is fixed at a point to create the boundary. The sentences that fall above the boundary are treated as relevant and others as irrelevant to the given query.

3   Support Classification

A heaps of information is available from various sources in diverse nature. Categorizing the obtained information becomes very difficult task. Task 2 of the CHIS track aims to identify whether the information obtained is supporting or opposing or neutral to the user query.

Identification of support of a sentence towards the query is viewed as a three class problem where the sentence has to be classified under any one of the three class labels namely "support", "oppose", "neutral". The model designed make use of C-Support Vector Classifier (C-SVM) which was a special class of support vector machines that uses "C Factor" for multi class problem. Basically support vector machine is a binary classifier but to obtain the class of "neutral" a special category of C-SVM is used from libsvm [7] package. The goal of the classifier is to build a model based on the training data which can be viewed for prediction on the test data.

The model of C-SVM is designed as follows:

1. Identification of feature vector using Tf-Idf.
2. Radial Bias Function (RBF) kernel is used.
3. Grid search is used to find C and γ values.
4. 15-fold cross validation is done to find best C and γ values.
5. Obtained C and γ values are used to train the entire training data set.
6. Fit the model to prediction on test data set.

The first step of C-SVM used frequency of word occurrence to build the feature vector. The next step identified whether the feature should be made of a word or with a character of n-gram. The lower and upper boundary of the range of n-values were extracted for different n-grams for all values of n such that n lies between $min\_n \leq n \leq max\_n$. Building a vocabulary that consider top max_features ordered by term frequency across the dataset. Next a learning method was applied to learn vocabulary, IDF and return term document matrix.

We have used parameters C and γ as penalty parameter of the error term. Kernel type used is Radial Basis function (RBF). When training C-SVM with RBF kernel, the parameters required is C. Lower the value of C makes the decision boundary. Grid search is used to find the better C and γ values. Coarse grid first technique is used to find the better region on the grid. After finding the best (C, γ) values the whole data set was trained on the training data set to obtain the final classifier. C-SVM method makes use of fit function to perform probability prediction on test data set.

C-SVM is considered as supervised learning task, in which a model is built to learn from the training data and to predict the class label for the unseen data. Support Vectors constructs a hyperplane or set of hyperplanes in high dimensional space which is used for identification of support [1, 2].

4 Working Model

A model was provided for the CHIS track related tasks. Figure 1 explains the overall process performed to implement the process involved in each task.

The steps followed to complete the implementation of CHIS task1 were as follows, where the user accepts the set of training document as input. On the given inputs pre-processing steps were applied. The pre-processing steps include stop word elimination and case conversion before performing actual tasks of CHIS.

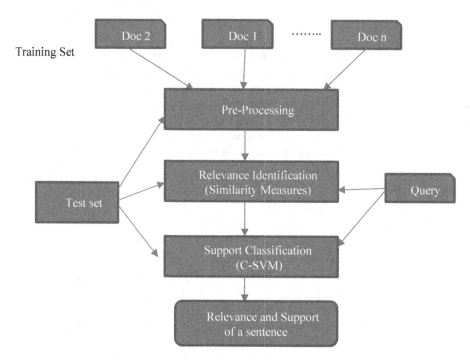

Fig. 1. Working model for tasks defined in CHIS track

Thus pre-processed data is used for Relevance identification task that find whether a given sentence is relevant/irrelevant to the query. To achieve this task, similarity measure between the given query and each sentence from the document collection is computed using the techniques namely cosine similarity, Jaccard coefficient, TF-IDF similarity and semantic similarity using word overlapping. The overall similarity is considered as the average of the above all similarity measures. After computing the overall similarity between each pair of query and sentence from the document collection, a threshold value is fixed at a certain point. If the similarity measure exceeds the threshold value, then the sentence in the document collection is considered as relevant else it is considered as irrelevant.

After finding the relevant nature of the sentence, these sentences are given for support calculation that is done by C-Support Vector Machine (C-SVM) classifier to predict the class label for the test data. It make use of term frequency to frame the feature vector. v-Fold cross validation with grid search are used to find the effective C and γ parameters. These parameters are used to train the model which further helps in predicting the test data.

5   Results

In order to implement the tasks provided in CHIS track, the organizing committee has been given with training dataset of five documents consisting of 400 sentences approximately in each document. Five queries were given that relates to at least one of the document. Training dataset consisting of total of three attributes, in which attribute1 consists of sentence, attribute2 consists of relevant or irrelevant and attribute3 consists of polarity of the sentence towards the query as oppose, support or neutral. Figure 2 gives an overall statistical summary of the training data set.

The given queries were as below:

1. Can e-cigarettes cause lung cancer?
2. Can Vitamin C prevent common cold?
3. Does Sun exposure cause skin cancer?
4. MMR vaccine leads to Austin?
5. Women should Take HRT_Post Menopause?

Query	Support	Oppose	Neutral
E-cigarettes are safer than normal cigarettes (EC)	93	165	155
Sun exposure leads to skin cancer (SC)	105	78	158
Vitamin C prevents common cold (VC)	111	68	99
Women should take HRT post menopause (HR)	42	136	68
MMR vaccine can cause autism (MR)	72	94	93

Fig. 2. Statistical summary of CHIS training data set

The test dataset is given in five different files each of which consists of around 80 sentences to check relevant or irrelevant to the query and for checking polarity of each sentence. The statistical summary of the test data is provided in the Fig. 3.

query	total	support	oppose	neutral
ecig	64	21	15	28
Sun exposure	88	34	3	51
Vitamin C	74	19	21	34
HRT	72	31	20	21
MMR	58	17	32	9

Fig. 3. Statistical summary of CHIS test data set

The model with the name JNTUH was developed for task 1 and task 2 and were evaluated by the CHIS organizers. The results of accuracy were compared with the accuracy obtained by the models submitted by other team members for the same task.

The comparative results for task 1 were shown in the table shown in Fig. 4 and the comparative results for task 2 were shown in the table shown in Fig. 5.

TASK 1										
Task 1										
Query		Amrita_fire_CEN	JNTUH	Fermi	JU_KS_Group	Techie challangers	SSN_NLP	Amrita_cen	Hua Yang	Jainisha Sankhavara
skincare		54.54545455	62.5	78.4	48.86363636	68.18181818	79.54545455	48.86363636	53.40909091	52.27272727
MMr		87.93103448	56.8965517	79.31	89.65517241	87.93103448	81.03448276	88.88888889	84.48275862	87.93103448
HRT		70.83333333	38.8888889	88.88	93.05555556	75	87.5	75.86206897	90.27777778	91.66666667
Ecig		71.875	57.8125	65.62	71.875	71.875	64.0625	76.5625	46.875	54.6875
Vitc		55.40540541	58.1081081	72.97	63.51351351	62.16216216	78.37837838	60.81081081	71.62162162	64.86486486
		68.11804555	54.8412097	77.036	73.39257557	73.03000297	78.10416314	70.19758101	69.33324979	70.28455866

Fig. 4. Comparative results for task 1

Task 2										
Query		Amrita_fire_CEN	JNTUH	Fermi	JU_KS_Group	Techie challangers	SSN_NLP	Amrita_cen	Hua Yang	Jainisha Sankhavara
skincare		56.81818182	64.7727273	73.8	44.31818182	62.5	0	23.86363636	46.59090909	37.5
MMr		32.75862069	65.5172414	44.82	32.75862069	68.96551724	0	34.72222222	63.79310345	46.55172414
HRT		26.38888889	48.6111111	54.16	22.22222222	37.5	0	43.10344828	48.61111111	27.77777778
Ecig		37.5	67.1875	51.56	29.6875	60.9375	0	39.0625	60.9375	46.875
Vitc		39.18918919	31.0810811	50	39.18918919	32.43243243	0	32.43243243	50	31.08108108
		38.53097612	55.4339322	54.868	33.63514278	52.46708993	0	34.63684786	53.98652473	37.9571166

Fig. 5. Comparative results for task 2

On comparing the results in Fig. 4, it is shown that the model developed for task 1 has resulted a poor accuracy of 54.84% which gave least performance when compared with accuracy obtained for others model. The analysis of the results obtained for task 1made it evident that the similarity score does not work for simple/small query. In general the feature of similarity scores work well for complex or large size queries. Figure 5 shown that comparative results of the model developed for task_2. The C-SVM classifier has resulted in a higher accuracy level of 55.43% which resulted in the top position when compared with the accuracy obtained by other models submitted for task 2.

6   Conclusion

Consumer Health Information Search (CHIS) was a track organized in FIRE 2016 that consist of two tasks for competition. Task 1 is to identify whether the retrieved sentence is relevant/irrelevant to the query. Task 2 is to calculate the support (support/oppose/ neutral) of the sentence with respect to the query. A framework has been designed to achieve this tasks. Task 1 is solved by computing several similarity measures that finds the syntactic and semantic similarity between the sentences retrieved for the given query. The relevant sentences retrieved need to be further classified as support/oppose/ neutral towards the given query needs to be achieved in task 2. To achieve task 2 a special type of C-support vector classification is used. It uses a Tf_Idf feature and incorporate the n gram approach to learn the vocabulary. Using these feature vectors, cross-validation with grid search, the training data is used to learn the model and prediction is applied on the test data to calculate the support of retrieved sentence for a given query. The results obtained from the CHIS organizers shown that the method adopted for finding the relevance factor in proposed work was not producing effective results when compared with other models submitted for this task. In the results obtained for task 2 were found to be working better and stood first in the accuracy when compared with the other models developed for this task 2. In future the relevant nature of the sentence is intended to be viewed as a binary classification problem. To test the results by applying the support vector classification to achieve task 1.

References

1. Liu, B.: Sentiment analysis and opinion mining. Synth. Lect. Hum. Lang. Technol. **5**(1), 1–67 (2012)
2. Pang, B., Lee, L.: Opinion mining and sentiment analysis. Found. Trends Inf. Retr. **2**(1–2), 1–35 (2008)
3. Li, Y., McLean, D., Bandar, Z.A., O'shea, J.D., Crockett, K.: Sentence similarity based on semantic nets and corpus statistics. IEEE Trans. Knowl. Data Eng. **18**(8), 1138–1150 (2006)
4. Metzler, D., Bernstein, Y., Croft, W.B., Moffat, A., Zobel, J.: Similarity measures for tracking information flow. In: Proceedings of the 14th ACM International Conference on Information and Knowledge Management, pp. 517–524. ACM, 31 October 2005
5. Grossman, D.A., Frieder, O.: Information Retrieval: Algorithms and Heuristics. Springer Science & Business Media, Heidelberg (2012)
6. Huang, A.: Similarity measures for text document clustering. In: Proceedings of the Sixth New Zealand Computer Science Research Student Conference (NZCSRSC2008), Christchurch, New Zealand, pp. 49–56, 14 April 2008
7. Chang, C.-C., Lin, C.-J.: LIBSVM: a library for support vector machines. ACM Trans. Intell. Syst. Technol. **2**(3), 1–27 (2011)

Entity Extraction of Hindi-English and Tamil-English Code-Mixed Social Media Text

G. Remmiya Devi(✉), P. V. Veena, M. Anand Kumar, and K. P. Soman

Centre for Computational Engineering and Networking (CEN),
Amrita School of Engineering,
Amrita Vishwa Vidyapeetham, Coimbatore, India
remmiyanair@gmail.com, veenakrt27@gmail.com, m_anandkumar@cb.amrita.edu,
kp_soman@amrita.edu

Abstract. Social media play an important role in today's society. Social media is the platform for people to express their opinion about various aspects using natural language. The social media text generally contains code-mixed content. The use of code-mixed data is popular in them because the users tend to mix multiple languages in their conversation instead of using their native script as unicode characters. Entity extraction, the task of extracting useful entities like Person, Location and Organization, is an important primary task in social media text analytics. Extracting entities from code-mixed social media text is a difficult task. Three different methodologies are proposed in this paper for extracting entities from Hindi-English and Tamil-English code-mixed data. This work is submitted to the shared task on Code-Mix Entity Extraction for Indian Languages (CMEE-IL) at the Forum for Information Retrieval Evaluation (FIRE) 2016. The proposed systems include approaches based on the embedding models and feature-based model. BIO-tag formatting is done as a pre-processing step. Extraction of trigram embedding is performed during feature extraction. The development of the system is carried out using Support Vector Machine-based machine learning classifier. For the CMEE-IL task, we secured second position for Tamil-English data and third for Hindi-English. Additionally, evaluation of primary entities and their accuracies were analyzed in detail for further improvement of the system.

Keywords: Social media text · Entity extraction · Code-mixed text
Word embedding · Trigram embedding features
Support Vector Machine

1 Introduction

Entity extraction has been a primary task in most of the Natural Language Processing (NLP) applications and it is defined as a task of extracting the named entities from any text. Entities of major categories are Person, Location, and

© Springer International Publishing AG 2018
P. Majumder et al. (Eds.): FIRE 2016 Workshop, LNCS 10478, pp. 206–218, 2018.
https://doi.org/10.1007/978-3-319-73606-8_16

Organization. The other entities are count, artifact, year, entertainment etc. The social media text, although unstructured contains informative content like the review about a product or a movie or opinion about a person or organization. Extracting entities from such informative content is the most challenging task. Moreover, the posts or comments in social media generally contain text in conversational nature which is in code-mixed format. The users also tend to type the text of their native language as Roman script instead of unicode characters.

An example for code-mixed Hindi-English text is given below:

chalo pehli baar **corporate** *mei bhi* **rainy day** *hoga.*

In the above example, English words are in bold letters and Hindi words are in italics. It can be seen that the Hindi words are in Roman script. Communication in social networking platforms like Facebook and Twitter are usually in code-mixed language.

This work is an extended version of the work submitted to shared task of CMEE-IL in FIRE 2016 [1]. In this shared task, we deal with Hindi-English and Tamil-English code-mixed dataset and the objective is to develop a system to extract entities from the content in code-mixed language.

Our proposed system for the task includes three approaches. The first approach is developed using word embedding features obtained from wang2vec model [2]. The second approach utilizes word embedding features from word2vec model [3]. The major difference between wang2vec and word2vec features lies in the inclusion of word order information in wang2vec. In the third approach, stylometric features were extracted from the training data. Extracted features from these three systems are used to develop three separate models using Support Vector Machine (SVM)-based classifier [4].

A brief description of previous related works is given in Sect. 2. Section 3 discusses on the code-mixed entity extraction task. The dataset statistics is explained in Sect. 4. Section 5 gives a brief overview on the word embedding models used in this paper. The methodology proposed is explained in Sect. 6. Discussion over experiments and results are explained in Sect. 7. The conclusions derived from the work is given in Sect. 8.

2   Related Work

In recent years, several researches were carried out in the field of text processing using code-mixed data. POS (Part-of-Speech) tagging was performed for code-mixed data of social media content in English-Hindi language [5]. A language identification task was carried out for Facebook data which is code-mixed between Bengali, English and Hindi [6]. A paper was published on thematic knowledge discovery for Facebook chat messages in English-Hindi using topic modeling [7]. Question classification system for code-mixed social media text in Bengali-English was developed using Bag of Words (BOWs) and Recurrent

Neural Networks (RNN) embeddings [8]. A hybrid approach of machine learning with rule based system was proposed for entity extraction in code-mixed English-Hindi and English-Tamil text [9].

Several works and shared tasks have been carried out in the field of entity extraction in social media platforms and few of them related to Indian Languages are enlisted here. In the Named Entity Recognition (NER) Task by Forum for Information Retrieval (FIRE)-2014, entity extraction for Indian languages like Hindi, Tamil and Malayalam was performed using rich features like context words, POS tags, root word, length and position [10]. FIRE 2015 entity extraction task focused on extracting named entities from social media text containing English, Malayalam, Tamil and Hindi content [11]. This work on entity extraction was implemented using SVM-based classifier in [12]. A Conditional Random Field (CRF) based approach was also implemented for the ESM-IL task of FIRE 2015 entity extraction task [13]. Another CRF-based system was proposed to perform named entity recognition for Indian Languages for Twitter based social media text [14]. With the popularity of code-mixed language in social media, a task on entity extraction from code-mixed social media data for Indian Languages (CMEE-IL) was conducted by AU-KBC Research Centre in FIRE 2016 [15]. In the CMEE-IL shared task, entity extraction for code-mixed data was implemented using neural networks [16]. A context-based character embedding was also implemented for the same entity extraction task [17]. International conferences for the shared task on entity extraction are listed below. An overview of Named Entity rEcognition and Linking in Italian Tweets for the task (NEEL-IT) was organized at EVALITA 2016 [18]. The Workshop on Noisy User-generated Text (WNUT16) conducted a Named Entity Recognition shared task for Twitter data in English language [19].

3 Code-Mixed Entity Extraction Task

The shared task on entity extraction of code-mixed languages was conducted by Computational Linguistics Research Group (CLRG), AU-KBC Research Centre, Chennai in FIRE 2016. The data for the task was collected from Twitter and other few microblogs. Hindi-English and Tamil-English code-mixed dataset was provided by the task organizers. Nine teams participated for entity extraction task in Hindi-English and five teams for Tamil-English entity extraction task. An example of Hindi-English and Tamil-English code-mixed tweet is shown in Table 1. The aim of the task is to extract named entities from the test data provided by organizers. Named entities in the dataset include Person, Location, Count, Organization, Year and so on. The number of users in social media platforms using code-mixed languages have increased predominantly today. Hence this task involving code-mixed language holds a significant relevance. The task evaluation was based on overall Precision, Recall, and F-measure. Since the individual entity-wise accuracy was not provided by the organizers, the participants could not figure out for which entity, the accuracy goes wrong and the reason why recall is less although precision value is more.

4 Dataset Description

Hindi-English and Tamil-English code-mixed text were used for the shared task. The three fields of the training dataset are Tweet ID, User ID, and the tweets. Each training file has a corresponding annotation file. The annotation file contains 6 fields namely Tweet ID, User ID, Length, Index, Entity tag and the entity chunks in the train data. Unlike Hindi-English dataset, Tamil-English dataset is not in complete code-mixed language, instead, some of the data are in pure Tamil script. To train the word embedding model, additional code-mixed text were used for both datasets. Data from the POS tagging task by International Conference on Natural Language Processing (ICON) 2015 [5], Mixed Script Information Retrieval 2016 (MSIR) [20], and some twitter data were the sources for the additional dataset for Hindi-English. The additional dataset for Tamil-English code-mixed language is from Sentiment Analysis in Indian Languages (SAIL-2015) [21,22]. The total number of tweets, average tokens per tweet and the number of entity chunks present in the training and testing data is tabulated in Table 2. On considering Hindi-English dataset, the number of tweets in test data is high compared to train data. Even though the number of tweets in Hindi-English train data is less than Tamil-English, the count of entity chunks is high in the Hindi-English dataset. The average tokens per tweet is high for Hindi-English than Tamil-English. This is due to the fact that the words in the Tamil language is generally agglutinative in nature.

The size of the additional dataset collected for Hindi-English and for Tamil-English is tabulated in Table 3. Since the time to complete the task was limited, we could not collect a surplus amount of Tamil-English code-mixed text.

Table 1. Example code-mixed text

Language	Code-mixed text
Hindi-English	Her reply pe muje smile Ati hai and I've the worst smile ever
Tamil-English	Intha padam parthe piragu than ennoda romba pudicha actor aanaru

Table 2. Number of tweets, average tokens per tweet and the number of entity chunks present in train and test data

	Train data			Test data		
	Tweet count	Avg tokens per tweet	No of entity chunks	Tweet count	Avg tokens per tweet	No of entity chunks
Hindi-English	2700	16.76	2413	7429	16.49	-
Tamil-English	3200	11.94	1624	1376	12.11	-

The Table 4 lists the six major entities present in the training data and their respective count. It can be observed from the table that one of the major entity, ENTERTAINMENT is covered more in Hindi-English code-mixed text.

Table 3. Size of additional utterances used

	Dataset size
Hindi-English	20617
Tamil-English	1625

Table 4. Major entity chunks and their count in the train dataset

Entities	Hindi-English	Tamil-English
Person	712	661
Location	194	188
Organization	109	68
Entertainment	810	260
Year	143	54
Count	132	94

5   Word Embedding Models

Word embedding is the vector representation of words. The purpose of word embedding is to map a word from a higher dimension to lower dimension through vector representation. Word2vec is a popular model used for retrieving word embedding features from text [3]. It includes two architectures. They are Continuous Bag of Words (CBOW) model and Skip-gram model. The improvised package of word2vec has been developed with additional features and named as wang2vec [2].

Sentences serve as input for training word embedding model. Vector representations acquired from the model of each word are based on the syntactic pattern in which the words lie in training sentences. The aim of the skip-gram is to predict the context word that has maximum likelihood given the neighboring words. So the aim is to maximize the value of X which is equated as in Eq. 1 where N is the total number of words, a is the window size and $p\left(y_{n+k}|y_n\right)$ is the output probability.

$$X = \frac{1}{N}\sum_{n=1}^{N}\sum_{-a\leq k\leq a}\log p\left(w_{n+k}|w_n\right) \tag{1}$$

To predict the context words $O \in w_{-a}, \ldots w_{-1}, w_1, \ldots w_a$ provided the center word w_0, the skip-gram utilizes a single output matrix $R \in |V| \times d$ where d is the embedding dimension.

The additional feature that improvised word2vec model to wang2vec model is the word order information. The sentences are fed to the neural network layer present in the word embedding model. The words are learned with respect to their position in the sentences. This enables the word embedding model to get trained in a better way. This, in turn, provides the system a better understanding of the syntactic pattern of each word. A set of $a \times 2$ output predictors $O_{-a}, \ldots O_{-1}, O_1, \ldots O_a$ of size $O \in |V| \times d$ [2].

The probability score of each word depicts the level of its relevance to the input word. The probability function used is softmax classifier and the corresponding equation is shown below in Eq. 2.

$$p(w_o \mid w_i) = \frac{e^{o_{w_i}(w_o)}}{\sum w \in V e^{o_{w_i}(w)}} \tag{2}$$

where, V is the vocabulary words and O_{w_i} corresponds to the $|V|$ dimensional vector.

6 Methodology for Entity Extraction

The preprocessing task is an essential step before analyzing and processing social media text. Initially, tokenization is performed on the given training data. The tokens obtained after the tokenization process is converted into conventional BIO format. This leads to BIO tag information for each word in the training data. Generally, BIO tag stands for Beginning, Inside, Outside tag. For example, consider the sentence, *"Sundar Pichai is the CEO of Google"*. In general, the entity *'Sundar Pichai'* indicates PERSON and *'Google'* indicates ORGANIZATION. Since the word *Sundar Pichai* has two parts, it is tagged in BIO format

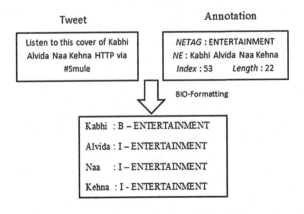

Fig. 1. Illustration of BIO-formatting

as beginning and inside. Outside tag is for the words that do not belong to any named entity. With the usage of BIO tag, words in the above example sentence, *Sundar* is labeled as B-PERSON, *Pichai* as I-PERSON and *Google* as ORGA-NIZATION. This BIO tag information is utilized in the three systems proposed in the paper. An illustration of BIO-formatting is given in Fig. 1.

The illustration of the proposed word embedding based models are shown in Fig. 2 and feature based method is shown in Fig. 3.

6.1   Entity Extraction with Wang2vec Embedding Features

The wang2vec model is an advanced version of the word2vec model with respect to the architecture of the models. The skip-gram model in the word2vec has become Structured Skip-gram model in wang2vec. The main improvement in this model is the fact that the word position information is taken into consideration. The wang2vec model is used to obtain the word vector features using structured skip-gram model. The vector size n is defined during the training of wang2vec model. Here, vector size n, for each word is set as 50. The word embedding features of each word in the given dataset are retrieved from the resultant vectors.

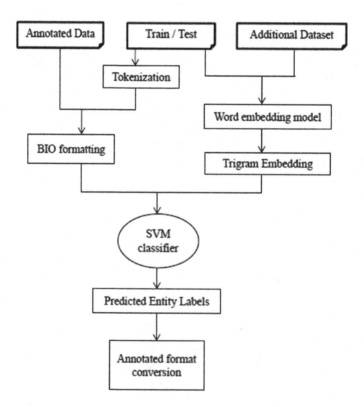

Fig. 2. Methodology of the entity extraction system using word embedding models

The neighboring context features from these vectors were retrieved and combined with the original embedding features. This, in turn, forms a feature set of size 150. Trigram embedding features are formed by appending original features to the context features. Finally, each word in the training data holds its corresponding BIO tag information and trigram embedding features. This serves as an input to train the SVM classifier. Hence an SVM model corresponding to this system is obtained. Wang2vec embedding features for test data were extracted in the same way. For testing, each word along with its trigram embedding feature set is given to the classifier.

6.2   Entity Extraction with Word2vec Embedding Features

The vector representation for each vocabulary word in the dataset can be retrieved using the well-known word embedding model called word2vec. Input for word2vec are sentences, as the extraction of word embedding solely depends on the syntactic pattern which is retrieved from the context words of each sentence. Word2vec uses the skip-gram model to obtain the vectors of each word in the training data. The entity extraction system is developed using these features. Similar to the system using wang2vec, this system also utilizes trigram embedding features of word2vec features.

Each word of the training data are merged with its feature set containing BIO tag information and the trigram embedding features. These features are integrated to form a feature set which is given for training the machine learning based classifier, SVM. Each word in the test data is merged with the trigram embedding features and is given for testing. The SVM classifier learns the different syntactic pattern in which each word lies from training data and performs recognition of entities from the dataset during testing of the system.

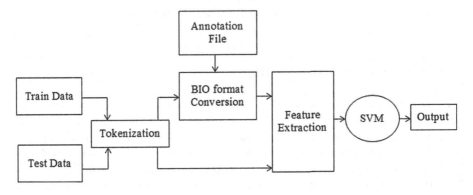

Fig. 3. Methodology of the entity extraction system using stylometric features

6.3   Entity Extraction with Stylometric Features

The third approach uses a conventional feature extraction method implemented using stylometric features. The stylometric feature set contains features like Prefix, Suffix, Length, Number, Lower case/Upper case and so on. The features used in our system are tabulated in Table 5. Each word in the training data is targeted and its corresponding stylometric feature set is extracted. The BIO tag information is joined with the conventional feature set to form the input for training SVM. For predicting the output tag, the stylometric features extracted are merged with the words in test data and given for testing.

The proposed methodology results with three SVM models for the three systems using wang2vec features, word2vec features and stylometric features.

Table 5. Stylometric features extracted from train and test data for feature based system

Features	Representation
Lower case	Lower case representation
Hyperlink	1 if hyperlink present
Hash (#), apostrophe (')	1 if word starts with #, ' symbol
Numbers, punctuation	Marks 1/0 if present/absent
Prefix-suffix	P3/P4: first 3/4 characters
	S3/S4: last 3/4 characters
Length and index	No of chars & position of word
4-digit numbers	1 if Token is a 4-digit number
First character upper case	1 if an upper case character
Full character upper case	1 if entirely an upper case word
Gazetteer features	Person, location, organization, entertainment

7   Experiments and Results

The procedure for wang2vec based embedding and word2vec based embedding models are similar. The difference between these two models is that wang2vec embedding features takes the word position into consideration using structured skip-gram model. The skip-gram model is utilized to retrieve word embedding features. The additional dataset is also taken along with the training data to train the two word embedding models. The vector size is set as 50. According to the user defined vector size, the trigram embedding feature set is extracted. The train data, after tokenization, is converted to BIO-formatted text. The words in the training data is merged with its trigram embedding vectors of size 150 and BIO-tag information serves as an input to the SVM classifier. Test data is also subjected to similar steps for retrieving trigram embedding feature set. After tokenization, the trigram embedding features of length 150 is given to SVM for predicting label of test data.

The third approach uses stylometric features for entity extraction of the code-mixed data. From the tokenized train data, features listed in Table 5 are extracted. BIO tag information along with the stylometric feature set of these words are given to the classifier to train the system. The tokenized words are appended with its corresponding feature set and given to the classifier for testing.

The systems were trained with 10-fold cross validation. Table 6 shows the cross-validation results obtained for Hindi-English and Tamil-English dataset for wang2vec, word2vec, and feature based models. The accuracy for unknown tokens is better in wang2vec based embedding model.

From the results by CMEE-IL task organizers, for Tamil-English we have obtained the second place and for Hindi-English we ranked in the third place. Tables 7 and 8 tabulate the results of the top five teams for Hindi-English and Tamil-English data respectively. From the table, it can be inferred that the

Table 6. Cross validation results for Hindi-English and Tamil-English

	Hindi-English			Tamil-English		
	wang2vec	word2vec	Features	wang2vec	word2vec	Features
Known	92.99	91.10	94.26	97.27	97.38	97.49
Ambiguous known	83.09	78.32	86.56	83.81	83.84	85.97
Unknown	91.03	90.95	86.94	93.67	93.44	92.46
Overall accuracy	**92.47**	**91.03**	**92.37**	**96.15**	**96.25**	**95.98**

Table 7. CMEE-IL results by the task organizers for Hindi-English

Team	Run 1			Run 2			Run 3		
	P	R	F	P	R	F	P	R	F
Irshad-IIT-Hyd	80.92	59.00	68.24	-	-	-	-	-	-
Deepak-IIT-Patna	81.15	50.39	62.17	-	-	-	-	-	-
Amrita_CEN	**75.19**	**29.46**	**42.33**	**75.00**	**29.17**	**42.00**	**79.88**	**41.37**	**54.51**
NLP_CEN_Amrita	76.34	31.15	44.25	77.72	31.84	45.17	-	-	-
Rupal-BITS_Pilani	58.66	32.93	42.18	58.84	35.32	44.14	59.15	34.62	43.68

Table 8. CMEE-IL results by the task organizers for Tamil-English

Team	Run 1			Run 2			Run 3		
	P	R	F	P	R	F	P	R	F
Deepak-IIT-Patna	79.92	30.47	44.12	-	-	-	-	-	-
Amrita_CEN	**77.38**	**8.72**	**15.67**	**74.74**	**9.93**	**17.53**	**79.51**	**21.88**	**34.32**
NLP_CEN_Amrita	77.70	15.43	25.75	79.56	19.59	31.44	-	-	-
Rupal-BITS_Pilani	55.86	10.87	18.20	58.71	12.21	20.22	58.94	11.94	19.86
CEN@Amrita	47.62	13.42	20.94	-	-	-	-	-	-

overall accuracy of the Tamil-English is less than the Hindi-English. The reason for this might be the fact that the dataset of Tamil-English is not completely code-mixed and partially in pure Tamil script. In the results obtained by our system, we observed that the recall value is less compared to precision. This may be because less unlabeled data were collected for word embedding models.

Table 9. Precision, recall and F-measure obtained for major entities of Hindi-English code-mixed text

Entities	Precision	Recall	F-measure
PERSON	56.52	21.31	30.95
LOCATION	64.29	36.00	46.15
ORGANIZATION	50.00	23.81	32.26
ENTERTAINMENT	47.30	32.11	38.25
YEAR	60.00	20.00	30.00
COUNT	55.00	31.43	40.00

Table 10. Precision, recall and F-measure obtained for major entities of Tamil-English code-mixed text

Entities	Precision	Recall	F-measure
PERSON	50.00	35.24	41.34
LOCATION	77.77	26.92	40.00
ORGANIZATION	22.22	20.00	21.05
ENTERTAINMENT	35.29	24.00	28.57
YEAR	100.00	20.00	33.33
COUNT	55.88	55.88	55.88

After the shared task, we decided to perform detailed entity-wise error analysis. Since the gold-standard dataset is not available, we divided the training data further into train and test data. The analysis was performed on the feature based system only because compared to word embedding based systems, the system using traditional features has given better accuracy. Tables 9 and 10 shows the entity-wise performance of the six major entities in the dataset. The precision value for ORGANIZATION is very less in Tamil-English text. The recall value of PERSON is less in Hindi-English text. It was also observed that most of the entities were wrongly tagged as O tag.

8 Conclusions

The users in social media communicates to one another by mixing multiple languages. People tend to deliver their views in social media using such code-mixed language. At business point of view, extracting opinion and discussion about a product from social media text has a greater importance. Extracting entities like Person, Location or Organization from such code-mixed dataset is a tedious task. The dataset provided by the CMEE-IL organizers is from Twitter and other few microblogs for the code-mixed languages like Hindi-English and Tamil-English. Our submission for the task included three different approaches. To perform the entity extraction task, first two approaches used the word embedding features of wang2vec and word2vec. Training of the word embedding models utilized the training data along with some additionally collected dataset. The third system uses only traditional stylometric features. Training and testing of the three approaches were carried out using SVM. The result for the system using stylometric feature was better than the word-embedding based systems. From the results of the task organizers, we can observe that the accuracy of Tamil-English is less and recall is less for all the systems. An entity-wise evaluation for the major entities is also illustrated in this paper. An increase in the size of additional unlabeled data will increase the capability of the word embedding models to capture the syntactic similarity of the sentences, more accurately. Hence, as future work, we are planning to collect more unlabeled data for approaches using word embedding models. We will also be focusing on character based embedding models with deep learning techniques and investigate whether including POS tag information with stylometric features will improve the performance of the system.

References

1. Remmiya Devi, G., Veena, P.V., Anand Kumar, M., Soman, K.P.: AMRITA_CEN@ FIRE 2016: code-mix entity extraction for Hindi-English and Tamil-English tweets. In: CEUR Workshop Proceedings, vol. 1737, pp. 304–308 (2016)
2. Wang, L., Chris, D., Alan, B., Isabel, T.: Two/too simple adaptations of word2vec for syntax problems. In: Proceedings of the 2015 Conference of the North American Chapter of the Association for Computational Linguistics: Human Language Technologies, pp. 1299–1304 (2015)
3. Mikolov, T., Sutskever, I., Chen, K., Corrado, G.S., Dean, J.: Distributed representations of words and phrases and their compositionality. In: Advances in neural information processing systems, pp. 3111–3119 (2013)
4. Joachims, T.: SVMlight: support vector machine. Cornell University (2008). http://svmlight.joachims.org/
5. Vyas, Y., Gella, S., Sharma, J., Bali, K., Choudhury, M.: POS tagging of English-Hindi code-mixed social media content. In: Proceedings of the 2014 Conference on Empirical Methods in Natural Language Processing (EMNLP), pp. 974–979. Association for Computational Linguistics (2014)
6. Barman, U., Das, A., Wagner, J., Foster, J.: Code mixing: a challenge for language identification in the language of social media. In: Conference on Empirical Methods in Natural Language Processing (EMNLP) 2014, p. 13 (2014)
7. Asnani, K., Pawar, J.D.: Discovering thematic knowledge from code-mixed chat messages using topic model. In: Proceedings of the 3rd Workshop on Indian Language Data: Resources and Evaluation (WILDRE3), pp. 104–109 (2016)

8. Anand Kumar, M., Soman, K.P.: Amrita_CEN@MSIR-FIRE2016: code-mixed question classification using BoWs and RNN embeddings. In: CEUR Workshop Proceedings, vol. 1737, pp. 122–125 (2016)

9. Gupta, D., Shweta, Tripathi, S., Ekbal, A., Bhattacharyya, P.: A hybrid approach for entity extraction in code-mixed social media data. In: CEUR Workshop Proceedings, vol. 1737, pp. 298–303 (2016)

10. Abinaya, N., John, N., Barathi Ganesh, H., Anand Kumar, M., Soman, K.P.: AMRITA-CEN@FIRE-2014: named entity recognition for Indian languages using rich features. In: ACM International Conference Proceeding Series, pp. 103–111 (2014)

11. Rao, P., Devi, S.: CMEE-IL: code mix entity extraction in Indian languages from social media text @ FIRE 2016 an overview. In: CEUR Workshop Proceedings, vol. 1737, pp. 289–295 (2016)

12. Anand Kumar, M., Shriya, S., Soman, K.P.: AMRITA-CEN@FIRE 2015: extracting entities for social media texts in Indian languages. In: CEUR Workshop Proceedings, vol. 1587, pp. 85–88 (2015)

13. Sanjay, S., Anand Kumar, M., Soman, K.P.: AMRITA_CEN-NLP@FIRE 2015:CRF based named entity extraction for Twitter microposts. CEUR Workshop Proceedings, vol. 1587, pp. 96–99 (2015)

14. Pallavi, K., Srividhya, K., Victor, R., Ramya, M.: HITS@FIRE task 2015: Twitter based named entity recognizer for Indian languages. In: CEUR Workshop Proceedings, vol. 1587, pp. 81–84 (2015)

15. Rao, P., Malarkodi, C., Vijay Sundar Ram, R., Devi, S.: ESM-IL: entity extraction from social media text for Indian languages @ FIRE 2015 an overview. In: CEUR Workshop Proceedings, vol. 1587, pp. 74–80 (2015)

16. Bhat, I., Shrivastava, M., Bhat, R.: Code mixed entity extraction in Indian languages using neural networks. In: CEUR Workshop Proceedings, vol. 1737, pp. 296–297 (2016)

17. Skanda, S., Singh, S., Remmiya Devi, G., Veena, P.V., Anand Kumar, M., Soman, K.P.: CEN@Amrita FIRE 2016: context based character embeddings for entity extraction in code-mixed text. In: CEUR Workshop Proceedings, vol. 1737, pp. 321–324 (2016)

18. Basile, P., Caputo, A., Gentile, A.L., Rizzo, G.: Overview of the EVALITA: named entity rEcognition and linking in Italian tweets (NEEL-IT) task. In: CEUR Workshop Proceedings, vol. 1749 (2016)

19. Strauss, B., Toma, B.E., Ritter, A., de Marneffe, M.-C., Xu, W.: Results of the WNUT16 named entity recognition shared task. In: Proceedings of the 2nd Workshop on Noisy User-generated Text, pp. 138–144 (2016)

20. Banerjee, S., Chakma, K., Naskar, S., Das, A., Rosso, P., Bandyopadhyay, S., Choudhury, M.: Overview of the mixed script information retrieval (MSIR) at FIRE-2016. In: CEUR Workshop Proceedings, vol. 1737, pp. 94–99 (2016)

21. Patra, B.G., Das, D., Das, A., Prasath, R.: Shared task on sentiment analysis in indian languages (SAIL) tweets - an overview. In: Prasath, R., Vuppala, A.K., Kathirvalakumar, T. (eds.) MIKE 2015. LNCS (LNAI), vol. 9468, pp. 650–655. Springer, Cham (2015). https://doi.org/10.1007/978-3-319-26832-3_61

22. Shriya, S., Vinayakumar, R., Anand Kumar, M., Soman, K.P.: AMRITA-CEN@SAIL2015: sentiment analysis in Indian languages. In: Prasath, R., Vuppala, A.K., Kathirvalakumar, T. (eds.) MIKE 2015. LNCS (LNAI), vol. 9468, pp. 703–710. Springer, Cham (2015). https://doi.org/10.1007/978-3-319-26832-3_67

Author Index

Printed in the United States
By Bookmasters